Sound Me⌐·

Everyday life is full of soundscapes created by professionals. *Sound Media* considers how music recording, radio broadcasting and muzak influence people's daily lives and introduces the many and varied creative techniques that have developed in music and journalism throughout the twentieth century. Lars Nyre presents the contemporary cultural engagements in the field of sound studies, and works back from the soundscapes of the present day to the 1870s.

The first part of the book, 'The present time', devotes five chapters to contemporary digital media, with particular focus on the internet, the personal computer, digital radio (news and talk) and various types of loudspeaker media (muzak, DJ'ing, clubbing and PA systems).

In the second part, 'Backwards history', Lars Nyre examines the historical accumulation of techniques and sounds in sound media. The history is told backwards, to peel off layers of technologies and practices, with a particular focus on multitrack music in the 1960s, the golden age of radio in the 1950s and back to the 1930s, microphone recording of music in the 1930s, and the experimental phase of wireless radio in the 1910s and 1900s, concluding with the invention of the gramophone and phonograph in the late nineteenth century.

Sound Media is a book for media students and scholars, music lovers and media pundits, as well as journalists, musicians and audio engineers. It includes a soundtrack CD with thirty-six examples from broadcasting and music recording in Europe and the USA, from Edith Piaf to Sara Cox, and is richly illustrated with figures, timelines and technical drawings.

Lars Nyre is an Associate Professor at the University of Bergen and Volda University College, Norway. He is chair of the research network Digital Radio Cultures in Europe (www.drace.org) and has published articles about mass media in research journals including *Journalism Studies* and the *Journal of Radio and Audio Media*.

Sound Media

From live journalism to music recording

Lars Nyre

Routledge
Taylor & Francis Group

LONDON AND NEW YORK

First published 2008
by Routledge
2 Park Square, Milton Park, Abingdon, Oxon OX14 4RN

Simultaneously published in the USA and Canada
by Routledge
270 Madison Ave, New York, NY 10016

*Routledge is an imprint of the Taylor & Francis Group, an informa
business*

© 2008 Lars Nyre

Typeset in Bembo by
Book Now Ltd, London
Printed and bound in Great Britain by
The Cromwell Press, Trowbridge, Wiltshire

British Library Cataloguing in Publication Data
A catalogue record for this book is available
from the British Library

Library of Congress Cataloging in Publication Data
Nyre, Lars.
Sound media: from live journalism to music recording/Lars Nyre
    p.cm.
Includes index
I. Title.
TK7881.4.N97 2008
302.23—dc22   2008003198

ISBN10: 0–415–39113–X (hbk)
ISBN10: 0–415–39114–8 (pbk)

ISBN13: 978–0–415–39113–9 (hbk)
ISBN13: 978–0–415–39114–6 (pbk)

Contents

List of figures

The figures are vital to the book's pedagogical argument. They present condensed information about sound media, and can be studied more or less independently of the written argument. The book contains three types of figures: artistic tableaus of life with sound media at different times in history, timelines of the media platforms that are analysed in a given chapter, and models of their functional properties. The medium models contribute noticeably to the backwards history of the book. As the book progresses towards the past the medium models become simpler in quite a visible way.

Note

Atle Skorstad created all the artwork, including the tableaus and the sketches of audio equipment and distribution platforms. Lars Nyre created the timelines and constructed the medium models based on Skorstad's sketches. Kjetil Vikene supplied the screen shot of haltKarl's composition for chapter 3. The map of New York City in chapter 4 is reprinted with the kind permission of Johomaps.

Soundtrack

This book enquires about techniques of communication in sound, and this is exactly what the soundtrack demonstrates. It is a chain of sounds including pop, rock and classical music, montages, machine sounds, live news, documentary, quiz shows and studio entertainment. You can listen to the soundtrack without reading the book, but you cannot read the book without listening to the soundtrack. If the soundtrack does not support the claims made in the case studies the critical reader/listener will be the first to know.

Note

Duration: 54:00. All tracks compiled by Lars Nyre. Copyright clearance administered by Sigmund Elias Holm. Sound engineering and mixing by Reidulf Botn. Executive producer: Sverre Liestøl. CD design: Thomas Lewe. Published by Routledge 2008. More details can be found in the soundtrack supplement at the end of the book.

Acknowledgements

If you got ears, you gotta listen.

(Captain Beefheart, 1980)

This book started as the doctoral thesis 'Fidelity Matters: Sound Realism in the 20th Century' (2003). Professor Anders Johansen at the Department of Information Science and Media Studies in Bergen supervised my studies of auditory perception and the mass media, not just for the doctoral thesis but also for preliminary studies as a bachelor and master student. What is good in this book I owe to his creative scepticism, and what is poor I owe to my not being able to overcome it.

The works of the phenomenologist and technology philosopher Don Ihde have inspired me since I first picked up *Listening and Voice* in the mid-1990s. In 2000 I was a visiting scholar and regular attendant at the Technoscience Research Seminar on Long Island, New York. Here I learnt to appreciate the links between American philosophy of technology and media studies, and this helped me to vindicate Marshall McLuhan as a serious scholar of the media.

In 2004 I was a visiting scholar at the Department of Media Arts at Royal Holloway College in London, and my conversations with John Ellis about the nature of broadcasting were a great inspiration. I also want to thank Colin Sparks, who directed the work in the European research network COST A20 'The Impact of the Internet on the Mass Media in Europe', and Paddy Scannell, who headed the commission that evaluated my doctoral thesis in 2003. I am grateful for the personal kindnesses they have showed me, and the intellectual vigour of their different approaches to media studies.

I am in great debt to the members of the research network Digital Radio Cultures in Europe (www.drace.org) for extended discussions and collaborative work on a range of issues relevant to this book. Thanks to Marko Ala-Fossi, Markus Appel, Alexandros Baltzis, Oliver Hahn, David Hendy, Henrik Hargitai, Per Jauert, Stephen Lax, Brian O'Neill, Susana Santos, Helen Shaw, Jon Peder Vestad and Nada Zgrabljic.

Thanks to Volda University College for a generous fund to pay the copyright fees for the CD for the Routledge edition. Chief engineer Sverre Liestøl has twice saved this sound media project from itself, and I am eternally grateful to him. Thanks also to the Department of Information Science and Media Studies at the University of Bergen for allocating funds that made it possible to check all the copyrights for the CD.

Since 2003 I have worked closely with professor Barbara Gentikow in the Cultural Techniques project, and I want to thank her for a very productive collaboration, and for allowing me to spend a lot of time writing this book while I was employed on her project. Thanks also to Hallvard Moe for being such a good reader. Atle Skorstad made all the drawings for the book, and Sigmund Elias Holm administered the copyright clearance for the CD. I am grateful to them for doing such good work.

Kjetil Vikene has been a fast friend in conversation and computerization since the mid-1990s, and his haltKarl project has become an integral part of the musical arguments in this book. Linda Eide has been my radio companion since the 1980s and a co-writer of texts about sound in the media since the early 2000s. Whole arguments of this book are developed in dialogue with her.

This book is dedicated to my family – Barbara, Nils, Isak and Agnes – whom I love. Without their noisy influence I could not have worked with this material for ten years.

Lars Nyre
Bergen, June 2008

Chapter 1

Theoretical introduction to sound media

What you hold in your hands is a book, and consequently you are now immersed in its sensory environment. Your eyes follow the argument line by line and page by page; you can skip between chapters at your leisure; and once in a while you may find yourself thinking new thoughts. Reading and writing are efficient techniques of communication, and they have been fostered around the book (and scroll and clay tablet) for thousands of years. The experience of sound media is entirely different from the experience of the book. You tap your foot half-consciously to the funky beat of the music, and you imaginatively share the adventures of the foreign correspondent on radio while doing the housekeeping.

This book is all about sound media, and this chapter clears the ground for an analysis of altogether ten different set-ups of the sound media that are widespread at the present time, or were influential earlier in history. The book is organized according to my version of the research tradition called medium theory. Joshua Meyrowitz has given a lucid definition of medium theory that I will start from:

> Medium theory focuses on the particular characteristics of each individual medium or of each particular type of media. Broadly speaking, medium theorists ask: What are the relatively fixed features of each means of communicating and how do these features make the medium physically, psychologically, and socially different from other media and from face to face interaction?
>
> (Meyrowitz 1994: 50)

By my lights Meyrowitz sets up a reasonable ambition for the media researcher, and indeed dozens of prominent researchers have studied more or less exactly what he prescribes without actively thinking about themselves as medium theorists (for example, Ellis 2000 and Scannell 1996). Briefly stated, my version of medium theory has four dimensions: 1) a description of sound and listening; 2) a theory of what a medium is; 3) a method for a backwards history of media; and 4) a method for rhetorical analysis of journalism and music.

I SOUND AND LISTENING

The *Concise Oxford Dictionary* (1975) defines sound as an experience of the ear caused by vibrations in the surrounding air; an event that is being or may be heard; the act of giving forth sound or causing to sound. But you don't need a dictionary to know what sound is. Your body hears long before you can read a dictionary, since from the first day of your life you have navigated through the world with the aid of the sense of hearing. You don't have earlids like you have eyelids, and even the deaf can feel sonic vibrations in their bodies. Hunters in the jungles of New Guinea relate to bird song, insect noises, and trees and plants moving in the wind. City dwellers relate to sounds of transportation, large masses of people, ventilation systems and fire engine sirens. R. Murray Schafer ([1977]1994: 274) coined the term 'soundscape' to capture this never-ending presence of sound in people's everyday lives.

Natural sound

Natural sound is my term for all the sounds that are non-mediated – that is, they occurred before sound media were invented, or they occur without any form of transmission or recording at the present time. Natural sound is crucial to public life in all civilizations of the world, especially in the form of oratory and song. Imagine Enrico Caruso (1873–1921) performing in San Francisco in April 1906, on the night before the great earthquake. The concert hall is packed with well-to-do citizens in starched shirts and gowns, their senses trained on the operatic singer and the orchestra. With eager expectation they hear sound waves emanating from Caruso's mouth at 340 metres per second. The sounds inform us about certain features of the actions of Caruso and the orchestra that the other senses do not, but at the same time the other senses give access to visible, touchable and odorous aspects of the same events.

My approach takes the sensory richness of communication into account. It is concerned not just with the sounds in isolation, but also with the things that vibrate – the singers and speakers and their equipment and the wider sur-roundings. Think of Caruso's body, which is the entire basis of his expressive voice, and imagine his beautiful clothes, his jewellery and the other accessories. These other things also have a communicative influence. Indeed, all five senses must be thought of as one exploratory entity, and in pursuing this thought I am inspired by Merleau-Ponty ([1945] 1992), Gibson (1966) and Ihde ([1976] 2007). On the basis of these influential works, I identify four existential char-acteristics of sound that guide the individual's communication effort, and these characteristics are also integral to the visible and touchable materials of communication:

- *time* (duration, chronology, causes and effects)
- *space* (directions, shapes, volumes, distances)

Figure 1.1 Caruso in the concert hall.

- *personal expressiveness* (emotions, moods)
- *coded message* (for example, news and love song).

Firstly, sounds always tell us something about time. A performance always happens right now, in front of those present, and for Caruso this means he is under social pressure to perform well. It is the same thing in the theatre, the opera and vaudeville. The real-time progression of sound events causes such phenomena as the nervousness of live performance, whether in the concert hall or at the political rally, where the performers have only one chance of making an impression, and nobody will forget it if they make a fool of themselves because they were ill-prepared. Sound events are ephemeral; they last for only a second, and at most around fifteen seconds in the extreme reverberation of a mountain pass. When the energy is expended a particular sound is gone forever. Some sound events appear to last for a long time, for example the constant roar of a waterfall or a tedious political speech that goes on for hours, but these consist of a continuous generation of sounds that all wear off immediately and are never heard again.

Before the invention of recording all the sound events were by definition continuous with the progression of the world at large. Caruso represented a new era with his famous recordings, which he released from the early 1900s (Day 2000). Many San Franciscans had listened to his records the night before the opera; over and over again they had listened to his tenor voice rising and falling, and the experience must have heightened their expectations. Tonight I will hear and see him in the flesh! And this is partly why Caruso is nervous. Unlike the recording session, a concert has no second take. Reviewers from San Francisco newspapers would be listening carefully and publish their reviews the next morning.

Secondly, sounds always tell us something about space. Caruso is singing in a modern concert hall, which is sound-proofed, with a rich and precise resonance created by expert acousticians. A concert hall is a sound technology, but it is not a mediation technology. It can be compared with the ancient amphitheatre and arenas in Greek and Roman times, except that the biggest arenas did not have a roof and had less well-controlled acoustics. Over 50,000 people could be in attendance at a Roman arena, and the sounds from the stage could reach even the cheapest seats with a measure of clarity, at least when the audience was silent. In a telling phrase Theo van Leeuwen (1999: 14) calls sound a 'wrap-around medium'. Referring to the same experience, Rick Altman calls sound a 'three-dimensional materiality'. He beautifully describes a woman speaking in an auditorium: 'Radiating out like a cone from the actress's mouth, the sound pressure soon fills up the entire auditorium, bouncing off the walls, the floor, and the ceiling, and bending around audience members, chairs, and posts until it is finally completely absorbed' (Altman 1992a: 21). Sound is never located at a singular geometrical point; it is always in the process of spreading further into the surroundings, and therefore the environment resounds with events from above or below, far away and too near, all the time. The bang of a closing door goes through the walls and resonates up the stairs, for an instant filling the corridor or even the street with its impatient movement. Great waterfalls can be heard miles away. In more technical terms the resonance in a given surrounding is related to the volume of the sounds (the louder, the greater the area of coverage), their frequency characteristics (low frequencies spread out in all directions, high frequencies go in a precise direction), and the texture of the things involved in the movement (waves are absorbed by soft materials and bounce off hard materials).

The environmental function of sound is important because humans live with it all their lives, perhaps coping well but perhaps also being stressed by it. Schafer ([1977] 1994) vividly describes the low fidelity sound of the modern West, where mechanical and electrical noises of all kinds make sure that there is never a moment of real silence. He perceptively points out that in such an environment sound does not come towards the listener but is present everywhere. Tony Schwartz (1974: 48) argues that 'acoustic space is more like something we wear or sit in than a physical area in which we move. A listener is wrapped in auditory space and reverberates with the sound.' To clarify the concept of environment I will set up a contrast between the general environment and the ambient environment. The general environment really consists of an average, and takes into account all the auditory experiences that a person could have while moving around in a given city or country, while the *ambient environment* refers to the actual sounds and other sense impressions that individuals have in their everyday locations, where they go about their lives as usual. This book focuses on the individual experiences of the sound environment, but it must be said that it is quite impossible to make empirical descriptions of them (I do not have access to their perception), and therefore it is nevertheless a general description of individual experiences.

Directional hearing developed as an early-warning system for physical danger – for animals just as much as for humans. Hearing surveys the soundscape and helps us to direct our eyes to a particular source of sound. This is simply human awareness, the ability to react quickly to new information (see Plomp 2002; Handel 1989). Wandering around in the soundscape of their city or village, people can easily discern the difference between locations based on sound. Sounds are the raw material for the orientations and explorations in which human beings constantly engage. In San Francisco in 1906 it started with a low rumbling that was different from all the familiar sounds of the city; it was soon accompanied by all kinds of things falling down, and the creaking and whining of wood, concrete and metal being dislocated, things crashing down on them. Finding yourself in an earthquake in the middle of a big modern city awakens your survival instincts. This is perception at its most acute.

Thirdly, sounds always tell us something about the personality of the performers. Simon Frith (1998: 191) claims that the singing voice 'stands for the person more directly than any other musical device'. Song and speech sounds spread out from the mouth, with the hands and body often helping the words to achieve their intended meaning. When Caruso sang 'The Siciliana', a complex ensemble of tongue, jaw, teeth, lips, nasal cavity, larynx and breath were involved, all trained to perfection by the great tenor. Beyond the talented timbres of 'The Siciliana' is the person Enrico Caruso. How did he interpret the intended passions of the song? Did he sound vulnerable or aggressive; and were any of his emotions particularly authentic because of a desperate love affair in his own life? The personal and private resonance of communication became very important with the emergence of sound media, and its historical development is at the heart of this book.

Finally, sounds often tell us something about the world by carrying a coded message. After all, the main reason why humans carry on vocalizing and melodizing is that these sounds can communicate messages to other humans very efficiently. There is no end to the uses to whcih language and melody can be put, and the resulting communication varies with, for example, the mother tongue used (Italian versus Norwegian), the social setting (formal or informal) and the speaker's skills (eloquent or clumsy). Let me stick to my case, and inform you that during the fateful night in San Francisco Caruso sang an aria from the opera *Cavalleria rusticana* (1890) by Pietro Mascagni. As the opera begins a young villager sings 'The Siciliana (O Lola, lovely as the spring's bright blooms)', a tormented love song to a young maiden. The villager has returned from military service and found that while he was gone Lola abandoned him and married the prosperous village teamster. This act of treason is sweetened by the fact that she is still in love with the young man. From this starting point the love story evolves. Please imagine the rich cultural analysis that could be made of Caruso's performance by combining operatic history with Italian cultural history and the great immigration surge to the USA during the early 1900s. Although the larger cultural context of these messages is not pursued actively in my book, it is all the time a background feature.

Mediated sound

Since the 1870s the messages in sound have been not only a natural but also a mediated phenomenon. Strange things are accomplished through recording, telephony and broadcasting. These media separate sounds from their occurrence in one place only and allow them to be projected in many unassociated places at the same time, or be repeated indefinitely later on (this has been pointed out by a host of authors, for example Jones 1992; Chanan 1995; Millard 2005; Katz 2004; Lax 2008). In millions of homes people have listened to the music of Caruso on the gramophone, have struggled with the weak transatlantic telephone connection, or have worried at the stern sound of Margaret Thatcher's voice on the radio. The fact that sounds were repeated outside the time and place of the original performance caused confusion in private and public life. In a typically modern way both producers and listeners have explored all conceivable opportunities to communicate with each other, slowly creating new provinces of meaning in sound communication (Bull and Black 2003).

I will analyse in this book a series of mediated sounds quite closely all of which are contained on the accompanying soundtrack CD. The first track is symbolic of the theoretical tradition from which I write. The LP is called *The Medium is the Massage* and was released by Columbia Records in 1967 as an accompaniment to the book of the same title (McLuhan and Fiore 1967). These sounds could only be made with modern, professional stereo tape equipment (8 or 12 track). The production is typical of the media environment in New York City in 1968, in the midst of psychedelia, the Vietnam War and the 1960s cultural revolutions. The book version of *The Medium is the Massage* is, by the way, a beautiful example of creative typography, and the pages are filled with unusually large and small type faces, drawings, photographs and facsimiles that support the argument of the volume.

My intention in analysing the McLuhan LP is to clarify the difference between the properties of mediated such as and the properties of natural sound such as Caruso singing in the concert hall in 1906. In order to be systematic, I will present the McLuhan track according to the same four characteristics as

Figure 1.2 McLuhan in the control room.

before: time, space, personality and message. McLuhan's aphorisms are transcribed for legibility, but most of the sounds are completely untranscribable.

Track 1: Marshall McLuhan: The Medium is the Massage, 1967 (1:42).

– Until writing was invented, man lived in acoustic space, boundless, directionless, horizonless, in the dark of the mind, in the world of emotion, by primordial intuition, by terror. Speech is a social chart of this bond.
– The medium of our time, electric circuitry, profoundly involves men with each other. Information [verbal loops and effects throughout].
– There are no grammatical errors in a non-literate society.
– All media work us over completely. They are so pervasive in their personal, political, economic, aesthetic, psychological, moral, ethical and social consequences that they leave no part of us untouched, unaffected, unaltered. The medium is the massage.
– Any understanding of social and cultural change is impossible without the knowledge about how media work as environments.
– Everything we do is music.

Firstly, the temporal existence of recorded sound is quite different from that of natural sound. Recorded sound is a material object fixed in time that can be bought and sold on the market. A recording has no continuity with the world, and that is why we can hear McLuhan and his companions today, even though they spoke in 1967. People can record important events such as the birth of their first child for the family history archive, and in doing so they bring the event into the future as something that can be experienced again and again.

Secondly, the acoustic space of a recording is in a sense double (Altman 1992a: 27). The sounds from the loudspeaker have their own acoustic space that is safely contained on the recording. The weird electronic noises that McLuhan and company made in 1967 can be played back in a number of different acoustic settings, and when they fill the listeners' room they are affected by the characteristics of that room. Since the technically produced acoustic space fills up a domestic space, the result is a double space. Notice that the acoustic space of the recording is unchangeable, except that the listeners can adjust the volume and place the loudspeakers in different ways to influence it slightly. If you move closer to the loudspeaker the sound gets louder, but you don't move closer to McLuhan. And there is obviously no way of entering that recorded space and moving around in it. Furthermore, the acoustic space of mediated sound is transportable. It can be played back in all kinds of public and private places. People can play the sound on their private stereo system, and this allows them to share the experience with friends. Since the Walkman was introduced in the early 1980s people have been able to take the mediated acoustic space with them wherever they go. If they like, they can be completely immersed in their own private experience.

Thirdly, personality in sound media is quite an elusive matter. Clearly, there is no direct contact between speakers and listeners as there could have been between Caruso and his fans. The performances are already complete when people hear them. Listeners cannot interact with McLuhan in a reciprocal way. There is, for example, no way to ask him what the heck he is trying to tell us. This means that in recording and broadcasting the relationship between producers and listeners is asymmetrical. The producers are absent from the listeners' locale, and the listeners are absent from the producer's locale. Never the twain shall meet. But despite the division there is obviously a process of contact between them, since mass communication works fine across the years and over large distances. There is an industrial distribution of messages to a dispersed public instead of a dialogue between interlocutors (Scannell 2005: 130). Anthony Giddens argues that the mass-produced address requires a specific form of trust. Since media events are substantially absent from the listener's perspective, people are forced to trust the persons who make the claims in quite an open and risky way: 'Trust presumes a leap to commitment, a quality of "faith" that is irreducible.' It is specifically related to the account of events from which people were absent in time and space, Giddens stresses (1991: 19). An implication of Giddens's argument is that there is little need for trust in events that are constantly in view, and which can be directly monitored and intervened in if necessary. Consequently, there is a great need for trust in the mass media.

2 MEDIUM THEORY

As already stated, I subscribe to a long tradition of scholarship that is often called medium theory, and it comes as no surprise that Marshall McLuhan is a crucial influence on my work. There is a large literature of interpretations of McLuhan's work; see, for example, Miller (1971), Grosswiler (1998), Genosko (1999), Levinson (1999) and Moss and Morra (2004).

There is one sentence on the McLuhan LP that is very helpful in pointing out what medium theory is about: 'Any understanding of social and cultural change is impossible without the knowledge about how media work as environments.' I take McLuhan's proposition to be profoundly true. The media are environments on a level with railways, road systems, airports and other gigantic technological infrastructures in society, although they are indeed many other things also. It is worth sticking with the material dimension, as McLuhan does when he argues that 'technological media are staples or natural resources, exactly as are coal and cotton and oil' ([1964] 1994: 21). The humans have set about refining their natural environment with electronic technologies, and are planning to live with these arrangements for a really long time. McLuhan describes what happens during such a long exposure to a technology: 'Physiologically, man in the normal use of technology (or his variously extended body) is perpetually modified by it and in turn finds ever new ways of modifying his technology' (ibid. 46). His theory acknowledges that this is a flexible relationship, but he nevertheless stresses that man is not completely in control of his technologies. He argues that 'technological environments are not merely passive containers of people but are active processes that reshape people and other technologies alike' (McLuhan [1962] 1992: i). For example, there are environmental aspects to flying across the Atlantic, and they will affect all passengers more or less equally in the long run, but the passengers are probably more concerned with the short-term effect of getting home quickly. I find it fruitful to apply this environmental theory of change on the mass media.

A medium cannot work as an environment without lots of people using the same equipment and practising the same techniques for a long time. A technology that has just left the laboratory cannot be said to work as an environment. The concept of media environment presumes industrial production of equipment in many countries and millions of people who have become accustomed to using it over a long time, perhaps during their entire life. And, most importantly, the concept of a media environment presumes that the medium quite regularly appears as a social background in people's everyday engagements.

Materiality up front

Notice how strongly my theoretical approach stresses the material dimension of the media (this perspective is inspired by Innis [1951] 1991; Winner 1986;

Ihde 1990; Gumbrecht and Pfeiffer 1994 and Mitcham 1994, among others). The media are results of scientific research under Western capitalism, and its combination of high-tech precision and desperate competition has produced great things. Most types of media equipment were first painstakingly engineered as prototypes in the secret laboratories of large corporations. The historical development of the equipment has had a direct relevance for the social history of the mass media. Many factors propel the industrial production of equipment and make sure that society becomes ever more saturated by the media. There is a regular replacement of equipment in private homes and company offices whenever a new and more efficient version has been launched on the market. Electronic stores such as PC World and Dixons are full of new equipment that promises to give the buyer improved efficiency and greater pleasure within a given context of use. In attics and museums discarded equipment piles up, for example cassette decks from the 1970s and 1980s. The wind-up gramophone has been discarded so completely that in 2008 you can really only listen to one if you go to a museum. In addition to the regular replacement of equipment there is an increase in the number of technological platforms that are used at the same time.

Not only do we regularly throw away old versions of the equipment and buy improved versions, we also possess more and more different types of equipment. This process propels the mass production of equipment and innovation in technology. When a new medium is introduced, it never really replaces an old medium but begins to exist alongside the old ones, partly replacing some functions and partly introducing completely new ones (Briggs and Burke 2002: 5). Consider that, during the period from the early 1970s until now, at least two major new technical configurations for communication have been erected: the personal computer, with broadband internet as an important feature, and mobile phone networks with text messaging of many kinds. Lab engineers have developed an endless amount of appliances and plug-ins that go along with them. Consider that before 1970 there were many mature media configurations, for example multitrack stereo music, colour television, 3D movies and voicemail for the telephone.

McLuhan postulated that the materiality of a medium has long-term effects on perception, while the content in the traditional sense is of minor importance. A medium's core characteristic is that it changes the ratio of the senses in public communication, compared to the ratio typical of previous media. After becoming prominent the medium promotes and cultivates some perceptual activities more than others, and in this indirect way it causes social change. McLuhan boldly formulates a law about the relationship between technology and communication:

> For the 'message' of any medium or technology is the change of scale or pace or pattern that it introduces into human affairs. The railway did not introduce movement or transportation or wheel or road into human

society, but it accelerated and enlarged the scale of previous human functions, creating totally new kinds of cities and new kinds of work and leisure.

(McLuhan [1964] 1994: 8)

This statement should not be rejected too hastily. Despite its deterministic ring it is a fruitful starting point for investigations of the changing relationship between humans and media. With refinements McLuhan's proposal to investigate the change of scale or pace or pattern can become a useful tool for analysing media history, as I hope to show in the empirical chapters of this book (and as I have also tried to show in Nyre 2003).

The notion of an influence from the medium *itself* has caused strong theoretical resistance towards medium theory. It seems to clash head-on with a more widespread way of theorizing the role of technologies in the media, namely the position that is often called social constructivism (see, for example, Tuchman 1978; Douglas 1987; Metz 1985; Marvin 1988; Winston 1998; and Lastra 2000). These approaches postulate social needs and aspirations as the driving force of historical development in the media. If such positions are incommensurate with mine it is not because of disputes about the historical facts, but because they do not give the material features of these historical facts sufficient attention. Carolyn Marvin has made a claim about the history of the media that I will label 'social constructivist':

Media are not fixed natural objects; they have no natural edges. They are constructed complexes of habits, beliefs, and procedures embedded in elaborate cultural codes of communication. The history of media is never more or less than the history of their uses, which always leads us away from them to the social practices and conflicts they illuminate.

(Marvin 1988: 8)

From my perspective it is hard to agree with this way of thinking. Consider the sound of Neil Armstrong's statement 'A small step for man, a giant leap for mankind', in July 1969. It was uttered in a helmet in outer space and transported back to earth at the speed of light, and then it was heard live by almost a billion people all over planet earth. The Apollo 11 broadcast goes to show that the mass media certainly have natural edges. The many technologies that made it possible for Armstrong to be heard conform to the laws of gravity, they run on electricity, they take advantage of electromagnetic radiation, and they put sensual constraints on users. It seems that the history of the mass media may just as well lead us towards these natural edges as away from them.

This book argues that a historically new form of social communication came about with microphones and loudspeakers from the late nineteenth century. There were no credible precursors to the experiences created in and around these media; there were only weak approximations such as the mechanical piano and the click of the telegraph inker. Edmund Carpenter says that each medium, if its bias is properly exploited, reveals and communicates a unique aspect of reality. Each offers a way of seeing an otherwise hidden dimension of reality. 'It's not a question of one reality being true, the others distortions. One allows us to see from here, another from there, a third from still another perspective; taken together they give us a more complete whole, a greater truth' (Carpenter [1960] 1979: 371). It is safe to say that electronic media had been 'properly exploited' when they allowed humans to study the earth from the perspective of the moon.

While a new medium certainly creates a new reality, it does so by its specific way of limiting human experience. For example, the telescope introduced the human eye to very large objects very far away, but these objects could not be heard or touched or tasted. They could only be experienced through the lens. The philosopher Don Ihde refers to this as a technology's non-neutrality. Technologies reveal and conceal, magnify and reduce, amplify and mute. Technologies transform experience, and this is an important aspect of their non-neutrality, Ihde argues (1990: 49). Again it follows that a medium is not 'constructed complexes of habits, beliefs, and procedures', as Carolyn Marvin would have us think, but rather a system of constraints on the senses that makes all messages similar in a systematic way, and leaves out other things just as systematically. An opportunity for action always carries with it constraints on action. Until replacements have been made the medium works *only like this*, and all experiences and interpretations in the culture will be framed by it for the duration. This goes to show that a medium is not a machine for transporting persuasive messages; it is a form of persuasion in its own right.

Documentary realism

It is well known that sounds, like moving images, seem to communicate more directly to our senses than written texts. There is a profound difference between experiencing the sound of a real gun at 1 metre's distance and experiencing the word 'bang' displayed on a piece of paper at 1 metre's distance. Media theorists have tried to capture the perceptual character of sound and moving images in many ways. Joshua Meyrowitz (1985: 75) argues that television involves 'an access code that is barely a code at all', and John Ellis (2000: 9) writes that radio and television present a 'quasi-physical documentation of specific moments in specific places'. I will refer to this as documentary realism, and I will demonstrate documentary realism in sound media with a detailed sound example. For classical music the recording medium has had the same communicative purpose throughout its history, namely to convey the musical performance as vibrantly and realistically as possible, and nothing else. The characteristics of this type of documentary realism come across if we compare three recordings of the same music score over a period of sixty years.

La Valse by the French composer Maurice Ravel has been interpreted and re-recorded endlessly since it was composed in 1920 (Larner 1996). It is often interpreted as a metaphor for the demise of the Austrian and German cultures that led up to World War I, embodied in the waltz. At the end the orchestra unleashes a terrifying energy that shatters the waltz and ends in an unsettling crescendo. My comparative case study comprises three different recordings representing the digital, magnetic and electric versions of the recording medium. First a 1991 recording made on DAT tape and released on CD.

Track 2: Cleveland Orchestra: La Valse, 1991 (1:13).

We hear the great musicianship with clarity because microphones are well placed to pick up the sounds from the instruments: some are placed near the instruments to pick up direct sound, others are placed in the ceiling or at the back to pick up the reverberations. The recording has a great sense of spaciousness and distinction of detail, and it is not an exaggeration to say that we can hear each musician's contribution to the whole. A number of complex skills are needed among the production staff to create this good sound, plus of course the musicians' talented efforts.

Moving twenty-one years backwards, we stop at the next version of *La Valse*, which was produced on magnetic tape and released on stereo LP in 1970. There may be a little less spaciousness and distinction of detail in this version than in the CD from 1991, but the difference is in no way substantial. They both sound very good. What should be noticed, however, is that in 1970 stereo had just become a standard feature of home equipment and the aesthetics of recording. Stereo sound greatly enhanced the sense of documentary realism, at least in classical music.

Track 3: London Symphony Orchestra: La Valse, 1970 (1:18).

The experience of stereo music was powerful and impressive *in the room*. Roland Gelatt (1977: 314–15) says that no one hearing stereo tape recordings for the first time could fail to be impressed by 'their sense of spaciousness, by the buoyant airiness and "lift" of the sound as it swirled freely around the listening room'. The listener could both locate sound sources horizontally from the left speaker to the right speaker and use the balance knob on the stereo to create a spot where the sounds from the two loudspeakers reproduced the intended acoustic architecture in a 'sweet spot' with maximum accuracy.

From 1970 we move another thirty-nine years backwards. The oldest version of *La Valse* is a mono recording, and really cannot be said to have a sweet spot at all. It was recorded and released on 78 rpm disc in 1931. At this time the audio quality was distinctly less clear and spacious than what could be created by later platforms, but this did not limit the sense of documentary authority in the recording.

Track 4: Orchestre Lamoureux: La Valse, 1931 (1:02).

The recording sounds thin and shrill compared to the two others. There is less clarity and therefore it becomes much more difficult to make out individual instruments in the mix, and there is also less spaciousness and 'lift' in the acoustics. But although the sound quality is very poor according to modern standards, this does not reduce the sense that we are hearing a live musical performance. On the contrary, any knowledge of recording practices in the 1930s will convince the listener that this recording is indeed more realistic than the others. The 1991 and 1970 recordings both sound almost clinically perfect, as if they had been modified and mixed without us being able to hear it, and without the producers informing us about it. In contrast, the 1931 version sounds truly indexical, as if there were no creative manipulations at all, only a great sluggishness in the medium that the musicians and producers managed to overcome.

These three versions of *La Valse* demonstrate a remarkable stability in the recording medium's function – namely to record music and other performances with as great a documentary authority as possible. Seemingly there is no real influence from the medium itself.

Figure 1.3 displays a model of how the recording medium works, and it is traditionally known as the linear communication model. The sounds of voices and instruments enter the medium at the microphone; the signals are recorded on tape or another storage medium; the recording is thereafter copied industrially and distributed on LP or another type of disk or file; and finally the recording is played back on a domestic record player and the sounds of voices and instruments are re-created through a loudspeaker. The notion of media neutrality has been widespread in classical music and much of journalism for the better part of a century. The truth claims of the news, the presumption that singers are authentic, and other expectations of realism rely on the idea of medium neutrality. It doesn't matter what is between the microphone and the loudspeaker, since it is in any case without substantial influence.

I consider the idea that a medium is a neutral transmission channel to be misleading. In popular music and rock there have been no ambitions of documentary realism since the 1960s, and radio reports had been edited together on tape long before that. The McLuhan LP, which was recorded at the same time as the 1970 version of *La Valse*, demonstrates this clearly. There is almost nothing in the McLuhan recording that comes from the world outside the studio and which could be represented with documentary realism (or lack of it). In the early twenty-first century it is increasingly obvious that there isn't really an indexical link back from the recording to an original event. Instead, there is a huge pile of interfaces and storage platforms and transmission platforms with a variety of different functionalities, and they are combined in different ways that vary greatly through history. How can this confusing mix best be approached?

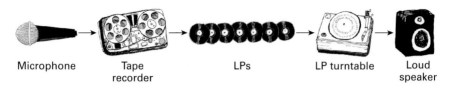

| Microphone | Tape recorder | LPs | LP turntable | Loud speaker |

Figure 1.3 Model of the 'neutral' medium.

The medium itself

The medium model in figure 1.3 is a good starting point for descriptions of different sound media, since it shows all the components that are necessary for mediation to occur. Notice, however, that each single component influences the character of communication, and when one of them is replaced a change in the perceptual conditions for the users occurs. Notice also that many more components than those displayed in figure 1.3 can be a part of the medium. Imagine drawing up the components that make up the computer, mobile telephony or satellite transmission, not to speak of hand-held devices that incorporate all three of them. Clearly, a medium is not a compact, self-contained entity, but a series of interconnected technologies where most components are regularly replaced without the basic lines of communication breaking down.

In this book I will discuss the functionalities of the history of sound media in a consistent vocabulary. A sound medium consists of *interfaces* where sound is expressed and listened to by humans, *platforms* that control, store and transmit signals to the public domain, and *signal carriers* that effect the physical transportation of the signal. The vocabulary is strongly inspired by Albert Borgmann's *Technology and the Character of Contemporary Life* (1984).

The interface is the point of contact between humans and technology (Johnson 1997: 14). It is designed specifically to be handled and related to by humans, typically with the hands, the mouth and the ears, and through visual perception. The microphone interface is crucial because it translates sound expression into signals that can thereafter be technically manipulated, and the loudspeaker is crucial because it translates signals into sounds that humans can hear. An interface is a point of simultaneous contact and division, meaning that it also makes us aware of how far away from other people we are when we communicate with them, for example, on the telephone.

A platform is a device that controls the storage and/or transmission of the signal. When, for example, an AM radio signal has been broadcast it can be received by all devices that contain a reception platform for AM radio signals. The platform is the publishing and distribution component of a medium, and it depends on the interfaces for something to publish and the signal carriers for efficient transport of the product. At the producing and receiving end there may be different but compatible platforms, so that a conversion process is necessary. This was the case in the 1960s, when pop music was produced on magnetic tape but distributed and enjoyed on stereo LPs. Notice also that a medium may consist of a whole series of interconnected platforms. The internet could be said to be a platform for websites, but in any case it relies on the computer platform for domestic access and the telephone platform for online connection. It could furthermore be argued that every piece of software on the internet that can distribute messages systematically is a platform – such as podcasting, web radio and file sharing.

The signal carrier facilitates the actual contact between separate but compatible platforms, and this involves transportation of the signal across large geographical distances as well as over a long historical period. The carrier contains analogues of sound events in a material form that is suitable for mass distribution. The signal can be carried 1) through the air by electromagnetic waves; 2) through landline wires strung between houses and offices; or 3) on a revolving disc or other tangible container. The signal carrier is by definition transportable, and in the case of radio transmission it moves at the speed of light.

Finally, I will comment on what could be called *the machinery*. The interfaces, platforms and signal carriers obviously rely on electrical power, and this comes from batteries or mains electricity. Electricity powers the tube or transistor amplifiers, the computer disc drives, the microphone and loudspeaker diaphragms and all the other electronic equipment. The machinery drives the equipment in a stable and inconspicuous way because the functions that demand manual labour and attention have been automated. The machinery's delicate movements are protected behind metal or plastic covers, and this process is often called 'blackboxing'. Although I do not analyse the machinery in any systematic fashion, it is absolutely crucial to modern media. Just imagine the severe disruption of the media environment that occurs during a power cut.

3 BACKWARDS HISTORY

It is time for a proper introduction to the historical perspective of this book. Medium theory presumes that the emergence and improvement of the media occur in history – that is, in a complex interconnection with all kinds of human endeavour, ranging from the trivialities of life without tap water to the political revolutions of the two world wars.

Media behaviour must be thought of as historically contingent; it is taught, conserved and translated inside a given technological system, and will die out if the equipment is removed or if better and more efficient techniques are introduced. Jonathan Sterne (2003: 2) describes the slow process: 'It is not that people woke up one day and found everything suddenly different. Changes in sound, listening, and hearing happened bit by bit, place by place, practice by practice, over a long period of time.' This book traces the emergence and disappearance of these cultural techniques in different sound media (Gentikow 2007).

Sound media form a global, modern phenomenon, one that is obviously very complex. The main purpose of the backwards history approach is to separate and identify all the cultural techniques in a systematic fashion. The complexity of the issue is unnerving. Each mass medium is made with different user interfaces and different cultural purposes in different countries, historical periods and social groups; and the process has been going on for at least 4,000 years. Faced with this great panorama, medium theorists study the media according to their material differences from one another (Schudson 1991; Zielinski 2006).

McLuhan, in *Understanding Media* ([1964] 1994), devotes one chapter each to several dozen media (including roads, weapons and other technologies that would not normally be labelled media), and he tries to explain how they are different from each other in sensory and functional ways. He is very sensitive to cultural meanings rooted in the specific ways in which a technology is designed and used. Friedrich Kittler writes about *Gramophone, Film, Typewriter* (1999), and Walter Ong writes about *Orality and Literacy* (1982) with much the same presumptions. Brian Winston's *Messages* (2005) also separates the mass media from each other in a systematic fashion, and describes them from the introduction of the printing presses in the 1450s into our own time. My book essentially describes two media, namely recording media and live media. The telephone is an important backdrop, as is the internet, the television, sound film and books, but none of these other media will be analysed with the same level of detail.

My backwards narrative of individual sound media has two dimensions: the composition of the medium at a given historical time, which will be displayed in medium models and timelines, and the chronological changes from one stable state of things to another, which comes across when the models and timelines from different chapters are compared.

The term 'break boundary' clarifies both these dimensions, and makes them applicable to systematic narration (Blondheim 2003: 179). Firstly, there are break boundaries between the characteristics of media existing at the same time, for example between newspapers, film, music recording, radio, television and the internet in our time. This is the synchronous dimension. Secondly, a medium exists in a definite historical period that comes after its invention and lasts until it has become obsolete. This is the diachronic dimension, and from this perspective one can describe break boundaries between the different historical phases of a medium's development, as well as the boundaries towards other media developments that may influence its course. My narrative has a well-delineated historical span which simply goes back to the invention of the first sound media in the 1870s.

Figure 1.4 is a timeline of all the live sound media that will be analysed in this book (in the black rows). Notice that the newest media come at the top and the oldest at the bottom. Below the timeline I have located other important electronic media that are part of the contemporary setting – in this case telegraphy and television, which are also live media. The live storyline goes back to

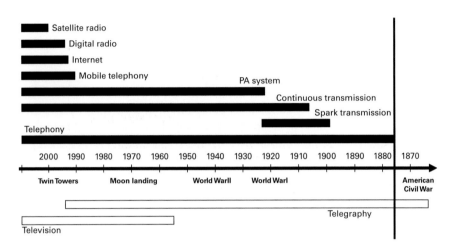

Figure 1.4 Timeline of live sound media.

Alexander Graham Bell's invention from 1876. It is important to note that private telephony and internet media are also live, although that is not how they are commonly presented. The figure helps us to notice that a new live medium does not make the others obsolete – except for Marconi's ur-technology, which I will describe in chapter 10. There is a noticeable accumulation of different live media as history progresses.

Figure 1.5 is a timeline of all the recording media that will be analysed in this book. The storyline goes back to the start of recorded sound, with Thomas Edison's invention from 1877. Looking back, four basic platforms can be found building on each other: computer sound, magnetic sound, electric sound and acoustic sound. It is noticeable how quickly the platforms replace each other; and it is clear that the platforms have a tendency to make each other obsolete, which is a quite different structure of development from live media. Below the timeline I have identified sound film, television programmes and music videos, which are all highly influential audiovisual recording media.

When going backwards, it is soon revealed that people who live now possess many technologies that previous generations did not have, but that our technologies are nevertheless to a large extent built on theirs. Backwards storytelling tries to untangle these dependencies in a systematic fashion, and in this sense it resembles archaeology. In fact all historical research can be thought of as a kind of archaeology. The researcher begins every investigation in the present and digs their way layer by layer into the past. But when the digging is over the researcher will most often turn this process on its head, and let it start in the distant past and narrate it towards their own time.

However, by starting the narrative in the present and progressing towards the past I write a history of disappearance. The further back we go in history, the

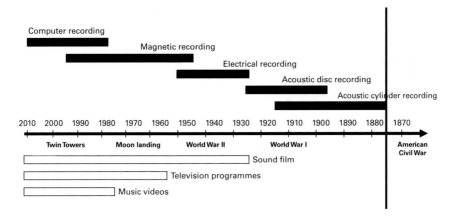

Figure 1.5 Timeline of recorded sound media.

fewer of the techniques are widespread. The number of people who regularly handled a computer to log into the internet in the 2000s could be measured in the billions, but if we go back to the 1960s the number of people using a computer could be counted only in the dozens. The infrastructure of television in the USA in the 2000s is enormous, but in the 1930s television was found only in a few laboratories in Berlin, London and New York, and there were no cultural techniques associated with it.

The further back we go, the fewer are the countries and cities in which the medium is located. And the further back we go, the more manual are the processes of mass communication, because the functionalities have not yet been protected in automatized systems. The timelines and medium models are drawn up to aid in this backwards history telling. In different ways they demonstrate how the technological configuration gets smaller and less complex until there is really nothing left to analyse.

4 AUDITORY RHETORIC

This book is a long series of studies in auditory rhetoric, and here I will clarify the method involved. Rhetoric is often called the *art of persuasion*, that is, the art of attempting to convince people to think or act in ways that suit the speaker's interests. A famous example is when Cicero was consul of Rome, in 63 BC, and he denounced Catiline as a dangerous enemy of the Roman republic. Greatly aided by his oratorical powers, Cicero managed to get Cataline sentenced to death and himself praised as a true republican (Fafner 1982: 79).

This high-stakes political rhetoric is dangerous for those involved, but there are fewer dramatic rhetorical situations in everyday life. In the 1940s the literary theorist Kenneth Burke changed the emphasis in a direction that suits the communication in sound media perfectly. Instead of being concerned with deliberation in an explicit sense, he deals with 'an intermediate area of expression that is not wholly deliberate, yet not wholly unconscious. It lies midway between aimless utterance and speech directly purposive' (Burke [1950] 1969: xiii). He refers to it as the rhetoric of identification. It is an attraction towards other persons and groups, and it is of vital importance for public life. Burke mentions the rhetoric of courtship as a case of such semi-conscious rhetoric in everyday life, but street concerts and political speeches rely on it too. In his perspective, rhetoric is the act of appealing for identification with a person or a group on the grounds of a claim or an idea (ibid.: 21).

The nature of rhetoric is well described by Lloyd Bitzer, who writes that 'rhetorical discourse comes into existence as a response to a situation, in the same sense that an answer comes into existence in response to a question, or a solution in response to a problem' ([1968] 1991: 9–10). 'Kairos' is an ancient term referring to this response, and it describes the happy situations where a speaker says exactly the right words at the right time, or the year when exactly the right pop sounds dominated during the summer. The competence needed by the producer is to be able to give a 'fitting response to a situation which needs and invites it' (ibid.: 10). My approach to rhetoric relies on Burke's and Bitzer's definitions, which I believe are well suited to the manifold techniques of the sound media, but it does not incorporate the vocabulary of the rhetorical tradition in a strict sense (see, for example, Foss 1996; Brummett 1991).

Auditory rhetoric consists of appealing to the public ear, making the best out of every microphone event, encouraging the studio staff to be creative, securing a big budget for the production, and gaining access to the best possible equipment. Based on these resources the producers manipulate acoustic spaces, time chronologies and voices to create experiences for people. A list of the stakeholders would include radio stations, record companies, electronics companies, celebrities, politicians, journalists, musicians and technicians. I will point out three strategies that resonate with the existential characteristics of communication defined earlier in this chapter:

- acoustic architecture
- time effects
- persuasion in person.

I presume that basically sound media communicate through all manner of moods, but mostly through inviting, pleasing and attractive ones. Paddy Scannell (1996: 88) argues that the moods are public in character, and disclose a climate of feelings, opinions and attitudes. The moods are made to fit into the individual's domestic setting. 'When I turn on the TV set I am "in the mood" for watching or listening', Scannell says. 'I am in the mood for a bit of entertainment, or relaxation or for finding out about what's going on in the world, or even just for having the telly on as a bit of company' (1998: 22). The dimension of mood makes up the primary social link between listeners and producers – in journalism by telling credible stories about reality, in music recording by playing enjoyable music. Consequently, the creation and maintenance of audience moods must be considered the primary task in radio and recording. These deliberate moods must be studied as the outcome of a historical process where journalism and music have continually adapted to the national and global conditions.

Acoustic architecture

Grandeur matters just as much now as it did in the time of Louis XIV at his Versailles palace. Locales are built with the skills of architects and decorators, to impress people, to make them feel at home. Architecture is about designing buildings and structures, and often also the design of the total built environment, such as town planning, urban design and landscape architecture (Carter 1995). It can be attuned to many different types of sociability among people, from the massive authority of the Pentagon in Washington to the serenity of an ancient Greek temple. And of course well-organized locales are just as important in radio, recorded music, film and television, although the techniques of construction are quite different (Connell and Gibson 2003; Blesser and Salter 2007).

Sound media rely on public acoustics, and this acoustics has been made in order that thousands and millions of people can listen to it in their domestic settings. Producers design the acoustic properties of their products in a very careful fashion, and this can be called the acoustic architecture of sound media. Ross Snyder ([1966] 1979: 350) thinks of the producers in broadcasting as architects of a spatial habitat 'in which contemporary man will live and move and have his being'. We no longer read about the larger world of history and politics only in textbooks, he says; rather, 'we are present in it' (ibid.: 353). Tony Schwartz (1974) claims that radio and television communicate by 'resonating' inside people's homes and in their social surroundings. When you walk though the city you will encounter many different media sounds; they resonate from a shop, a passing car, or from a window on the fourth floor of a building in a side street.

The production acoustics is created with a combination of two techniques that are quite particular to audiovisual media. The first technique is called *microphone placement*. It is of great importance how near or far away from the sound source the microphone is located. Edward Hall (1969) identified four spatial zones around the individual's body that carry different communicative implications. Social distance is so short that the interlocutors almost touch each other's lips; personal distance is an arm's length or two; social distance is across the room or round a table at a café; while public distance is across an auditorium, a concert hall or a town square. These distances can easily be replicated in the sound media, and they give much the same social impression that Hall stipulated for natural surroundings (Meyrowitz 1979: 58). The second technique is called *volume control*. Producers can adjust the volume and pitch of everything they record and transmit, and they can mix the sound so that all sources are blended to be just right for the purpose. Arnt Maasø (2002) describes how the Norwegian TV2 made a promo where soft female whispering is mixed very loud. It creates a strangely attractive address with a volume typical of an important public message and the distance of a very intimate relationship. The two techniques of microphone placement and volume control are crucial to at least eight types of production acoustics:

- voice acoustics
- inaudible studio acoustics
- resounding studio acoustics
- multitrack acoustics
- synthetic acoustics
- telephone acoustics
- outdoors acoustics
- equipment acoustics.

Sound events can be produced in *voice acoustics*. A high-quality microphone picks up a voice in a sound-proof studio. There is only one source of sound in a highly controlled space and, depending on the performance, the address can feel very intimate (a whisper), personal (a soft pleading tone of voice) or social (lively shouting). This acoustics is only used in broadcast journalism, and not in music production.

Sound events can be produced in *inaudible studio acoustics*. Several microphones are rigged to pick up several sound sources in a controlled studio environment. It can be a series of musical instruments for a music recording or several speakers for a journalistic programme. There is little sense of an identifiable locale, although the room's resonance may sometimes be mixed to create the feeling of a warm room, a large room, etc. All the sound sources are well shielded from each other, and are also fed separately into the mix.

Sound events can be produced in *resounding studio acoustics*. Several microphones are rigged in a large studio, and the performance takes place in front of a live audience. The event is arranged and mixed to balance the performers and the audience reactions, and also to convey the size of the hall and its atmospherics. Notice that this is nevertheless a very controlled environment, where producers also supervise the behaviour of the live audience. These events are typically marked by social or public distance.

Sound events can be produced in *multitrack acoustics*, which did not exist before the 1960s. Many recordings are edited together in an audible way. The producer can make use of sounds recorded especially for a session or select suitable archive sounds. Montage techniques are commonly exploited in this acoustics, and the producer can make the acoustic signature change all the time, jumping for example from the voice alone, to parliament, to the studio sound of the Eagles. A two-minute recording may have dozens, even hundreds, of different elements, each implying their own acoustics. Multitrack acoustics can be brutal for dramatic effect or gentle for emotional effect.

Sound events can be produced in *synthetic acoustics*. The most radical version is where no microphones are used, and music is created with MIDI programming. There may be an ice-cold metallic sound that does not resonate with any known space outside the medium.

Sound events can be produced in *telephone acoustics*. Telephone acoustics imitates or simply channels sounds of mouthpieces of telephones. There are often technical noises that disturb communication, and the frequency range is limited to just about the range of the human voice. However, there is very little complaining about the poor sound of telephones on radio, probably because we are all so used to this soundscape from our private lives that we recognize it as familiar.

Sound events can be produced in *outdoors acoustics*. One or more microphones are used to capture events in their natural surroundings. There will typically be several controlled sound sources, such as a reporter and some interviewees, but there will always be uncontrollable events in addition, for example heavy traffic or a crowded swimming pool, and these events are integral to outdoors acoustics. The events that are mediated can be planned or spurious, and they can take place in private or public settings. This acoustics is frequently used in broadcast journalism, but not in music production except for concert albums. In Hall's terms, outdoors acoustics typically has social or public distance.

Finally, sound events can take place in *equipment acoustics*. The equipment itself makes sounds that can be very telling of how well or bad the equipment works. There are, for example, interruptions, static, hiss, pop and crackle. Equipment acoustics is essentially the sounds of resistance to mediation, and they can be stressful for the producers and listeners alike.

Reception environments

Earlier I stated that the acoustic space of sound media is double – that is, it is presented from loudspeakers in a domestic setting. The listeners experience this in a range of lifeworld settings that they can, to a large extent, organize as they wish. In parallel to the craft of the producers, listeners learn two basic techniques that affect the sound: loudspeaker placement and volume control. The listeners decide in which directions the sounds will go, and can for example organize a sweet spot for their stereo system or 5.1 surround sound. Regarding volume control, the listeners can adjust the volume of the sound to suit the situation – for example by turning up the volume in a noisy environment or turning it down if they are tired and edgy. The two techniques of loudspeaker placement and volume control are used to project sound into all the regions of everyday life. Most people in Western countries are likely to be familiar with these five reception environments:

- the home
- the car
- earphones
- public arenas
- outdoors.

The *home environment* is stationary, and the radios and stereo set typically have set positions in the kitchen, the bathroom, the bedroom, the living room, and so on. The rest of the family is never far away in the home environment, and most of us can relate to the constant negotiation among family members about what should be on: the TV or the radio, rock music or hip-hop, loud music or quiet music, and so on (Morley 2000).

The *car environment* is portable, and the stereo, radio and loudspeakers are built into the interior of the vehicle. It is a small enclosure with very little resonance, but speakers are custom made and there can be fabulous fidelity in a well-equipped car. The driver typically decides what will be played, and also controls the volume, and passengers with a preference have to negotiate with the driver (Bull 2003).

The *earphone environment* is wearable, and this means that it can follow the individual wherever he goes (Bull 2000). Notice that there is a distinction between earphones and headphones. While earphones are inserted into the ear cavities, headphones only cover the outside of the ears. The latter have been in use throughout history, while earphones were introduced in the 1980s. The earphone environment can be fully controlled by the individual, who can start and stop and adjust the volume entirely to his own liking.

The *public arena environment* is an umbrella term that covers all kinds of organized settings for sound reproduction, such as cafés, restaurants, pubs, clubs, sports arenas and shops. The listener can influence the volume only by leaving the place.

The outdoors environment is also an umbrella term, and it points to a range of ways in which sound can be radiated into the surroundings without prior agreement. Teenagers play basketball in a back alley and a boom box blasts out hip-hop music, or a crew of carpenters listens to Kiss FM at the work grounds. There are two positions towards outdoors sound: that of the people who control the sound and those who are exposed to it. The people who get exposed have little control over the volume, except by confrontation. They may not even be in a position to leave (if the noise is on their street), and may in the worst case feel threatened.

Time effects

The temporal characteristics of radio and recording are simple, as I have explained. Radio is fundamentally an ephemeral medium, and programmes are mostly heard only once, with a steady flow of new instalments. Another way of saying this is that live media present events in real time instead of recording them for later publication. Recording media repeat already completed events, a long or a short time after they have happened, and typically with heavy editing in between (Wurtzler 1992; Auslander 1999).

Regardless of the difference between live media and recording media, their presentations are very often felt to be live (except for those made with multi-track acoustics), and this effect comes about because listeners are prone to conceive of human sounds as taking place in some kind of simultaneous presence (Ellis 2000; Scannell 1996). This perceptual tendency is inherited from face-to-face situations, and it can be called the liveness effect of sound media. It is actually not very puzzling that we can hear Winston Churchill as a living person long after he is dead, because this is how we always hear human sounds. This liveness effect is an important part of media soundscapes, and it has been exploited strategically from day one.

I have a systematic focus on the material features of time experience in the media, and this can be distinguished from the ideological approach. Nick Couldry (2004: 356) argues that liveness is not a natural category but a constructed term. It is 'a category whose use naturalizes the general idea that, through the media, we achieve a shared attention to the "realities" that matter for us as a society' (see also Feuer 1983). I agree with both of them that the public sense of time is laboriously constructed, but there are limits to which aspects of temporal experience can be constructed. An LP can never be live in the way a news bulletin is, and a news bulletin can never be recorded like an LP. This distinction has far-reaching consequences and leads me to treat live media separately from recording media throughout the book, while the ideological concept of 'liveness' is less important to my argument.

First, I will describe the temporal character of the recording media. According to my analytical method, recorded sound can be arranged in two basic ways:

- live-on-tape (pre-production)
- edit-on-tape (post-production).

A performance can be recorded from start to finish without any interruptions, and this is often called live-on-tape recording. I have already presented this technique, which can also be called pre-production, in detail in relation to the three versions of Ravel's *La Valse*. Microphones send the signal directly to a disc (or a broadcasting transmission station), and there is no editing of the signal on the way. The producer can only start and then stop the recording. Everything about the performance must therefore have been planned and rehearsed in advance, and the musicians would do new takes until everyone was satisfied. In a very long period from the 1870s to the 1930s, because of the limitations of the gramophone disc, this was the only way producers could publicize sound. The technique of pre-production is now more or less outdated because of tape and computer editing.

In strong contrast to live-on-tape, there is edit-on-tape recording. Here the technique can also be called post-production (Moylan 1992). In a studio environment the producer selects partial performances from many different times and localities and creates a carefully dramatized entity. The finished product is often called a master, and it can be a music recording for LP or CD, or a programme for radio or some other publication platform. There are great variations in complexity, for example, between the hundreds of edits and overdubs in the McLuhan track and the relatively few edits in a reportage for a news bulletin. Indeed, it is possible to use the resources of post-production to make a record that sounds completely untouched, so that most people would believe it was pre-produced. This strategy is called continuity recording, and will be discussed in chapter 7.

Moving on to a discussion of the temporal character of live media, I will stick rather closely to journalism in radio (and television), but notice that the telephone and the internet are also live media. Anyhow, radio and television are live at the point of transmission (Ellis 2000: 31; Hendy 2000: 120), and this means that the programme can always be interrupted with a message if, for example, there is a terrorist attack in a city. The main purpose of journalistic techniques is to present the country or city's organized life as it progresses through the day, every day. If recorded sound relates to an inner, imaginative time, then live sound relates to the outer, directly shared time.

Think about the dramatic hours on the morning of September 11, 2001, American time, to which I will return in chapter 4. Imagine that you live in New York City and, as the reporter describes the first of the twin towers falling down, you too can actually see it falling, from your penthouse window. This would be a strong case of real-time mediation. John Ellis makes the fundamental point: 'Transmission is live, even when the programmes are not' (2000: 31). There are at least four basic ways of experiencing real time through electronic media, and they are all raw materials for liveness effects:

- station flow
- live programmes
- being on the internet
- speaking on the phone.

All stations have a continuous organized flow of sound elements. There are typically news updates at the top of the hour, and jingles, promos, advertisements and all kinds of pre-recorded programmes inserted at various times. Recorded programmes can be inserted in the station's live flow, and 'are able to claim the status of liveness for themselves simply because the act of transmission attaches them to a particular moment' (ibid.). The flow can be more or less automated, and it will typically be organized according to the time of day. In the morning the pace and intensity of music and speech is different from shows that are aired in the afternoon or during night-time.

In live programmes the main events obviously progress in real time, with the responses of speakers and other attendants being audible and taking place in human time. There are few or no recorded elements, except for some that are quite audibly recorded. Examples can again be jingles, promos and advertisements, which very few people would mistake for live programming. Over time several genres have developed, mainly live outside reports, for example from a dramatic accident, and live studio shows with guests and telephone conversations and quizzes. There are also specially staged media events, such as sports events, royal weddings or big political rallies (Dayan and Katz 1992). The most spectacular type of live programme is the unexpected event which gets relayed in the form of breaking news.

When people are logged on to the internet they engage in a live communication activity, although often it does not feel especially live. Being on the internet is basically a private activity. People are connected at their own leisure, for a short or long period governed by themselves, and they can download and upload all kinds of information during the session. With broadband it has become more and more common to be constantly online, so that the hook-up feels less live than during the more precarious modem age. Notice that people can contact radio and television stations when they are online, especially through email and posts at chat rooms associated with stations. This is an ever-growing resource for public life.

When people speak on the telephone they obviously engage in a live communication activity. The speakers will never hear their conversations again (unless they are under surveillance, and end up hearing them again as evidence in court). Phone conversations enter into the ongoing flow of life, and skilled phone callers know how to talk to the right people at the right time of day. We all know that we should call our business partners in the daytime and friends and family in the evening, and nobody at all in the middle of the night unless there is an emergency. Regarding the character of telephony, the only exception to live exchanges are the pre-recorded answering machine messages, which nobody would mistake for a live conversation (except if they are intentionally made to confuse people). Notice that live telephone calls are an important resource for talk radio, and people can also use the mobile phone to send a short text message (SMS) to a quiz show or other programme (see chapter 5).

These real-time experiences have something that a record album lacks entirely, namely the special allure of feeling that what you are hearing is actually happening right now. Gary Gumpert (1979: 294) argues that, when the listener knows that something is live, there is an implicit belief that they can influence the future outcome by participation. He describes how the sports fan yells, perhaps pounds the table or strokes his lucky charm, in an effort to make his team score a goal. In a similar vein Shingler and Wieringa (1998: 106) write, 'A listener tuning into a live broadcast can feel that they too are part of the process of "life", that they are part of history *as* it is being made, rather than being consumers of the past.' Although we cannot be absolutely certain that we hear a live event, we all nevertheless think of it as outer time, real time. The listener wants to feel 'the aura of uncertainty in which he can cast his evil spell, dispense a blessing, or merely hope' (Gumpert 1979: 294).

Persuasion in person

Electronic media have a bias towards the personal and private, the welcoming voices, cosiness and fun (see, for example, Langer 1981; Johansen 1999). Listeners can forgive and forget almost anything if they are emotionally attached to the performers. For musicians and journalists alike it is crucial to know how to present oneself in an appealing context. Indeed, personal credibility, or 'cred', is one of the greatest values of the mass media. Think of the PR strategies that brand a new folk artist as 'authentic' or the glamorous life that many celebrities stage for themselves in order to get press coverage. The techniques in question here are largely intuitive strategies for making listeners feel a certain connection, of giving credibility to oneself in the media setting. It could be called persuasion in person, and it is a craft that has been studied under many names both inside and outside the media (for example, Goffman [1959] 1990; Schutz 1970; Sennett [1974] 1988).

Programmes and recordings alike require careful planning and execution. This is to say that sound media rely heavily on scripts and rehearsals of the different elements in those scripts (Ytreberg 2002, 2004). A script can be of many types, for example a poem to be read out, the piano notation of a melody, or the wording of a news bulletin. The performers' behaviour can be analysed on a continuum ranging from completely script-based to completely improvised performance. The script is a way to control what gets recorded or what gets on air. Erving Goffman points out that the notion of 'speaker' is often discussed in a confused manner, and he presents a threefold definition of its intentionality structures. Speaker means *animator* – the sounding body from which utterances come. It means *author* – the agent who puts together, composes or scripts the lines that are uttered. And it means *principal* – the party to whose position, stand and belief the words attest (Goffman 1981: 226). Based on these distinctions I have identified four inflections of personality that will be used prolifically in the analyses of later chapters:

- reciting speech and song
- eyewitnessing
- role play
- projecting your personality.

Firstly, there is the technique called *reciting from a script or score*. In this type of address the speaker functions as a skilful animator of a script. In radio this strategy was inspired by the public authority of newspapers and telegraphy, and radio journalists tried to create an auditory version of this by speaking in a neutral and solemn tone of voice. Individual characteristics of the speaker, such as sex, age, dialect and voice timbre, are therefore suppressed, and supposed to be without importance. This script-driven address may easily be submitted to prior censorship. Although the message should be vivid and lively, there should be as few traces of the speaker's personality as possible. It should be possible to replace one actor with another without communication being affected by the replacement. This technique is used by singers and journalists alike. The good reader is relaxed, has forgotten about the microphone, and knows how to imagine the audience as a single person. In journalism the author of the script is often the person who reads it, and they have written the script in the way they like to read it. But in music and theatre the author is typically somebody else, for example a composer, a writer, a poet. In journalism the reader often has a strong ethos, for example, being recognized as a journalist with a good reputation. There are many ways of infusing the reading style with authority. For example, educational programs address listeners in an authoritative way, and the sound of the address *as such* implies that the speaker is an expert in a field, and that they have all the personal credibility and scholarly integrity needed for listeners to trust them.

Secondly, there is the technique called *eye witnessing*. The speaker is or has been present at the scene of some important event, and the listeners are presumed to acknowledge the speaker's presence there. The eyewitness describes the event as best they can, and the public expects a realistic description. Very often eyewitnessing is live at the scene, and in these cases the words have to be improvised. Only other persons who were present at the event could replace the current speaker. When someone witnesses and recounts an event it is in a sense the event itself that speaks. It demands a realistic description of its properties, and the speaker is in what Erving Goffman (1981: 233) calls a 'slave relation' to it. However, to witness something has two faces: the passive one of *seeing* and the active one of *saying*. Witnessing in the rhetorical sense is therefore 'the discursive act of stating one's experience for the benefit of an audience that was not present at the event and yet must make some kind of judgment about it. Witnesses serve as the surrogate sense-organs of the absent' (Peters 2001: 709). Remember that the listener is in no position to challenge the truth claim since they are not present at the scene, and they are likely to trust it. This technique is used only in journalism, and not in music.

Thirdly, there is the technique called *role play*. In this type of address the speaker plays a role that the listeners are supposed to recognize as unique. The performer pretends to be a character that is described in a score, a fictional play, a radio script or an ad-libbed situation. The interpretation of the role is crucial, and the character of Hamlet has been presented in as many shades as there are actors who have played him. Role play often implies quite strong emotional display, and the behaviour is more lively and exaggerated than in other genres. This is demonstrated, for example, in a stand-up show or talk show. In Goffman's scheme the speaker is an animator only, and most often the author is another person – a long dead composer, etc. Role play relieves the performer from any expectation of trust-worthiness, since everybody knows that an author or composer put the words in the speaker's mouth. But there is indeed something about the individual performer's unique existence that plays a part in the experience of credibility. There are many borderline cases between role play and being oneself.

Lastly, there is the technique called *projecting your personality*. Politicians, celebrities and journalists have engaged in this technique for a hundred years, and it is intimately related to the presence of the microphone. First I will point out that all humans of course project their personalities in everyday life; we do it in tactical and spontaneous ways, on the phone or face to face. But this is not what I am referring to here. When people project their personality in public there is a necessary awareness of the way in which they comport themselves – a kind of meta-consciousness that is not as noticeable in completely private settings. As I have suggested, there is a sliding scale here, from a weather forecaster reciting in a mechanical voice to the celebrity who suffers a psychological breakdown on prime-time television (Tolson 2006; Salamensky 2001).

The intended effect of the technique I call 'projecting your personality' is to come across as honest and unaffected, although this effect can be difficult to achieve. Emotional qualities such as charisma, charm and character are the main communicative tools. The speaker tries to come across as a unique individual, so that nobody else could replace them. A side effect of this impression is that listeners can also hold the speaker personally responsible for their words and actions, since, unlike the weather forecaster, they presume to be speaking only in the capacity of being themselves. They can rightfully be blamed or credited for all aspects of their presentation. This technique is used by singers and journalists alike, but it is most common in journalistic settings. In Goffman's scheme the projection of personality implies that the speaker incorporates the three functions of animator, author and principal.

At the end of the chapter I will briefly reconnect the lines of investigation that this book is built on. As I have already mentioned, my theory of sound media has four dimensions: 1) a description of sound and listening; 2) a theory of what a medium is; 3) a method for a backwards history of media; and 4) a method for rhetorical analysis of journalism and music. These methods will now be applied to cover the sound media in Europe and the USA for 130 years. From this detached perspective I hope to show that the media are a joint venture of electro-mechanical resources and human creativity. As a hint about the balance of forces in this venture I will quote McLuhan again: 'All media work us over completely. They are so pervasive in their personal, political, economic, aesthetic, psychological, moral, ethical and social consequences, that they leave no part of us untouched, unaffected, unaltered. The medium is the massage.'

Part 1

The present time

Chapter 2

The acoustic computer
Nervous experiments with sound media

The computer has rich opportunities for experiments in journalism and music, and my history must begin here. It is truly interesting that much of this experimentation takes place among ordinary people, at their home computer. Innovation takes place not just in the celebrated media companies such as the BBC, and not just in the laboratories of global corporations such as Microsoft, IBM or Xerox.

I have selected some of the innovations that have been made in sound media due to the computer, and will analyse them in detail. All the examples were found on the internet, through a process of browsing and searching. There is a vocal outburst from a Tasmanian headphone user on YouTube in 2007, there is a little song from a group called God vs. the Internet, which was issued on the music-publishing site Acidplanet.com in 2005, there is a professional radio reportage from bbc.co.uk in 2004, and finally there is a podcast from the US media site This Week in Tech in 2006. But first I will lay out the technological background in some detail.

The multimedia landscape

Already in the 1970s the computer was so central to Western societies that the notion of the information society had taken hold in public (Briggs and Burke 2002: 260). Alongside the computer the internet emerged as a military communication structure built to withstand a nuclear attack from the Soviet Union, but it was not taken up by the general public in the same way as the PC. The internet was really introduced to the public only in 1993, with the emergence of the world wide web (Gauntlett 2000; Miller and Slater 2000; Herman and Swiss 2000). The combination of the computer and the internet introduced an entirely new communication infrastructure into people's lives.

The internet is a multimedium. It is a collection of cultural achievements that constantly mix with new interfaces. Among the old media that the internet emulates are letters in the post (email), the typewriter (word processing), newspapers (online newspapers), radio (web radio), television (web TV) and file cabinets, not to speak of all the commercial industries that established a strategic presence on the internet during the 1990s, and thereby created the online bookshop, the online library, and so on. This diagnosis is well known, and the process has been described as 'remediation' (Bolter and Grusin 1999), 'parasitic media' (Williams [1975] 1990) and 'rear-view mirrorism' (McLuhan [1964] 1994). Even now, thirty years after the personal computer was introduced and fifteen years after the world wide web became commonplace, the parasitic development of new media continues.

As I stated above, my analysis relates quite particularly to internet experiments among ordinary people. An example can be the uploading of private photographs to Flickr, where people have found the strangest new ways of organizing and presenting photographs to each other. Indeed, a fair number among the population in Western countries are regularly trying out ways of using computer interfaces and software, at night, after work and during the weekends (Rheingold 2002; Manovich 2001; Turkle 1997). And it is not even necessary to know machine language to do so, because software nowadays always has a user-friendly interface where all functions are explained and can accommodate your preferred combinations. There is a solid dose of entrepreneurship lurking in the domestic sphere, and there is a genuine desire to contribute to the better functionality and more meaningful content on the internet (Delys and Foley 2006; Nyre 2007a). If you are clever you can even invent a new killer application, as American teenagers did with Google and Napster.

Domestic life also has much else to offer in the way of mass media. For relaxation, the average Western household has flat-screen TV, perhaps also a surround-sound system, not to forget the good old stereo set. These media are all immersive; the users lie back in their easy chair and surround themselves with the sounds and images. People also have portable equipment for media consumption, such as the car stereo and radio, and wearable equipment such as the iPod or Walkman. The strange acoustic space of the mobile phone is also relatively new. All these media create what Todd Gitlin calls a 'torrent of images and sounds that overwhelms our lives' (Gitlin 2002).

Figure 2.1 shows the audio platforms that I will discuss in this chapter (see also Nyre and Ala-Fossi 2008). Notice that the newest technologies are at the top. Below the line are the two important communication technologies on which the five sound platforms are built – namely the personal computer and the world wide web. It is easy to see that all the developments in question are quite recent, since none of the interfaces for sound on the internet were developed until the early 1990s.

The late arrival of sound on the computer implies that the sound interfaces are anchored in the graphical user interface on the screen and the hand–finger interfaces on keyboards and mice. It is impossible to locate a sound file and play it on the computer without using these basic interfaces. In the future it seems that sound will invariably be embedded in a textual–graphical–visual mix.

User-publishing sites, the newest platform on the list, are a splendid example of the textual–graphical–visual mix. The system is for videos, but it relies strongly

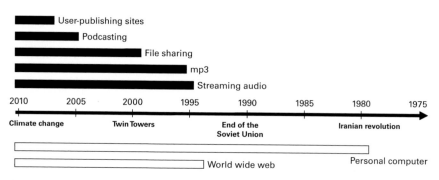

Figure 2.1 Timeline of computer sound.

on sound communication in the form of music and speech, and also on graphics, flash animations and written text. YouTube had its breakthrough in 2006, just a year after podcasting had been the new and hot platform. In the early 2000s the portable iPod and mp3 player were introduced, and people's use of computerized sound soared. The mp3 format had been introduced in the 1990s, before file sharing and portable players, and people could start copying their LPs and CD's to the computer and manage their music collection entirely on this new platform. The first commercially viable platform for sound on the internet was streaming audio, from the early 1990s, and it led traditional FM and AM stations to start streaming their station flow on the web (Simpson 1998).

Making contact with the public

From the 1980s to the late 1990s people in the Western world used modems to connect from their home computers to the internet. After they had turned on the computer, they would painstakingly log on to the internet by calling up the internet service provider (ISP) on a phone number. Now, with broadband connection, the computer is automatically logged onto the internet. But in order to emphasize the live character of the internet, the modem hook-up is a good place to start. The modem hook-up has an acoustics of its own, the strange beeping and whining noises while the modem is trying to synchronize the contact and bring people online. You can hear what it sounds like on track 5.

Track 5: Modem Sounds (0:27).

This is a good example of what I call equipment acoustics. The sound does not have an explicit purpose, but it nevertheless means a lot. It resembles computer game sound, and it also resembles punching the dials of the telephone and waiting for the connection. We can imagine the absolutely live transmission at the speed of light – 300,000 kilometres per second. The modem sounds have a crucial function but no cultural meaning, while techno sounds by artists such as Kraftwerk and Autechre are equally technological on the surface, but have both melody and rhythm, and are rich in cultural meaning.

John Naughton (1999: 16) argues that the wire snaking out of the back of the machine to the modem has changed computing beyond recognition, because it has transformed the computer into a communicating device. The modem makes it possible for the user to hook up with the public in a broad sense. Remembering that the internet consists entirely of modem and broadband connections, it is clear that these connections make the computer into a live medium. At least technically speaking it has the same temporality as radio, television, telephony, and satellite communication, and can contribute to the public sphere in the same way. When the connection is on, we can dispatch messages and read incoming mail, news, etc., but when it is off we have no contact with the wider public, and we must repeat the material we have already stored on our computers.

The fact that the internet is a live medium is an important feature of its public success. The domestic user can monitor public events as they unfold, and the internet also makes it possible for users to cultivate a strictly personal circle of communication, for example on Facebook. The social value of instant connection with others is great, and most people are curious to know what their communication companions have been up to since the last time they were in contact. They can keep track of developments in their field of interest month after month and year after year.

Bolter and Grusin (1999: 197) argue that, although almost everything changes on the internet, one thing remains the same, and that is 'the promise of immediacy through the flexibility and liveness of the Web's networked communication'. The stability of live interaction on the internet strengthens it tremendously as a social technology. Online interactive communities can gather from anywhere in the world and engage in what they presume to be a stable collectivity. The benefits of global connection were pointed out by Joseph Licklider *et al.* in 1968: 'They will be communities not of common location, but of *common interest*. In each field, the overall community of interest will be large enough to support a comprehensive system of field-oriented programs and data' (quoted in Rheingold [1985] 2000: 219–20). For example, the community of music lovers is large enough to support a great range of sub-communities, such as the fan sites for particular artists and sites dedicated to specific musical styles.

Outburst from Blunty3000

On the internet listeners and producers seem to consist of the same kind of people, instead of being neatly differentiated as active producers and passive

Figure 2.2 Youths with laptops at school.

listeners. If you have something to say in public, whether for personal or political reasons, the internet is at your fingertips. User-publishing sites present the user with more opportunities for expressing themselves in private and in public, and at lower cost of doing so than before. You can, for example, produce a video with software bought at the local computer store, and broadcast yourself on a user-generated website such as YouTube. There is also a general tendency for radio and television stations to capitalize on this engagement through reality TV with interactive websites, and email- and SMS-driven television (Livingstone 1999; Siapera 2004; Hill 2005; Enli 2007).

The first case study in this chapter is a video published on YouTube by a man in Tasmania. This is an example of public expression without editorial screening, something that was almost unheard of thirty years ago. Nobody else can stop you from publishing your stuff, although if it is considered harmful by the providers it will soon be removed from the site. Blunty3000 posted a video commentary on his YouTube area in April 2007. He sits in front of his webcam and argues vehemently that people who wear headphones in public should be left in peace, but all he does for visual effects is wave his arms and hold up a pair of headphones. Therefore the recording is fully comprehensible without the visual feed.

Track 6: YouTube: Blunty3000, 2007 (1:06).

You know, when you see someone looking like this in public, you see a person like me – remarkably like me, more like, maybe look, maybe look exactly like me – and wearing these things on my ears, and I'm in public, and I'm in a store, and I'm looking at a gang cover or something like that, or I'm in a frigging elevator. I mean, that's the international sign for 'I'm isolating myself from the rest of the world so I don't have to talk to you.' I want myself away, I'm listening to a podcast, or I'm listening to music or I'm listening to the sounds of baby seals being clubbed to death because it makes me giggle! Whatever! I've got headphones on, don't bother me; don't talk to me. You know I can't hear you; I've got frigging headphones on. These things – if you see a person in the street wearing these things – consider them a cloak of invisibility. Don't talk to that person, don't approach that person!

Blunty3000 presents a tirade against people who disturb headphone users. He is loud and rude and sarcastic, and sounds like the internet version of a cowboy, shooting at what he wants to shoot at, and abiding by his own laws. Blunty3000's behaviour resembles that of a stand-up comedian who plays a carefully rehearsed role, and indeed his exaggerated frustration and shouts suggest that this is a rehearsed monologue. In this sense it is quite professional after all. Five thousand visitors had heard this recording by the end of 2007, and some of them may even have thought about what he said afterwards.

Technically, it is a very simple production. A high-quality microphone picks up his voice in a domestic room, and it is recorded with audio software. In all likelihood this recording is pre-produced, which means that Blunty3000 performed his tirade in one take, and uploaded it to his space on YouTube without any editing other than starting and stopping the tape. His behaviour to the microphone is quite personal, at least in the sense that the indignation is his own. He does not purport to speak for anybody but himself, and listeners can hold him personally responsible for his words and actions. Although formally it is YouTube which publishes the material, people who listen to this performance will relate to Blunty3000 as the editor, journalist and technician, all in one person. Blunty3000 has published a number of monologues on YouTube, and his confrontational style has earned him a long list of derogatory comments from other YouTube users.

YouTube demonstrates that people have acquired techniques for public expression that were previously restricted to professionals. In particular, people are learning how to present themselves effectively in a public setting, using microphones, cameras and editing software to great effect. Thousands of people are in the process of developing rhetorical techniques that may in effect become new media, since journalists and other media professionals will ultimately adopt many of them for programme purposes. This parasitic activity is demonstrated well by news websites that now put great value on discussion forums, personal video submissions and photographs taken by ordinary people with camera phones.

The crucial novelty that makes people into journalists or, better, micro-editorial production units is the easy access to what is in principle a public sphere. It is very easy to publish your stuff on the internet. Maybe nobody bothers to listen, but you can in any case make yourself available.

Premature publishing

Young people in the 2000s are media savvy. They grow up with expressive interfaces such as microphones and cameras, not just loudspeakers and screens. Amateur publishing can also be found among music lovers, and many young people meddle with recording equipment, where they create more or less attention-worthy music. This can also consist of mash-ups, where people sample and edit works by other artists, and modify their original intentions for their own humorous or artistic purposes. If you are making a home movie you can import your favourite recorded music into the software and edit it to become a nice-sounding soundtrack. This craft has little or nothing to do with professional recording qualities.

On Acidplant, MySpace and other user-generated content sites, hundreds and thousands of files are accessible at a click. Most of these files can be thought of as demos, although professional artists use MySpace in particular as an advertising medium for their music. In the analogue era a demo tape was something that aspiring artists brought to a record company, and everybody knew it was of poor quality and would be re-recorded in a professional way if the record company was interested. Clearly the process of publishing music through file sharing and websites is parallel to the analogue demo-tape process, except that it is easier to produce the music with high quality and possible to publish it on a global level. Upload it to the internet, and it is there for everyone in the world to hear, in principle.

Steve Jones (2000: 217) argues that 'recording sound matters less and less, and distributing it matters more and more' (see also Jones 2002). The next case study involves a teenager who makes a music recording at home and distributes it on Acidplanet. He composes a melody and lyrics, and he invites a group of friends to accompany him. This has been a typical teenage thing to do ever since Bob Dylan first inspired youngsters to write their own material in the early 1960s. The band is called God vs. the Internet, and they sing a song with religious undertones.

Track 7: Acidplanet: God vs. the Internet, 2005 (0:48).

> Yeah. Here we go.
> May the circle be unbroken,
> My bottle bye and bye,

> I found Jesus taking all my troubles,
> Now he'll walk you side by side.
> And I feel alright.
> Together, together.
> I feel just fine.
> Oh Sweet Jesus.
> Ha, ha, ha.

Again the production technique is very simple. Several microphones are rigged to pick up several sound sources in a controlled studio environment. There are perhaps four persons performing. A man sings vocals, somebody plays acoustic guitar, there is a synthesizer (perhaps overdubbed), a trumpet and a tambourine. The acoustic architecture is simple: it has slight reverberation that resembles a domestic room, like a den, a teenage bedroom, or perhaps an office. There are no professional production values in this recording, no real balancing or mixing, and very bad audio quality.

Nevertheless, the melody of 'May the Circle be Unbroken' is beautiful, and the trumpet sounds especially vulnerable. There is a certain helpless charm to the song. It seems like the band addresses other young people, who are presumably more relaxed and optimistic than the adults, and the combination of ironic distance and sincerity in the lyrics might indeed appeal to teenagers. At heart this song illustrates the amateur enthusiasm that finds regular expression on all kinds of user-generated sites. But with respect, the threshold for publication is low in this case.

Notice that on the web listeners can often talk back to the producers. In October 2006 the following comment was posted on God vs. the Internet's area on Acidplanet by a person called Paul D. Richardson: 'Sorry if this is harsh, but that was the worst thing I've ever heard. I had to turn my speakers right up just to hear it, and when I did what I heard would have made the blues masters roll in the grave.'

The BBC's acoustic authority

Now there will be a stark contrast to amateur journalism and amateur music. The professional productions of broadcasters and the music industry have been under siege by the internet since the early 1990s (there are many analyses of this convergence; see for example Lowe and Jauert 2005; Leandros 2006; Kretschmer et al. 2001). Most notably, their traditional forms are being challenged by the amateur practices I have just described. The problem is that the internet's platforms are radically more interactive than the recording and broadcasting media, and a hundred years of asymmetrical cultural techniques have to be redirected.

Can public service broadcasting still offer something that is exclusive? It seems that truly professional sound journalism is the only thing that public broadcasting services still serve up as an exclusive product. For many decades public service broadcasting was the hallmark of quality journalism in Western countries. And when it comes to sound media, the stamp of quality was the compact news bulletin, investigative reportage, dramatic documentary programmes, and not least expensive programme formats such as radio plays (which you will never find on the internet other than those from radio stations). High-end radio production gave public service broadcasting an authoritative presence in the public life of the West, and it continues on the internet (Jauert and Lowe 2005).

If you enter the BBC's huge internet portal looking for high-quality radio programmes, you will be satisfied. The next case study is from BBC Radio 4, which brands itself as 'intelligent speech'. It is a thirty-minute science programme called 'Acoustic Shadows', which deals with the varied art of acoustic design. The blurb on the website reads: 'From the most reverberant room in the world to a chamber where sounds die the moment they almost leave your mouth, Robert Sandall takes a journey into the world of acoustics – its origins, its people and some of its amazing soundscapes.' When it comes to production values this programme is dramatically different from Blunty3000 and God vs. the Internet.

Track 8: BBC Radio Four: Acoustic Shadows, 2004 (2:02).

[Recordings of concert hall acoustics]
[Car door slams] – Okay, we're pretty near the Indian Hill site now, we've driven about two hours from San Diego, we're out in the middle of the desert. It's hot. Watch out for rattlesnakes!
[Acoustic guitar – Ry Cooder style]
– Steve Waller is a sound explorer in a literal sense. His field of research is the rapidly growing one of acoustic archaeology, which involves him travelling the world studying the connection between ancient rock and cave art and acoustics. Before they got the paints out Steve believes our ancestors selected the sites they wanted to decorate for their potential as natural echo chambers, a clear case of sound before vision.
– We're standing at the bottom of this mountain that's made out of basically house-size boulders. And in it is a fire-blackened cave that has Indian pictographs, which are basically painted rock art.
– Steve, we're heading for that small opening a hundred feet further up?
– Oh, yeah, it's one spot which they chose to decorate. That is where the echo's coming from. [Dahh!] It's as if the sound is coming right out of the mouth of that cave. If you think back to when the ancient peoples thought that echoes were due to spirits speaking back, you can see that it's as if the rock is speaking to you, as if voices are calling out of the rock, and they're calling out right from that place on the side of the hill where they chose to decorate. [Dahh!]

The programme is concerned with acoustic archaeology, and the reporter Robert Sandall has made recordings of indoors and outdoors acoustics which he uses rhetorically to demonstrate what acoustic archaeology is about. The listeners can sense the rocks and cliffs that the speakers walk between, and the reverberant 'dahh!' informs us just as efficiently about the topic as the speech by the two men.

The programme is post-produced, with careful editing together of three different types of sounds: the voice-over and outdoors speech; the environmental sounds of cars, walking, shouting in a reverberant space; and the guitar music. Seventy years of competence-building in radio journalism lies behind this reportage, and we can hear the accumulated skills of creating a seamless, well-dramatized entity out of a series of raw materials (see for example Herbert 2000: 193ff.; and McLeish 1999: 257).

When it comes to the protagonists' way of speaking this reportage also conforms perfectly to the demands of classical radio journalism. The BBC journalist reads from a well-prepared script, and in this type of address the speaker is expected to function as a skilful animator of the facts and explanations contained in the script. Although the reading should be vivid and lively, there should be as few traces of the journalist's personality as possible. In contrast, the interviewee should sound as if he is improvising his speech in a personal and intimate way, since he is after all not a professional journalist. But still, the behaviour of the interviewee should be harmonized with journalist's speech. At the end of the excerpt, when Waller says that it is as if 'voices are calling out of the rock', he speaks with exactly the kind of enthusiasm that the journalist needs to complement his own reading parts. Both speakers were well aware that what they said at the microphone would be edited before it was put on air, and this made their behaviour relaxed and quite natural-sounding.

There are two professional qualities here that are often lacking in amateur recordings on the internet: the smooth, inaudible editing of multiple strands of sound, and the seemingly effortless and highly informative speech. My point is that high-quality reportage is the hallmark of public service institutions on the internet, while user-published content is made with much less sophisticated production techniques, and would not readily be taken up by public service institutions. This is not a surprising division of labour. The big broadcasting institutions have created professional journalism for over seventy years, and this long-standing tradition keeps journalism from truly resembling the amateur initiatives on the internet.

Public service broadcasting is often seen as a protector of democratic values and as the narrator of personal and social stories with relevance for the citizens (Carpentier 2005: 208; Winston 2005: 251ff.; Williams [1975] 1990: 32ff.). In having such important functions journalism rises above the communication that ordinary citizens can affect between themselves. Journalists work in a well-defined profession with trade unions and interest organizations, and they possess complex expressive skills involving writing, camera work, styles of speaking and moving around, editing, checking sources, complying with ethical guide-lines, etc. In a cultural sense public service broadcasting will always consist of one-way communication, with a centralized editorial organization distributing their carefully made product to the masses. The BBC's website demonstrates that this asymmetrical relationship works fine also on the internet.

Podcast frenzy!

In a matter of a few years from 2005, podcasting has become a standard option for listeners (Levy 2006: 227ff.). By clicking on the 'subscribe' button on a website, listeners can regularly receive fresh instalments of their chosen audio or video programmes. I will go into the technical details of podcasting in a later section; here I will attend to the production values of podcasting.

The next case study is from a podcast-only service called www.twit.tv (the acronym stands for 'This Week in Technology'). The company produces its own original podcasts, and this makes it different from many of the podcasting services which distribute standard radio or television programmes on just another platform. I have selected a podcast that TWIT made about an event called the Podcast Expo in California 2006; it was made during the buzz and expectations of the big conference, and everybody is wandering around, test-ing, buying and selling podcast products.

There is an upbeat rock jingle at the beginning, and professional voices read the headings in a neutral style, sounding mechanical in much the same way as the voices that say 'Mind the gap' at underground stations. 'Netcasts you love (a man). From people you trust (a woman). This is twit (a man–woman duet)'. This soulless but informative way of speaking is a classical feature of American-style broadcasting. There are also several sponsored messages, and when the actual programme begins it resembles talk radio quite a lot. The similarity to the production values of American commercial radio is quite striking.

Track 9: This Week in Tech: Podcast Expo, 2006 (2:31).

– And we're live at Podcast Expo [– Yoohoo], I could say Netcast Expo, Doug Kay is here from IT Conversations, he's gonna hand his tiara off to me a little later on. [– Absolutely] Last year's podcast person of the year. And if you should fail to, it could, succeed in your duties, you'll be, I'll be runner up. [– Okay, thank you, yes] – Actually, Doug has a big announcement, so we'll get to that in just a second. Also with me Steve Gibson, another TWIT from Security now and GRC.com. Sitting next to Steve Gibson, the great Scott Warren from Mac Great Weekly in the Eyelifezone [– Hi everybody], he's also a great aperture expert, aperturetricks.com and pod-castingtricks.com. What we're gonna do today is talk to a lot of podcast-ers, as many as we can in half an hour before they take this stage away from us. Podcast Expo is, this is the gathering of the tribes for podcasting, the second year we've done it, about 25 hundred people, we've taken over a small part of the Ontario Convention Center, a lot of booths showing podcast software, podcast hardware. Broadcasters General Store is here and thanks to them we've got audio on this podcast, they let us [– Which is really handy for a podcast]. It certainly makes a difference, they let us their Alesis Multimix 8 Firewire.

TWIT produces mainly live-on-tape events, which are cheap and simple to create. In this case there is a row of industry men on stage, they are introduced by the host, and the host talks to them all in the course of the programme. This is an example of resounding studio acoustics. Several microphones are rigged on a stage, and the performance takes place in front of a live audience. The programme is mixed to pick up the performers and the audience reactions, and also to convey the size of the hall and its atmospherics. It all sounds authentically like the Ontario Convention Center in Los Angeles.

Podcasting is not a live medium like web radio, and among other things this implies that the raw material for a podcast can be heavily edited before it is launched to the public. Since the producers are well aware of this while taping the show, the mood of podcast programmes can be more relaxed and happy-go-lucky than traditional radio. But there are lots of similarities with radio, as I have already suggested. For example, podcasting mainly communicates in the form of twenty- to thirty-minute programmes, which happens to be the typical length of a traditional radio programme. Some podcasters make three- or four-minute instalments, which is the typical length of a radio commentary piece.

Listening to the message of the TWIT podcast, I have to say that it sounds quite partisan. By reporting so enthusiastically from the Podcast Expo, TWIT promotes its own platform every minute of the way. The speakers want recognition of podcasting as a medium, and this podcast is a good example of the intimate connection between equipment manufacturers and editorial production. This is not critical journalism, this is an expression of a common interest in expanding the market that is quite typical of new internet media. The podcasters try to sell equipment and programmes, and perhaps even establish a new medium with social practices of its own.

The Podcast Expo illustrates the driving forces of technological innovation in the media. The modern mass media are built on competitive lab experiments in the military-industrial complex and commercial enterprises, and the motivation is basically the same in the podcast industry. There is an intense pursuit of better functionality and greater efficiency and more diverse areas of use. Companies such as Microsoft, Apple, Nokia and Google try to create the next killer application, like the iPod was. You can ask who will win the competition, but the truth is that the competition will never end; it will only change into being about something else.

I will end this section on a critical note. It is important to consider that the optimistic moods of advertisers, PR companies and the broadcasting stations may be purposefully unrealistic. In the article 'The Mythos of the Electronic Revolution', James Carey and John Quirk argue that there is an idealizing rhetoric embedded in the very fabric of electronic communication, which they call 'the rhetoric of the electrical sublime'. This is, they say, an ethos 'that identifies electricity and electrical power, electronics and cybernetics, computers and information with a new birth of community, decentralization, ecological balance, and social harmony' (Carey and Quirk 1989: 114). In their view technological life includes a clever ideological and commercial staging of roles for people to believe in, where the various appliances are seen as necessary for succeeding in one's life involvements. Carey and Quirk refer to this as an ethos that goes like this: 'Everyman a prophet with his own machine to keep him in control' (ibid.: 117).

The computer sound medium, 2008

Now I will turn to a more precise analysis of the medium I am talking about: the 'computer with internet' medium. Regarding sound production, the computer medium is quite symmetrical in a technical sense. It is truly the same equipment that is being used by the important BBC journalists and the amateur musicians. Both of them can, for example, edit and mix their production on their laptop in the evening. Since all parties can in principle publish and distribute messages, it is difficult to say that it is a linear medium with production at one end and reception at the other.

But although the medium is quite symmetrical in access and opportunities, there is a big difference between the professional training of journalists and musicians, on the one hand, and the lack of it among ordinary users, on the other. As I have suggested earlier in the chapter, we can hear this by comparing the BBC's 'Acoustic Shadows' with the shouting monologue by Blunty3000 on YouTube.

Figure 2.3 shows the technical environment of sound communication on the internet. The mixing board at the production end symbolizes the great creative control that producers and journalists still typically have in comparison with listeners. The mp3 player at the reception end symbolizes the flexible ways in which listeners can use the sounds from the internet (and computer). Notice that for both parties almost all the vital functions are contained on the computer in the form of software. The figure shows that there are essentially two platforms: the personal computer and the network between those computers. I have argued that, when it is hooked to the internet, the computer is a medium of live distribution. But the issue is more complex. The computer has a storage and playback feature that always works, whether there is a connection to the internet or not, and this is simply the computer itself. In addition there is the live connection that can be turned on or shut off by the user.

The computer is sometimes called an *Überbox*, which refers to its tendency to contain all kinds of other media. And, indeed, all the traditional interfaces of

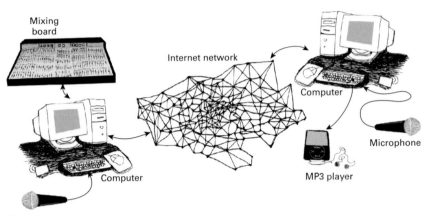

Figure 2.3 Model of computer sound media.

sound media are clustered around the computer, for example mixing boards, sound-proof studios, LP turntables, video cameras, microphones and synthesizers, and all these familiar interfaces could have been drawn up in the figure. This clustering is possible because the computer platform is what Alan Turing called a 'universal computing machine' (Rheingold [1985] 2000: 45ff.) that can run any arbitrary but well-formed sequence of instructions. It can, for example, encode and decode written messages, or sample and store photos, sound and video. Whatever it is, the computer can process it according to its basic algorithms, which rely on the numbers 0 and 1 in endless combinations. The rich acoustic and visual experiments at the computer are translated into binary signals during production and are converted back to the human realm during playback.

The digital signal carrier is so miniaturized and blackboxed compared to analogue signal carriers such as the LP that it almost seems to not exist as a material fact at all (Simpson 1998). It can be contained in all kinds of microchip devices; and it seems completely immaterial apart from the file icons that pop up on the screen when, for example, you put a memory chip in the USB port.

The most striking feature of the double platform of computers and the internet is the web of connections that it offers. It creates access between all parties that have a modem or broadband connection. Remember that the internet is based on the same principles as telephony, except that it does not transfer analogue voices, but digital information. That old network has been in operation in most countries for over a hundred years, and the wires are well established in the home. This feature to some extent explains the rapid rise of the internet. Users can also hook up to internet providers through mains electricity, satellite dishes or cable networks.

The processing capacity of the computer (with internet connection) can be considered a public resource. When you don't use your processing power it goes to waste since, for every second, hour and day that it lies inactive, it could have been used for some calculating purpose. The processing capacity could have been lent out at night – for example, to scientists who could use it to analyse raw data from radio telescopes that scan outer space for signs of intelligent life (see http://setiathome.berkeley.edu). Some people download music and films and podcasts all through the night and stockpile enormous amounts of cultural products that they will never consume in full, but which nevertheless serves the purpose of not letting their time-bound information resource go to waste.

I have already discussed the rhetorical potentials of web radio and podcasting. Here I will describe the two new platforms in comparison with traditional broadcast radio, in order to get their special features across as clearly as possible. Web radio and podcasting can be considered sub-platforms in the great multimedium which I call 'computer with internet connection'. However, since this mother medium has such a stable presence, the sub-platforms can for all practical purposes be treated as self-standing media platforms (just like email software, web browsers and other appliances).

Audio streaming was a groundbreaking live technology for the internet (Priestman 2002). Notice that this is not the same as downloading, since no files are transferred to the computer. The audio streaming player made it possible to listen to the sound while receiving it, and in effect this introduced radio on the internet. As I have already noted, all websites rely on visual guidance for the listener, and web radio is no exception. The listener must search the web to find web radio stations, and the streaming feature is packaged in a rich visual environment of news, schedule information, contact information, and so on. Nevertheless, web radio re-creates that fundamental quality of broadcasting which is called 'live at the point of transmission' (Ellis 2000; Hendy 2000), albeit in a telephonic network instead of through terrestrial transmission. Although there is a buffering process between the streaming servers and the listener's computer that can delay the signal by up to ten seconds, web radio in effect transfers sound in the same temporal manner that FM and AM radio has always done (Priestman 2002: 9). Web radio is a cheap form of publishing and distributing sound, and it has greatly lowered the threshold for establishing new editorial outlets. Services can, for example, be made without large initial investments for small groups scattered around the world (Coyle 2000). The internet has become the main delivery system for thousands of web-only radio operators and an important supplementary platform for practically all radio broadcasters.

In contrast to web radio, podcasting is not a live medium, because the message has to be completed in every facet before it is published and distributed.

There is no streaming process; instead, the file is automatically downloaded to the computer, and it must be actively deleted by the user. Because podcasting relies on downloading, nobody expects the podcast programme to be interrupted, for example, by breaking news. The podcast platform has no readiness to respond to current events, except that of course a new instalment can be published sooner than originally planned if some pressing event makes it opportune.

The subscription feature of podcasting is important to notice, since it is quite different from web radio's live streaming. The listeners get their radio in the mail, so to speak. This is very different from traditional radio, which has always been characterized by the here and now of the public sphere. The listener receives new programmes on a regular basis, for example once a week, and can bring the recordings out into their everyday surroundings and play them back on the iPod (Berry 2006). All the major radio stations offer this service for most of their programmes, and it has led to an increase in listening to talk and information programmes among people who would previously not listen much to the radio. Notice that mobile listening to podcasting contrasts with the way in which people listen to streaming audio, where (in 2008 at least) they are more strictly bound to the stationary computer or the laptop. Typically, the podcast user will listen while doing something else, just like radio programmes and music have always been enjoyed.

Meet the pirate

File sharing has led to great innovations in the art of listening – innovations that keep us in control of our music (Hacker 2000). Admittedly these innovations have taken place in dubious ways. Peer-to-peer networks have long challenged the music industry by allowing music to be shared without compensation to the rights holders, and without any sales of CDs or other physical media by the record companies. This alternative music industry was introduced with sites such as Napster in the late 1990s and the Pirate Bay in the 2000s (for elaboration, see Alderman 2001; Sterne 2006; Rodman and Vanderdonckt 2006).

Music lovers can make playlists for their Walkman or iPod, just like people made mixed tapes to play in the car in the analogue era. People's playlists typically have a single song focus rather than in-depth attention to whole albums. This also goes for podcasting, where you select your favourite shows instead of listening to a live flow. This reduces the producers' and artists' control of the role of the individual items in a larger album context. Playlists can be organized by genre, year of release and many other variables that give the music lover greater control over their act of listening than ever before.

Since there is so much music on offer on the internet, the listener can in principle cherry-pick their music and compile the perfect record collection. Once the music is downloaded to the computer it can be organized in an audio library. These activities have increased what Paddy Scannell calls the 'personalization of experience'. He argues that the media are 'something that individuals can now increasingly manage and manipulate themselves through new everyday technologies of self-expression and communication' (Scannell 2005: 141).

However, the cherry-picking by music lovers is not something new. As the historical part of this book will show, a highly sophisticated culture of listening to records had developed already by the 1930s, and it was strengthened with the arrival of stereo music on LP in the 1960s. This culture lives on among the LP and CD lovers who still listen to a whole album in one concentrated act of listening, and who have a solemn reverence for their albums.

In the context of file sharing on the internet, music lovers can build a really big music collection at low cost. This is what Jacques Attali (1985: 101) calls 'stockpiling'. People buy more records than they can listen to, and the pirate most definitely downloads more music than he can listen to. The storage capacity of computers in the late 2000s is great, and avid music lovers can have 20,000 to 30,000 songs in their file cabinet. Presuming that an average CD holds approximately fifteen songs, this equals something like 1,300 to 2,000 CDs. Although people basically create their own private record collections, they can of course share them with anonymous others through file sharing software. The music collection is a part of the public domain for as long as the user makes it available.

Some music lovers relate to music less as an expensive and fragile commodity and more as a huge standing resource. Some feel that it is so easy to download music that the actual file is not worth caring too much about. There is no need to build up a personal collection of files if you can serve yourself online at any time, the argument goes.

The search engines of the internet bring sound recordings to hand more easily than ever before in the 130 years of sound media. Amazon and eBay are places to look for CDs to buy, while iTunes and other companies present legal music. Of course, thousands of pirate sites distribute music to anybody for free. The internet functions as a standing reserve of sound, or, more precisely, of references for sound, that the listener can choose to launch or download. Websites such as Allmusic or Rhapsody have plenty of background information about songs and artists, and there are websites specializing in transcriptions of pop lyrics. Compared to the information that can be supplied on a CD cover, the internet has a radical potential for informing the user about the cultural and historical setting of the music they listen to. Very often people search in an open and curious way, limited only by their perseverance in pursuing their interests. Notice that a search can also be conducted through visual cues on a website – pictures of artists, logos for radio stations and other graphical material. Often a quick glance tells you what you need to know.

Sound browsing is also possible. Allmusic provides excerpts of 5.5 million songs which can be chosen from standard browse and search procedures, so people can listen to a thirty-second snippet and evaluate the music before they buy or download it. Notice that this is not really an auditory search, since this would imply that the user enters an excerpt of, for example, a guitar sound, and the search engine would find all the songs with the same type of guitar sound. But the Allmusic monitor after all means that you can steer your search for musical pleasures by attending to the actual music, and not to written recommendations or information that the graphical interface alone can supply.

The computer is a miracle

It is difficult for ordinary people to learn how the computer and internet actually work. You are confident that you could explain it comprehensively if you had the time and money to educate yourself and study it at length, but since that is not possible, or not in your interest, you have to rely on the functionalities by default.

Rather than interrogating it ourselves, we are likely just to accept it all as a functional fact of life. There is a tension in this way of living with things, an uneasy or hesitant or even reluctant acceptance of the great functionalities and increased opportunities. This is *trust in technology*. It does not come about by conscious thought processes in every instance of contact. On the contrary, it comes about because of withdrawal from explicit thematization (Nyre 2007b). Paddy Scannell describes this notion of habituation in the context of broadcasting:

> The language used to describe the invention of radio first and, later, television expressed over and over again a sense of wonder at them as marvellous things, miracles of modern science. Their magic has not vanished. It has simply been absorbed, matter-of-factly, into the fabric of ordinary daily life.
> (Scannell 1996: 21)

People don't think much about the computer's strangeness, and don't have time to study it in full technical detail. For most people the incomprehensible sediments into a habit and its complexity vanishes. Alfred Schutz (1970: 247) writes: 'The miracle of all miracles is that the genuine miracles become to us an everyday occurrence.'

Chapter 3

Synthetic music
Digital recording in great detail

Synthetic sound is all around. Even grandmothers listen to techno beats and weird sounds of synths, samplers and computers. Two innovations in particular have made these technological sounds possible, namely multitrack editing and the digital generation of sounds. These intricate cultural techniques have been around since the 1970s, but with the computer they have become a mainstream phenomenon (and only then, in my perspective, does a technique become truly interesting).

Three case studies will be presented, all of which in different ways demonstrate the hyper-technological character of modern music. First I will analyse a densely multitracked rock composition by the group haltKarl from 2007 and present two versions from different stages of the production process. Secondly, I analyse a completely synthetic techno beat by Autechre from 1995 where it sounds as if no microphones have been used at all. Finally I will analyse a passionate crooning performance by Beth Gibbons and Portishead from 1994. Her performance is just as human as the human voice can be, despite its being embedded in a dense flow of sampled sounds and drum machine beats.

The synthetic media landscape

Westerners in the 2000s are a media-savvy people. It seems that nothing can surprise us when it comes to hearing and understanding recorded sounds (and images). People can hear sounds from outer space, sounds from inside an ant hill, and sounds from the volcanic inferno of the earth's core. In the context of visual media, we have seen the insides of a womb and the hurricanes on Jupiter in colour. Impressive though these representations are, they are strictly documentary.

People are also used to another type of media experience: animations in sound and images that are created entirely inside the technologies, and which nobody would mistake for something that exists outside the media. When dinosaurs charge down the road in *Jurassic Park* (1993) there is no doubt that the images are non-documentary, and the same is the case for TV promos, commercials and programme intros that are often highly advanced when it comes to graphical effects. This type of animated reference is often used

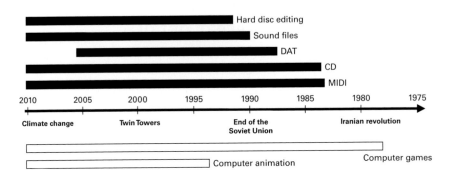

Figure 3.1 Timeline of digital recording media.

for entertainment and aesthetic effect, where there is no moral imperative to represent the world in a realistic manner. However, there is heated discussion about ethical problems in digital animation, since now the technical possibilities for manipulation are almost limitless (Kerckhove 1995; Gitlin 2002: 71ff.).

When describing the synthetic production of music I want first to connect to an ongoing cultural process that parallels the visual animations of TV and film. American and European music lovers enjoy the products of an industry with a joint creative history that goes all the way back to the cylinder phonograph in the late nineteenth century. This means that there are well-developed aesthetic sensibilities among the general public, and during the last three decades these sensibilities have shifted towards greater acceptance of technological sounds. Hip-hop, techno music, electronica – whatever trademark is put on the music, it has none of the acoustics of the concert hall, but all of the acoustics of the computer. These techniques of production have become influential on people's tastes in general, and are used in commercials, on film soundtracks, in computer games, and so on. The music lover has turned towards textures and timbres, and considers them enjoyable in their own right.

Figure 3.1 lists the main platforms that are necessary for the creation of synthetic music. There is clearly a thematic overlap with the platforms that were discussed in chapter 2, for example regarding file sharing and mp3, but this chapter focuses more strictly on high-quality music production. Underneath the timeline I have listed visual animation media – computer games and animation formats based on software such as GIF, QuickTime, Shockwave and Flash. These visual animations can be accessed on the internet and played on a computer. It is instructive to start my discussion of synthetic sound production on the background of visual animation. To create the illusion of movement, an image is displayed on the computer screen, then quickly replaced by a new image that is similar to the previous image, but shifted slightly. Each image can be constructed entirely on the computer or be a montage of real footage and animation. This technique is identical to the way in which the illusion of movement is achieved with traditional television and motion pictures, except that every pixel must be plotted by a programmer instead of being automatically registered by a camera lens. In principle, computer sound is designed just like the computer animation of images.

One of the really big changes in music recording happened quite recently. During the 1980s the introduction of the CD started a slow but ultimately complete replacement of analogue equipment. From the 1990s there was file sharing, and people started getting used to music in the form of computer files. The change created fruitful conditions for the development of synthetic techniques.

Audio editing software made it possible to manipulate the sound with graphical interfaces, particularly in the software layout as it appears on the screen. Cut and paste editing was a very important innovation, and it started influencing music production from the early 1990s. Before that it had become widespread in word processing software such as WordPerfect and Word (Manovitch 2001).

The MIDI standard for programming of music scores and instructions was the first commercially viable digital technology for synthetic sound creation in the early 1980s. MIDI stands for 'musical instrument digital interface', and this protocol enables items of electronic music equipment to communicate and synchronize signals with each other (Chanan 1995: 161, 357). In combination with samples of instrument sounds, a given MIDI composition can be played back in any type of sound, for example, the violin, the guitar sound or falsetto singing. Notice also that computer games such as Pac-Man and other stand-alone devices had their own sound-generating principles before the advert of MIDI.

Hard-working rockers

Before I describe digital recording in detail, I will remind you that recorded music is still a physical thing, despite its fugitive digital existence. Recording 'turned the performance of music into a material object, something you could hold in your hand, which could be bought and sold', argues Michael Chanan (1995: 7). In addition to the potential for making money, recording allowed musicians to hear themselves as other people would hear them. They could listen very carefully to several takes before they decided which was the best one, which they then released to the public. During the decades artists have cultivated this technique, and it is now a completely integral part of record production, as can be seen by the central location of monitor loudspeakers in the control room. The activity can be called analytic listening.

In this section I will attend to the way analytic listening influences the recording process, and my point is that it is crucial to the painstakingly careful construction of sounds, bit by bit, sample by sample, instrument part by instrument part. Musical events are first recorded straight through, and afterwards they are altered and combined with other musical events in the process of editing, to construct the desired musical rhythms, melodies and harmonies. All the time the producers listen carefully to the sound and discuss it among themselves. Layer upon layer can be added or removed according to the producers' changing creative vision. Even low-budget recording sessions in an attic involve a tremendous modification and manipulation of the musical sounds.

Track 10 is from a Norwegian recording in process. The group is called haltKarl, and since it has not yet released any CDs it is completely unknown to the wider public. The band will probably aspire to national fame sometime in the future. This song has actually been under development for around five years, and we hear two versions: the professional version from 2007 and a demo version from 2005.

Track 10: haltKarl: Almost Gills, 2007 and 2005 (1:51).

> Both my lungs are spoken for
> Breathing water in through the pores
> Hormones might get the best of me
> Black men might just have bigger feet
> All my girls got the same disease
> And all my girls want a better deal
> All my girls cry
> All my girls go
> Under water I can hear them.

The music is in rock style; it sounds rather like heavy metal with beach harmonies, or like a mix of the Red Hot Chili Peppers and the Beach Boys. The three-man band plays guitars, bass, drums and synths, sing solo vocals and harmonies, and use all kinds of digital effects.

The sound is highly controlled, which is a result of the slow composition method that has been used. It is as far from a live performance as one can get, although it actually sounds much like a live performance. The clarity and simplicity of the sound belies the immense depth of layers in the song and its production process. The band owns a large array of stomp-box effects for the guitar and bass, software plug-ins, outboard synthesizers and effect processors that can modify the signal from any type of source into whatever sound is wanted. haltKarl is exploiting the powerful computer processing capabilities of relatively cheap modern-day computers to the full.

Regarding its production technique, 'Almost Gills' has an interesting chronology which I will go into in some detail. The song has been recorded twice, in two completely different versions that nevertheless sound much the same at first hearing. haltKarl is a determined band, and in 2005 its members were satisfied with the melody, lyrics, harmonies and detailed instrument arrangements, but not with the production qualities of the song. With the

Figure 3.2 haltKarl in the studio.

structure of the song set in stone, they started preparing a new, professional version, where all parts, instrumental as well as vocal, were rerecorded. On the soundtrack we first hear the new but still unmixed version from 2007. It was recorded in a semi-professional studio with a relatively short production period, in contrast to the 2005 version, which has a far less professional sound and was recorded in basements, cabins, living rooms and even bedrooms over a number of years.

There are several reasons for analysing the strategies of an unknown rock group from Bergen. The production techniques used are now so typical as to be almost the industry norm, despite the fact that they are extremely time-consuming. The slow construction of a song, layer by layer, is just as common in pop as in rock or hip-hop or techno, among struggling artists at the home computer as well as the big established acts in expensive recording studios such as the Record Plant in Los Angeles. The process of improving the sound can go on for months or years before the artists are satisfied. The album *OK Computer* by Radiohead (1997) is a case in point. In fact, this construction process is now so widespread that it is the starting point for the cultural perception of music not just among the musicians themselves, but also among ordinary people. In other words, the entire public is well skilled in enjoying sound with these highly complex characteristics.

Techno acoustics

The next case study will relate to acoustic characteristics. Artists design the acoustic properties of their recordings very carefully, and this can be called the acoustic architecture of sound media. In chapter 1 quoted Ross Snyder ([1966] 1979: 350) referring to musicians as architects of a spatial habitat 'in which contemporary man will live and move and have his being'.

Acoustic architecture is intuitively understandable as relevant to concert recordings and other cases where an actual space is picked up by microphones. But there are more difficult examples. The electric guitar and the Hammond organ produce sound via internal electronics; so where are these sounds located? It would be strange to say that the sounds of the electric guitar resonate somewhere inside the instrument, as if it were just like a saxophone or a drum. This problem of reference became more pronounced with the synthesizer and its programming of tone-generators. Sounds then became internal to the technology in the simple sense that they did not resonate in a real room and were not picked up by microphones. They were created wholly on the inside of the equipment and sent directly to the tape or the loudspeaker.

The music of the German group Kraftwerk is a good example of at least partly synthetic music. Mark Cunningham (1998: 281) comments on this 1980s techno sound: 'If there was a shared emphasis among the varied styles thrown into the charts from the early to mid-Eighties it was one of unnatural sounds, created electronically by sequencers, drum machines, synthesizers and the advent of sampling.' Few if any acoustical instruments are played on Kraftwerk's albums; the only sounds that are definitely from the world outside digital construction are the voices of the singers.

'Dael' (1995) by the British duo Autechre is an example with fully synthetic acoustics. This English band is well known to techno freaks but virtually unknown beyond their hardcore audience.

🎵 *Track 11: Autechre: Dael, 1995 (1:09).*

[No lyrics]

It creates a very precise sound which is 'written' in layers of rhythmic elements speeding up and slowing down, with a dark melody behind. There are strange modulations that sound like a zipper being drawn and a repetitive rhythm, and the overall effect is metallic, sharp and cold. None of the sounds are analogue, and there are no vocals or analogue instruments such as a guitar or trumpet. Notice that the analysis of what the band has done to create the sound can only be based on speculation, since there are so many ways to make music with digital software (and MIDI plug-ins). It is really impossible for anyone to establish the production process of this type of music.

This has something to do with the fact that synths and MIDI signals have a purely technological acoustics; and this in turn implies that the recognition of spaces and sounds among music lovers is restricted to their knowledge of synthetic instruments. Notice that MIDI carries instructions written in a computer language that all modern synthesizers, drum machines and other digital processors can understand (Honeybone *et al.* 1995: 23). The proliferation of MIDI implies that popular music in general has ventured into a synthetic timbre-management. The activities at the mixing board and the computer can now be considered as important as the sounds of traditional musical instruments.

This development has concerned music lovers for several decades already. In 1990 Andrew Goodwin claimed that, with sampling and other digital developments, the authority of the artistic statement has been reduced: 'The most significant result of the recent innovations in pop production lies in the progressive removal of any immanent criteria for distinguishing between human and automated performance. Associated with this there is of course a crisis of authorship' (1990: 263). As I have suggested, it is difficult to identify the performers, and to point out what their musical accomplishments actually consist of. Goodwin claimed that sequencing and sampling technologies have cast such doubts upon our knowledge about just who is (or is not) playing what that some bands place comments such as 'no sequencers' on album covers to retain their status as 'real' musicians (ibid.: 268).

In the late 2000s it is another story altogether. Music lovers are now so used to the synthetic techniques that very few would consider them unreal or inferior to musical sounds picked up with microphones in the traditional way. Indeed, the members of Autechre are not at all afraid that their status as musicians will be compromised by the synthetic way of playing music. On the contrary, their reputation in the techno community is rock solid because of the seriousness with which they approach the art of computer music.

The passionate crooner

A third fundamental feature of recorded sound, along with space and time characteristics, is the personality of the artist. In the old days, with singers such as Edith Piaf and Vera Lynn, there was a strong emotional connection between listeners and artists. But can listeners relate to persons in such an intense way when the music is so marked by synthetics and computerization?

My next case study is a trip-hop song by Portishead from 1994. Portishead is an English band well known to lovers of contemporary Western pop and rock. They were part of the Bristol sound, named after the city in the west of England where such bands as Massive Attack originated. It was characterized by 'minimalistic arrangements, dub-influenced low-frequency basslines, samples of jazz riffs, keyboard lines or movie soundtracks, and drum loops – "breakbeats" characteristic of hip hop and rap from the ghettos of American cities during the 1970s and 1980s' (Connell and Gibson 2003: 100). In the song 'Glory Box', the lead singer Beth Gibbons makes her voice stand out as particularly human against a background that is particularly technological.

🔊 *Track 12: Portishead: Glory Box, 1994 (1:03).*

> I'm so tired, of playing
> Playing with this bow and arrow
> Gonna give my heart away
> Leave it to the other girls to play
> For I've been a temptress too long
> Just ...
> Give me a reason to love you
> Give me a reason to be a woman
> I just wanna be a woman.

This is a lush electronic sound. The band creates a dense flow of drums, bass, synths and electric guitars, and there is an LP sound effect that makes it seen as if the music is being played on a turntable. There is also a lingering reference to several other compositions, for example Tchaikovsky's 'Swan Lake' and the 1970s pop song 'Daydream' by Franck Pourcel's Orchestra. This goes to show that, although 'Glory Box' may sound very modern and alternative because of its technical aspects, the song follows a long melodic tradition. Notice that 'Glory Box' contains a sample from Isaac Hayes's 'Ike's Rap III' (liner notes on the CD). This is the most direct way in which Portishead refers to other musical works, since a sample is after all a little piece of a recording made by another artist (for implications of sampling, see Chanan 1995: 161 and Goodwin 1990: 258ff.). The listener would have to be quite familiar with Isaac Hayes's work to recognize the sample, though.

Beth Gibbons sings in a good voice, crooning just like pop artists have done since the 1930s (see chapter 9). As I have already suggested, she manages to sound like an especially vulnerable woman in this stark electronic setting. It is an outstanding case of a craft that appeared in the 1970s, where female singers such as Joni Mitchell and Kate Bush projected gentle human moods against a background of a complex rock production. By adding the LP sound Portishead signals a retrospective acknowledgement of this previous era in pop music history. My conclusion is simple: listeners can relate to singers in the digital age with as much trust as they did before. Listeners are likely to think of Beth Gibbons's exclamation 'I just wanna be a woman' as an expression of her autobiographical frustrations as a woman.

However, a conservative music lover might argue that these hi-tech recordings are not as authentic as the old recordings of Edith Piaf or Louis Armstrong. Singers nowadays are assisted tremendously by voice technologies, such as modulating the voice to be in the right key, while in the past artists always had to be good to sound good. But if artists lose their credibility by manipulating their voices and putting them into a technological context, then there is very little credibility in modern music. Clearly, since the human voice can be modified just as easily as any other sound, it cannot be denied authentic qualities any more than other modified sounds. The alternative would be to suspend one's trust in absolutely all sounds recorded after approximately 1970, since they have all been manipulated.

Among music lovers the traditional view has been that the human voice is untouchable. In the 1980s there was a certain pop design philosophy, practised for example by the Human League, that allowed all sounds *apart from* the human voice to be synthetically created (Cunningham 1998: 291).

There is something extra valuable about the untouched voice, it seems. Basically, a voice is personal in the sense that friends and acquaintances can recognize it as belonging to one unique individual among hundreds and thousands of other persons. In this way it points to a name, a set of personal characteristics, etc. To say that a voice is *recorded* means that people who know the person beforehand will recognize the recorded voice as belonging to that unique person. If the voice sounds alive and rough, with traces of whisky or drugs and the background of a nightclub coming through in the recording, the chances are that the artist will be felt to be authentically mediated. The human voice has an ethos of its own, an emotional, personal *appeal* that most musicians do not dare to disrupt. This conforms well to traditional ideas of 'authenticity' in pop and rock music.

Notice that, strictly speaking, a human voice cannot be synthetically created. With a synthetic voice the sounds have not been generated in the vocal chords and oral cavity of a flesh and blood person, and this remains the case regardless of the fact that the sound may resemble that of a human voice very much, and may even be mistaken for one if the processing is very clever. It still does not have a source reference outside the realm of digital construction.

But although a voice cannot be constructed, it can be modified. An example of this can be found on Radiohead's *Kid A* (2000), which contains all kinds of humanoid sounds and blurred transitions, from the obviously human to the obviously synthetic. The increasing use of voice modification technologies makes it interesting to enquire about the *limits* of the voice's trace back to a body and a personality. If the producer changes the frequencies, at what point does the sound stop referring to a unique individual? How much reverberation can a voice sustain before it becomes unrecognizable as a trace of a body? Is there a minimum duration for which the voice must be present in the mix in order for the listener to be able to relate to it as tracing a personality?

There are no definite answers to these questions, but there is a definite tendency among music lovers. During the 1990s this type of voice modification entered the mainstream of pop music, and famous artists had huge hits where their voices were heavily modified. In 1998 Cher released 'Believe', and took the risk of offending some listeners' sense of authenticity because of the way her voice was manipulated. Her producer correctly presumed that her 1990s fans would be able to hear her new recording as unproblematically representing the real Cher. In an age of widespread listener sophistication such a strategy is not a great risk to take for a popular artist. Danielsen and Maasø (forthcoming) have analysed Madonna's 'Don't Tell Me' as a good example of the specifically digital sound of modern music production. Another striking example is provided by the US artist Beck, who varies his vocal style so much that it is hard to ascribe to him an identity based on voice, and he is often associated with a postmodern pop style. On the CD *Midnite Vultures* (1999) Beck sings in at least three different ways. He has a kind of tough guy funky voice and a slick groovy voice, and also makes use of short bursts of a hoarse screaming voice. All these are obviously processed and overdubbed, and they are sometimes superimposed on each other.

The voice is regularly modified so much that it almost doesn't refer to a human, but becomes a sound in a strictly material sense. I will rely on Simon Frith to conclude how music lovers relate to this phenomenon. He argues that people engage songs by responding to the materiality of the body while singing: 'Singing is a physical pleasure, and we enjoy hearing someone sing not because they are expressing something else, not because the voice represents the "person" behind it, but because the voice, as a sound in itself, has an immediate voluptuous appeal' (1981: 164). This is the bottom line of modern music listening.

The recording medium, 2008

As in chapter 2, I will outline the infrastructure of the medium in question. If the professional studios are taken as the starting point, the recording industry is still based on a highly asymmetrical technical set-up. There are complex sound-proof studios and advanced computer systems that amateur musicians can only dream of using and that most ordinary music lovers do not even know exist. The asymmetry between production and listener techniques in effect makes up two highly advanced, but separate, sound environments. Just as there is high-quality music recording, there is high-quality domestic listening.

Figure 3.3 shows that there are two different distribution platforms in the current set-up of the recording medium. The CD distribution system relies on industrial copying of CDs, which are sold through music shops on the high street or through online services such as Amazon and shipped to the buyers in the post. Music lovers can listen to CDs in a range of settings, but the most advanced setting is still the high-quality stereo set with two loudspeakers centrally located in the living room. In addition to CD distribution, there is file transfer on the internet, either legally through services like iTunes or illegally on pirate services. While downloaded music can of course be listened to on the high-quality stereo set, listeners typically download music to an mp3 player and carry it with them in their daily life. This robust distribution platform seems to be taking over from the more vulnerable CD distribution system. Some music lovers still purchase LPs and play them on the old-fashioned turntable, but this platform is not included in the figure.

This chapter mainly revolves around synthetic sound, and this type of sound relies on digital carriers. I have stressed that recorded sound has become

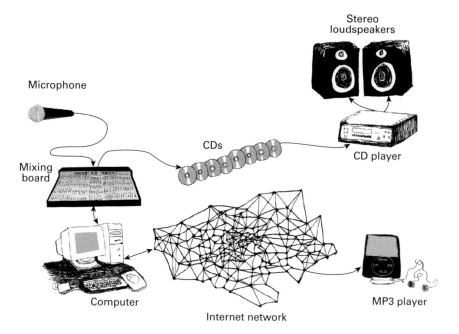

Figure 3.3 Model of the digital recording medium.

perfected to the extent that it need not refer to natural acoustic spaces at all in order to communicate. The track by Autechre demonstrates this in the simple sense that all sources are produced inside the computer, and can therefore be perfectly represented in the computer's code.

This synthetic quality can be explained by making a historical contrast. In both tape and digital recording the ambient sound is picked up by microphones and converted to electromagnetic impulses. Digital media have one more conversion process, namely the sampling and encoding of the electromagnetic signal into binary digits. This can be done optically by a laser head (CD) or magnetically with a spinning disc (hard disc), or with solid state electronics (memory chips). Not least, a programmer can write a sound signal entirely in code, without any external influences (White 1997).

In digital recording there is no physical contact between the microphone pickup and the code on the disc, and consequently no mechanical degeneration of audio quality. In comparison, the analogue signals of tape and LPs are like satellites in low orbit, and it is only a matter of time before they are destroyed. When rearranging a sound array on magnetic tape, the tape had to be physically cut or re-recorded to another tape deck. 'Every time it is copied or displayed, it suffers irreversible damage. Its signs are abraded and come closer to being mere and useless things' (Borgmann 1999: 167). It was not until the advent of digital coding that sound could be considered 'perfectly contained' in a storage medium.

The more often an analogue signal is sampled, the more accurate its digital representation and consequent reproduction will be. The coding standard colloquially referred to as 'CD quality' samples each second of analogue signal 44,100 times, and in professional recording there is typically a sampling rate of 96,000 Hz (Thompson and Thompson 2000: 321ff.). The sampling process ensures that 'there is no discernible difference between the sound recorded in the studio and the signal reproduced on the consumer's CD system' (Goodwin 1990: 259). In a technical sense at least there is a stable and 'perfect' signal equilibrium between the producing and the listening end. In the late 1980s the digital signal of CDs was marketed with the slogan 'Perfect Sound Forever' (Harley 1998: 255).

Sound on the screen

Musicians can create sound on synthesizers, and they are therefore liberated from the restrictions of studio acoustics. But they are also liberated from an enormous amount of wiring and apparatus that were necessary in the analogue era. Indeed, there are such a large number of plug-ins and digital devices that the entire work of production can take place in front of the computer screen. In this creative environment the features of the signal can be sculpted in enormous detail. Brian Eno has described the multitrack studio as a microscope for sound (Cunningham 1998: 334), and this description is highly relevant for contemporary audio software.

To illustrate the functionality of software audio I asked haltKarl to supply a facsimile of the composition 'Almost Gills' as it looks when spread out on a computer screen in Cubase. It demonstrates well the contemporary work environment for musicians.

At the bottom of figure 3.4 we can see the symbols for starting, stopping, pausing and winding back or forward, and for many producers they provide an immediate association with the obsolete interface of the magnetic tape machine. It is a standard strategy in graphical design to make new interfaces resemble the old ones wherever possible. Another example of this is the faders to the top right, which look very much like those on an analogue mixing board. The design also borrows structures from notational systems in acoustics with the curves that display volume and other physical characteristics. Other features that are not shown in figure 3.4 borrow the structure of musical notation systems, and the musician can plot notes directly into the interface.

To the left of the figure we can see that the tracks are organized in a series of horizontal rows (much like tables in Excel), and this is the main tool for multitrack production. Each track is an independent file, and this means, for example, that the volume, the frequency, the speed of reproduction, and all kinds of effects can be manipulated independently for that track.

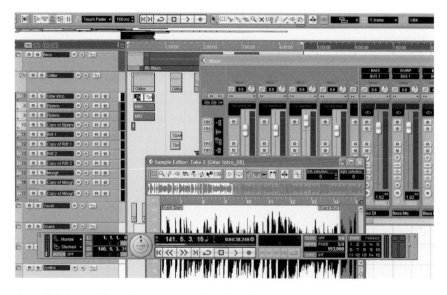

Figure 3.4 Screen shot of composition in audio software.

During the multitrack work process the software is alive with animation. The tracks that are selected for visual presentation will flow through the screen from left to right. In audio software there are many features that depend on the animated representation of sound in the graphical display. One of the most striking is the fact that each track can be zoomed into in great detail and processed accordingly. Each sound signal can be rearranged so that the chronology changes, the pitch and volume can be altered, and the recording speed can be slowed down or speeded up. All this can be done in minute detail. For each track the sound signal can be manipulated at the level of minutes, seconds, tenths of seconds, hundredths of seconds, or milliseconds.

My point is that digital sound production is anchored in computer graphics. The visual guidance has a radically creative influence, since the complex doctoring of sound in contemporary music could not have been achieved without it. The coordinate system and graphs that can be displayed on the screen have greater analytic detail than even the most skilled hands at the knobs of the tape recording machine could achieve. The combination of acute listening to the sounds and visual guidance on the screen becomes a powerful tool.

The mixing board is for many purposes embedded in this graphical interface. It has been an instrument in the recording process for several decades, and as I have stressed it has become an instrument almost in the same sense as the guitar or the piano. The mixing board is a blender, where any sound source can be channelled to an appropriate destination and all the signal streams can be manipulated independently of each other. For decades the mixing board forced technicians and musicians to develop skills in hand–ear coordination in order to work with sound. The mixing board was a huge electronic component, with hundreds of knobs and levers (see the cover of this book, where a Midas XL3 is depicted). Developments in the computer industry have greatly reduced the focus on such manual labour and increased the emphasis on hand–eye micro-movements.

Among producers there is now an expectation that they can do anything with sound on the computer. Paul Théberge says that the 'infinite malleability of the sequenced data mitigates against the idea of a single, finished product; indeed, many musicians complain that in the studio it is difficult to know when to stop working and rearranging the sequenced material' (Théberge 1997: 229). Since it is easy to make radical alterations even in the later stages of production, there is more decision-making than before, and recording becomes a question of initiative and the lack thereof. 'When faced with a stunning array of possibilities, it becomes difficult to determine exactly what decision to make, what choice is the right one', Steve Jones (1992: 153) observes.

Perfect sound

Finally I will focus on the way that music is consumed in domestic settings. Music lovers create a sweet spot in their living room by placing the loudspeakers so that they point to the same point in the room, and when they have adjusted the volume, bass and treble they lean back to enjoy the music. There is great public concern with the fidelity of sound, and it seems that CDs and the stereo system are still considered the best platform for sound reproduction. Poor sound is only a reflection of poor equipment. Less than perfect sound is somehow a result of one's economic situation and other factors completely external to the CD medium.

But sound perfection only takes us so far. Imagine that you have just rented a car, and have to drive for a really long time. In the glove compartment you find a cassette tape by Bruce Springsteen, and you put it on knowing well that the old cassette played on a cheap car stereo will not sound anything like your CD system. But you really like Bruce Springsteen, and you are delighted at this happy coincidence. The experience of recorded music as such is more important than any individual platform for it. My point is that, when digital recording arrived, music lovers were already satisfied, and some people consider the warm and round sound of 1950s and 1960s vacuum tube amplifiers to be superior to current CD equipment, which is often considered cold and sharp-edged.

Platforms that are not related to the computer suffer a decline, and become increasingly obsolete among the new generations of listeners. The sounds created by Frank Zappa on magnetic tape with LP distribution are only present to us with their sound signals, and not with the manual techniques that were used to record and play them. If they are available only as mp3 files on the computer, they must be handled with the techniques of mp3 files on the computer. The listener does not crank up the mechanical gramophone to listen to Enrico Caruso on the internet. In this way the production and listening techniques of obsolete platforms slowly disappear. Even the CD player is fast becoming obsolete because of file transfer on the internet, although the music industry is trying to counteract this development.

On the other hand, there is no difference in the strictly auditory experience of recorded music. Let us say you download the Frank Zappa music as an mp3 file, and then you play it back through the stereo set that you got for Christmas in 1994. Although the storage and distribution platform has changed, the auditory experience in front of the loudspeaker remains more or less unchanged. The acoustic drama has been greater in earlier times, for example when stereo amplification replaced mono sound in the 1960s.

Chapter 4

The mobile public
Journalism for urban navigators

Sound is very useful for mobile communication, and it is more useful than live images if you are driving a car or navigating in other ways. Urban dwellers in particular listen to the radio while they travel around the city. And there are professional news services that cater to this mobile public by constantly presenting updated information about relevant topics such as weather, traffic and public events in the city.

This chapter is concerned with the documentary realism in the programming of news stations. Their entire output is based on the implicit claim that this information can be trusted – that the navigators can continue their travel and rely on the station to present true and relevant information about crucial issues. To accomplish this big task, news stations have an efficient, centralized newsroom that is run according to strict journalistic procedures. Many people work in concert to create a constantly updated news service and a good flow in the programme. The case study for this chapter involves the news station, 1010 WINS in New York City, a station that has been run according to an all-news format since the 1960s and which is one of the oldest in the world of its type. I will analyse the main news and its distinctive sound as it appeared in the year 2001.

The mobile media landscape

Before I go into this type of broadcasting in detail, I want to sketch the wider perspective. Modern life in the West is full of urban navigation. People are walking, cycling, driving a car, taking the subway, going by train, going by boat, and flying aeroplanes, and we are all going somewhere in particular. As individuals move around the city, village or countryside they can only rely on their own skills of navigation. And information that media can supply is often very useful during these acts of navigation. Wireless communication is particularly interesting as a provider of relevant information for individuals.

Figure 4.1 shows that there is a wide array of wireless news media on the market. This chapter will focus on services that can be distributed on the platforms drawn in black: AM/FM radio, DAB radio and satellite radio. Although

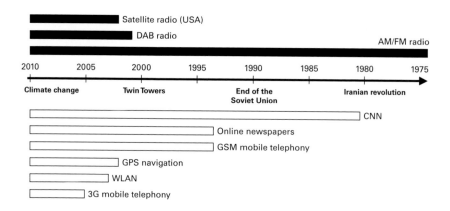

Figure 4.1 Timeline of wireless media.

I will analyse radio journalism's contribution, I will first describe the wider landscape in some detail.

Below the arrow I have listed a series of live media that have the potential to become potent news providers, or that have already been potent for many years, such as CNN. The advanced wireless technologies such as satellite GPS navigation are at the pinnacle of a hundred years' worth of innovation in the transmission of signals. Although GPS has enormous editorial potential, it has not been properly exploited yet, and it has unresolved issues about protection of privacy. I will discuss the potential of GPS journalism briefly at the end of the chapter.

The good old terrestrial radio stations still dominate the mobile media when it comes to news and current affairs, basically because the free and simple reception of the signal is a continuing attraction for listeners. However, subscription-based satellite radio has been available in the USA since 2001. It is used mainly for nationally syndicated programmes, and less for the kind of all-news services that I will analyse here. DAB radio was introduced in Europe at about the same time as satellite radio in the USA, mainly as a higher quality platform for traditional content (Lax *et al*. 2008). Notice, however, that both satellite and DAB radio can transmit meta-data and short messages along with the sound, and, for example, music information, traffic updates and news feeds can be piped through to the small text display screen.

The mobile phone is perhaps the most versatile tool when it comes to navigation, since it is a personal medium which few people lend out to others, and the user therefore always has it easy to hand. You can contact other people in a crisis, or you can browse through websites on WAP. A WAP browse provides the same basic service as a web browser, but the interface is simplified to operate within the restrictions of a mobile phone, for example the small screen and low bandwidth.

Online news sites are quite prominent in the mobile media industry in the 2000s. A website can present text and graphics of high practical value, for example maps, directions, alerts, and so on. But although the user can read websites on laptops in wireless hotspots while travelling, news sites on the internet are truly mobile only if the user has a broadband-equipped telephone serviced by a high-speed mobile network. In many Western countries there are such services which give you the entire internet on your mobile phone. Clearly these digital services can help you to navigate more efficiently through a big city and to socialize with other people in new ways (Rheingold 2002).

When considering to news services it is important to mention all news stations on television, since they are the strongest competitor for radio news. While travelling, people typically listen to the radio, but when they get home they immediately turn on the TV and forget about the radio until they leave the house again. The most famous all-news network in the world is probably CNN, which was started in the early 1980s but had its real international breakthrough during the Gulf War in 1991 (Gitlin 2002: 171). Later examples are BBC World, MSNBC and Bloomberg Television. But the idea of really quick updating of news was first established during World War II. Public demands for new information was a strong influence, and it forced the broadcasting stations both to have hourly bulletins and to become more professional at handling the news (Crisell 1997: 56). In the latter half of the twentieth century the process towards more frequent updating culminated with the 24-hour news format. In a time-bound medium this is the maximum limit.

All news all the time

1010 WINS is a 24-hour all-news radio station for the greater metropolitan area of New York. It compiles journalistic information about the following thirteen counties: Manhattan, Brooklyn, Queens, Bronx, Staten Island, Nassau County, Suffolk County, Fairfield County, Bergen County, Essex County, Long Island, Westchester County and Rockland County. This list alone tells us something about the level of detail in the station's journalism.

Before going into detail about journalistic production, I will describe the sheer sound of this type of radio. It ticks along like a clock through the day. Every full hour there is a high-pitched beep to signal the time, and then comes a brass fanfare over a Morse code-like percussive rhythm. A male voice says: 'All news all the time. This is 1010 WINS. You give us twenty-two minutes, we'll give you the world.' The ticking sound continues as the news reading commences. Notice that five different journalists speak during the first minute.

Track 13: 1010 WINS: Top of the Hour, 2001 (2:24).

– Good morning, 67 degrees at 7 o'clock, it is Wednesday May 2nd, I'm Lee Harris, and here's what's happening. Con-Ed reportedly wants to fire up the city's most polluting power plant to deal with the energy crunch, but environmentalists say that move is illegal.

– Say it ain't so, Joe Namath. Would the Jets really move to LA? This is John Montone, I'll have fan reaction from Carlstad.

[Back to Lee Harris]

– Police and prosecutors are looking into the fatal shooting of an unarmed Newark man by an Irvington police officer who killed another man during a traffic stop four years ago. Super model Nicky Taylor remains in critical condition with severe liver damage following a car crash in Atlanta. And you probably don't know any of them, but we are told millions of Americans are taking up yoga to deal with all the stress in their lives.

– This is Accuweather meteorologist Dr Joe Sobel. Sunshine will help temperatures get to near ninety today and tomorrow. Could be record highs.

– This is Steve Torre. The Devils win at overtime in Toronto, to grab a two–one lead in their second round series. The Yankees behind. Mike Michina shot out the twins. The Mets rally to beat the Astros at Shea.

– I'm Ron Emmeda, and Rupert Murdoch moves closer to buying Hughes Electronics from GM. And April was not a kind month for the nation's auto makers.

[Back to Lee Harris]

– WINS Newstime 7.01. [A synth marks the time, and a keyboard rhythm ensues] Traffic and Transit on the one's now. Sponsored by New Jersey Transit. Here's Pete Tauriello.

The excerpt ends with a long traffic report that I have not transcribed here, but it will be dealt with in detail in the next section. The most important thing to notice is the lively sound of the news flow. There is a clear rhetorical strategy behind it. The output is typically heard on car radios with poor reception, on clock radios in the bedroom, and on cheap mono radios in the kitchen. The station caters explicitly to this acoustic contact, processing the presentation to sound crisp and intelligible, but at the same time coarse, solid and sturdy. The news sound is kept up hour by hour, and year by year, and only the commercials create breaks in this endless flow of news. The characteristic sound means that regular listeners can easily find the station on the AM band.

The work environment in news stations is very different from that of recording studios. Broadcast studio environments are busier and more stressful for the producers and performers alike (see Herbert 2000: 22ff.). Instead of having all the time in the world to edit and mix the sound, they are organizing a never-ending live transmission. The idea of a second take is absurd, as it has always been in live radio.

The all-news format is not built to create sustained listening throughout the day but to create frequent revisiting whenever people might need an update (Crisell 1994; Shingler and Wieringa 1998; McLeish 1999). 1010 WINS typically completes a full circle of news, traffic and weather in around twenty minutes. All news stations present themselves as a standing reserve of updated, relevant, fresh information in a designated area, building their credibility on catering to the information needs and interests of their listeners at any time.

Since the format is trained towards news stories with short-term relevance, there is a sense of urgency and immediacy to the programming. This could be called *practically live* programming. The output has been scripted and read during the last ten to twenty minutes, and that is sufficient for a sense of real-time progression to be incurred.

Stations that choose to adopt this format are typically based in big cities, where the population is dense enough for it to be profitable to set up such an editorial service, and where the surroundings are actually complex enough that there is a real need for guidance among the inhabitants. The stations can draw on strong feelings of local community among their listeners and they can also cultivate this sense of community in their programmes. 'People's feelings about community, about territory, work and weekends, roads and traffic, memory and play, and what might be happening across town' are seized by radio so that it can 'map our symbolic and social environment' (Jody Berland, quoted in Hendy 2000: 188).

The message is very important on news stations. It might involve a suspension of the alternate parking rule, the name of the newly elected mayor, or a terrorist attack; and in no case is the sound produced as a background feature. This is different from much of the contemporary radio and music output, which is often produced as a comfortable living space for listeners. The practical implications of the information form the main issue for listeners, and consequently news production consists of detecting events that take place in the public sphere, describing them according to the relevance for the listeners, and radiating them back to the public sphere. The journalists talk about the features of the city in a way that presumes their listeners are familiar with its outline, and the common reference created in this way can metaphorically be called a map of the city. The suburbs are distinguished from the city centre; the seashore, rivers, bridges and roads are outlined, and within these implicit geographical borders the political and commercial organization of the city is followed up carefully.

Get mobile today

The car is an extension of the person's ability to walk, or, as McLuhan spectacularly states: 'it is an extension of man that turns the rider into a superman' ([1964] 1994: 221). The car is one of the few settings in which radio can get the listener's full attention. A British driver says: 'My best moments of radio happen in the car because I am stuck with it. Television and printed materials are out of the question and, unless I want to listen to tapes, radio becomes the central focus of my attention' (quoted in Shingler and Wieringa 1998: 111). When driving the listener is open to new information about the geographical area he moves around in.

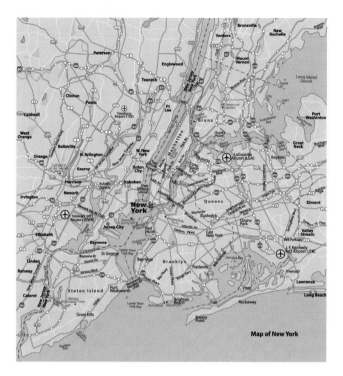

Figure 4.2 A map of New York.

The car listener is a splendid example of an 'urban navigator' and will be my main protagonist in the next sections. A navigator is simply a pilot or a guide. This is a person who is in transit from one place to another and checks the coordinates of an unknown or at least a confusing area by the use of instruments or memory, and he either carries other people with him or travels alone. The navigator's destination varies greatly through the day and the week, but some routes are driven very often, such as the route to work.

I will describe a scenario where a car driver who lives on Staten Island is about to go to work in Brooklyn. The navigator leaves home in a Staten Island suburb at 7 a.m. and turns on 1010 WINS. A slow drive to downtown Brooklyn lies ahead, first onto the Staten Island Expressway and then across the Verrazano-Narrows Bridge to Brooklyn. After crossing the bridge, if there isn't too much traffic, he can drive on the Gowanus Expressway all the way to downtown Brooklyn. During the morning rush hour this stretch of 20 to 25 kilometres will take approximately one hour.

People driving from Staten Island towards Brooklyn around 7 a.m. on Wednesdays will move slowly, especially on the Gowanus Expressway. On 1010

WINS Pete Tauriello says: 'Bumper to bumper delays in Brooklyn, Lee, on the Gowanus from the Belt right up to 38th Street, where we have a box truck broken down, blocking the left lane.' Since there is no mention of the Verrazano Bridge, the driver can presume that traffic on this stretch moves at a normal tempo, which is a good thing if there is trouble on the Gowanus. 'Bumper to bumper delays' is an unhappy word for everybody who has not yet passed 38th Street. It means that the speed may have slowed down to 5 or 10 kilometres an hour, which will at worst double the drive time.

By 7.30 our driver has entered the Gowanus Expressway. Hundreds of cars are standing almost completely still because of that accident on 38th Street in Brooklyn. With a touch of compassion Tauriello informs that traffic has completely stopped on the inbound Gowanus at 38th Street. As 1010 WINS moves towards 8 a.m., some listeners are so completely stuck in traffic that they do not really need more information. When traffic starts moving again they will notice without any help from the radio studio. And now a short message from our sponsors:

Track 14: Unknown artist: Get Mobilized, 2000 (1:00).

> Get up, get out, it's another day,
> You're on the road trying to make it pay,
> Too many things to do and not enough time,
> Don't want to find yourself sitting in line.
> Who wants to spend their life at the pump,
> We've all got somewhere to go.
> Fill her up fast and be on your way,
> Get mobilized, get Mobil today.
> Pick up the kids, pick up some bread,
> Gotta keep moving to stay ahead,
> Sometimes it feels like you live in your car,
> Seems like you drive all day and never get too far.
> Fill her up fast and be on your way,
> Get mobilized, get Mobil today.

This little tune was put on air in the USA by Mobil Oil. The unknown band tells an encouraging story about everyday life on the road, and the melody is reminscent of a thousand country-and-western songs. The purpose of this ad is to make listeners recognize the need to be on their way, and associate this important feature of their lives with Mobil Oil.

Advertisements such as this recommend people to act as navigators so that the oil company can earn money on petrol. The advertisement shows that the navigator is also a rhetorical phenomenon; it is a role that is staged in the public sphere in order to influence the citizen to behave according to the role, and it connects well with what James Carey calls the rhetoric of the technological sublime: 'Everyman a prophet with his own machine to keep him in control'

(Carey and Quirk 1989: 117). People are led to believe that the greater control and power they have over their lives, the better their lives are.

In contrast to the ad, 1010 WINS's editorial reports most definitely have use value. The traffic report may influence the pattern of traffic through the area and inspire reflections on strategic possibilities among listeners who are not in the middle of the tailback, but who know the routes. This is to say that the news station offers a pragmatic mapping of a given area. When 1010 WINS say they will give you the world, they mean the world within practical reach, which in this case is New York City. It would be absurd to syndicate this kind of programming on a national scale.

Breaking news

Suddenly, the breaking news jingle disrupts the routine progression of the day. Our driver on the Gowanus Expressway instantly knows that something bad has happened. When a local station presents breaking news, the news may be directly relevant for the navigator's next move, since it may imply that he or his family is in real danger.

Track 15: 1010 WINS: Breaking News, 2001 (1:23).

[Synth-based heading] 'Breaking news now on 1010 WINS.'
James Faraday: 'This just came into our news room: A plane has crashed into the World Trade Center. Let's get this live update from 1010 WINS correspondent Joan Fleischer. Joan, what do you see?'
Joan Fleischer: 'Well, I'm standing on the top of my roof and I'm looking at the World Trade Center and there is a huge hole in it, and there is a fire in the building right now, huge smoke pouring out of it and things are falling from the building itself [...]'
James Faraday: 'Allright, 1010 WINS correspondent Joan Fleischer on the scene in Lower Manhattan ... er ... any emergency personnel on the scene as of yet, do you see?'
Joan Fleischer: 'I can't see anybody but I hear the fire trucks ... and ... I heard the plane very close to the top of the buildings. I looked outside and I saw it hit and it exploded immediately.'
James Faraday: 'Did you manage to see what kind of plane it was?'
Joan Fleischer: 'I couldn't tell, it looked like a smaller plane but I couldn't tell, no I'm not really sure. I would say it wasn't a huge jet, but it was a plane that sounded like it was a fighter jet overhead and then I saw it explode close to the building.'
James Faraday: 'Are you able to see any wreckage on the ground from where you stand?'
Joan Fleischer: 'No, I'm too high up.'

Figure 4.3 Brooklyn, September 11, 2001.

We hear the very first attempt to describe the fact that a passenger plane has crashed into the World Trade Center, before anybody had really understood what was happening. The anchor is located in Midtown Manhattan where the studios are, while the witness, Joan Fleischer, speaks on a landline telephone from her apartment in Lower Manhattan. Her apartment overlooks the Twin Towers, and she is in the perfect position to describe what happens. Our driver in Brooklyn also has a perfect view, but from a much greater distance.

I will analyse the technique of journalistic eyewitnessing at length. The radio woman and the car driver are both witnesses to the events, but in two different ways. There are two meanings to the notion of witness; seeing something in a passive way, and saying something about what you see (Peters 2001: 709). Joan Fleischer is thrown into the latter role, and is charged with the responsibility of finding the words to describe this unexpected and harrowing event.

As the scale of the disaster dawned on people, the entire city ground to a halt. The moving public of New York was immobilized by traffic jams and overload in all communication systems. Drivers would be even more completely stuck in their cars when the mobile system crashed, with nothing better to do than listen to the radio news and ask themselves what will happen next.

As we all know, the September 11 events became global news in an instant, and all news companies in the world reorganized their schedules to capture what was going on in New York. The same is true for 1010 WINS. Along with other local news stations they were in a good position to report from the disaster. They had several roaming reporters who had to record on tape and drive back to the studio to publish them on air, because the wireless networks for telephony were down. John Montone at one point reported through a public telephone booth, playing his cassette recording close to the mouthpiece.

In New York on this particular day there were thousands of witnesses, but since the mobile phone network was blown out very few could give describe what they experienced there and then. If we compare their situation with that of Joan Fleischer at 1010 WINS, it is clear that most of the listeners in the greater metropolitan area were at a safer distance. Indeed, most New Yorkers would have no first-hand experience of the disaster, but only hear about it on radio and TV. John Ellis (2000: 11) points out two typical qualities of this experience: powerlessness and safety. The listeners on September 11 were powerless in the face of the attack, but could feel relatively safe (except that there was fear of more attacks in other locations).

But even at a distance they would be profoundly touched by what they saw. Paddy Scannell (1996: 101) distinguishes between witness and victim in a way that helps me to get the point across. The witness might have seen the whole thing first hand, but is nevertheless at a certain distance from the event. The victim, on the other hand, is at the centre of events in a far more volatile way. 'It's the difference between direct and indirect involvement, between something happening to oneself and seeing something happen to some others.' The implications of being a victim fitted the urban navigators in New York City during September 11 quite well. The victim engages in a self-oriented behaviour where he feels sorrowful or angry in and for himself (ibid.). This is how the drivers on the Gowanus Expressway and other New York arteries must have felt after some hours of gridlock, with new and disturbing events constantly being reported on the radio.

Eyewitnessing

Joan Fleischer is an administrator at the radio station, but as soon as the newsroom is made aware of her ideal location she steps in as an eyewitness. The authority of her report relies on the timbres of her voice. In her shock and dismay we have proof that this is actually happening, or at least the listener would have to be very suspicious if they were to claim that her eyewitness reports are staged.

In rhetorical terms, the eyewitness's credibility relies on making the listener believe that the speaker has direct access to an aspect of the world as it is currently developing. The eyewitness makes the listener believe that what is said is actual and real. This classical notion of documentary realism comes across in Harold Mendelsohn's 1962 claim that live news and information programmes 'allow the listener to participate vicariously in the great events of the day', and that the listener identifies more strongly with the speaker 'merely by virtue of having been a witness to the same happenings' (quoted in Fornatale and Mills 1980: xvii).

The next case study displays eyewitnessing at its most extreme. The listener is likely to be touched not only by the physical drama of the events that are described, but also by the psychological drama of the reporter's effort to describe it.

Track 16: 1010 WINS: The South Tower Collapses, 2001 (2:16).

> Lee Harris: '... called it quit while they were ahead there. And all of this, the World ...'
> Joan: 'Oh wait, oh my God there is ... [scream] ... oh my God, the building fell!!! Are you there? The building just fell!'
> Lee: 'Which, which building? ...'
> Joan: 'Oh my God! The south building fell, the south building just crumbled from the top [shaky voice] ohh my God, the building just fell! The entire World Trade Center, the south building, just fell. I just saw the whole thing. Oh my God! oh my God! I can't see anything, but the whole thing went down. Oh my God! Ohh, I saw the building crumble, it's all the way down. I can't see at what point it is still standing. Oh my God, ohhhhh ...' [several seconds of gasps and sighs]
> Lee: [shaky voice] 'If what Joan is saying is true, the tower has just collapsed ...' [Beeping sound – time signal at 10 o'clock]. This is 1010 WINS ...' [beeping sound]
> Joan: 'Ohh my God, the building just crumbled.'
> Lee: 'This is 1010 WINS, New York. One of the [Joan: ohh ... completely down] two towers, the south tower of the World Trade Center, has just ... crumbled, collapsed in a pile of dust [Joan: Ohh], this approximately one hour after it was hit by an aircraft.'
> Joan: '... the second building ... the second building completely down. [Joan speaks to a man] ... you heard the ... me too!'
> Lee: 'Uhh ... a situation that started bad just gets worse and worse and worse. The World Trade Center, south tower, that was hit by a plane and wrecked by an explosion, approximately an hour ago, has totally collapsed. The north tower is still standing, but the World Trade Center south tower has collapsed. Let's go live to CNN for a moment.'

Notice the effect of the outdoors acoustics that is picked up by Joan Fleischer's mouthpiece. There is a frantic wailing of fire engines, and clearly something very dramatic must be happening for so many to be in the same spot with their sirens going at the same time. This is a good example of how environmental sounds lend documentary authority to a news report.

Joan Fleischer's eyewitness account of the event is highly engaging. As suggested, the way she utters her words is in itself a symptom of something dramatic. The hesitation and stammering is completely different from the news reporter's regular way of speaking on air. She is emotional, hurt and shocked – all that a news journalist is supposedly not. Goffman (1981: 223) says that the traditional news reader's role 'requires the performer to set aside all other claims upon himself except that of presenting the script smoothly'. But this type of neutral address is impossible for Joan Fleischer, and her emotional reaction is of course exactly what makes the eyewitness report so convincing.

Lee Harris is safe in 1010 WINS's studios in Midtown Manhattan, but he nevertheless struggles to cope with the situation. He is almost unable to speak coherently, and he sounds quite distressed. When he says 'a situation that started bad just gets worse and worse and worse', we can easily hear how shaken he is. After summing up the disaster he says 'Let's go live to CNN for a moment', and it sounds as if he is in desperate need of time out.

How does his behaviour compare to the journalistic procedures? It is a rule of radio journalism that the news reader should sound lively, confident and sensitive so that he becomes even more credible as a source of information. 'The overall process should give the listener the impression that the broadcaster's *talking* to him rather than *reading* at him. It's prepared, of course, but it should *sound* spontaneous' (McLeish 1999: 65). Lee Harris demonstrates that in breaking news situations the speech can actually be spontaneous all the way down, and this makes the journalism highly credible. Sometimes, as the journalistic procedures break down completely, the trustworthiness of the production skyrockets.

The radio medium, 2008

It may seem strange that the medium of radio is not discussed until chapter 4 in a book about sound media. However, the computer with its internet connection and enormous possibilities for digital manipulation had to be presented first, because computers also influence the production values of radio in our time as well as the listeners' media behaviour. But radio is still a self-sufficient medium with the same strengths and weaknesses as it has always had.

There are four different platforms involved in the medium of 2008, all with their own gigantic distribution system. These are terrestrial transmission, satellite transmission, mobile networks and the internet. I will focus on the two platforms that are most directly important for traditional radio services, namely terrestrial and satellite transmission (the internet's functionality was discussed in chapter 2, and the mobile phone will be discussed in chapter 5).

Figure 4.4 shows the basic interfaces and platforms in modern radio. Programmes are created with microphones, mixing boards and computers. The signal goes to the transmission stations, where they are radiated out through satellite systems in the sky or radio towers on the ground. Imagine the great distance between the satellite in the sky and the radio receiver on the ground, and you see the scale of the operation. The signal is received on quite small and handy receivers, which are either portable (in the car, for example) or wearable on the listener's body. One of the key features of both satellite and terrestrial transmission is therefore that the listeners can roam around freely in the environment without having any reception problems. It is the same thing with mobile telephony, since this also relies on signal transport through the air.

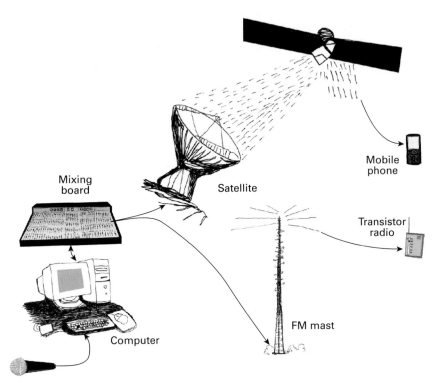

Figure 4.4 Model of the wireless sound medium.

Interestingly, the atmosphere around the earth is a most important carrier of information. It is used for military and commercial communication, and people are in fact constantly exposed to ultra high-frequency signals that criss-cross our bodies at the speed of light.

Terrestrial radio could also be called *ground broadcasting*. Whether they carry digital signals such as DAB or analogue signals for FM and AM, the waves spread in a line-of-sight fashion into the natural environment. The signals go straight ahead, and do not curve around hills and mountains; nor do they conduct along the ground as lower frequency waves do. There is no way to pick up American broadcasting in Australia late at night (except by web radio through the internet). It should be noted that ground broadcasting is therefore very precise and localized, and if a station has only one transmitter in a hilly area many people will fall outside the zone of reception. If a station has national coverage it is only because dozens of transmitters and hundreds of signal repeaters have been built all around the country. AM and FM broadcasting is especially suitable for local and regional media outlets. Terrestrial radio will be analysed at length in later chapters.

Satellite radio could also be called *sky broadcasting*. When the signal leaves the radio station it goes to an up-link antenna which maintains a link with the satellite, and is fed with new information all the time. Geostationary satellites have a very high data capacity, and can offer hundreds of stations simultaneously to potentially millions of people. The satellite orbits in the direction of the Earth's rotation, at an altitude of approximately 35,786 kilometres. For reception equipment on the ground a satellite with geostationary orbit always appears in the same location in the sky, and satellite is therefore a very practical platform for transmitting signals to the same geographical area over a long period of time.

Satellite reception allows a listener to roam across an entire continent, listening to the same audio programming anywhere they go. The antenna must have a clear view to the satellite, and in areas where tall buildings, bridges, or even parking garages obscure the signal, repeaters can be placed to improve it. The receiver interface resembles the TV receiver in many regards. There can be a recording functionality, programme pause and resume, and a graphical display of available services. An important difference is that there is no satellite dish with a fixed position, and the reception is therefore much more mobile.

The receiver for terrestrial radio looks much the same as that for satellite radio. This is especially true for DAB. Both satellite and DAB signals can carry radio text or dynamic label segments from the station, and can give journalistic information such as song titles, music type and news or traffic updates, and of course also commercial messages. Advance programme guides can also be transmitted. A similar feature also exists for FM in the form of the radio data system (RDS), which can transmit the station's ID and also retune the car receiver to stations that have regular traffic bulletins. These features are not very spectacular compared to those of a mobile phone, and it seems clear that much more experimentation is needed to achieve true innovation in terrestrial broadcasting.

GPS journalism

I will end this chapter with a comment on GPS, which may be the thing of the future regarding news and information services for urban navigators. The Global Positioning System (GPS) is based on a gigantic infrastructure of satellites in outer space. There is a constellation of at least twenty-four medium earth orbit satellites that transmit precise microwave signals, and the system enables a GPS receiver to determine its local time, location, speed of movement and direction of movement. This information is produced by triangulating the position and time of several satellites.

The ability to determine the receiver's absolute location allows GPS receivers to act as a surveying tool or as an aid to navigation for ships, cars, freight lorries, aeroplanes, and so on. Much of this communication is completely private, and there is little or no coordination of people via GPS. Museums and zoological gardens can use location data to present information about artworks or caged animals. The visitors carry a hand-held device and when they get near to the object in question a pre-recorded tape or video starts playing automatically; if they leave the zone the recording will stop. If the focus were changed to a more direct experimentation with social coordination, GPS journalism might be a rhetorical technique with great potential for the future.

Technically speaking there could be a GPS chip in every new radio receiver. Notice the resources that would be put at the disposal of journalism: the time, location, speed of movement and direction of movement of every single listener, registered continually. The journalistic potential of such a databank is enormous. Of course such a resource could also be exploited cynically for purposes of surveillance or blackmail.

There are no widespread journalistic techniques in this field yet, and no established listener techniques either. But the technology harbours features that would greatly empower the urban navigator. Imagine that you could log into a station community where all the topics and all the information is organized to assist you at your present location, and new batches of information are presented when you move into a new location. The listeners are likely to feel an even stronger identification with the community of which they are part than they do with what stations such as 1010 WINS are able to do now. With GPS journalism the station can administer the busy life of urban navigators in a safe and controlled way, at least during the calm period until the next breaking news turns everything upside down.

Chapter 5

Phone radio

Personality journalism in voice alone

Talk radio is a mixture of voices from the phone and voices from the radio studio. Radio has always had a bias towards personalities, and now it is stronger than ever. The radio industry thrives on the opinions, anecdotes, jokes and confessions of ordinary people.

This chapter is concerned with the centralized, editorial procedures of professional talk stations, and in particular focuses on what could be called personality journalism. I will analyse not just how journalists present themselves to the public, but also how lay participants do it. There are three case studies: an old lady in London calls a current affairs show on LBC Talk in 2004; two young girls from Crewe (UK) call to participate in a quiz on BBC Radio 1 in 2001; and a depressed husband calls the psychiatrist Dr Joy Browne on 710 WOR in New York. Their behaviour was diagnosed long ago: McLuhan ([1964] 1994: 299) wrote that 'radio affects most people intimately, person-to-person, offering a world of unspoken communication between the writer-speaker and the listener.'

The talk media landscape

Talking is a fundamental means of communication between people. It is among the first communication skills we learn, and is already well developed at the age of five. My point is that talking is not an expert activity like computer programming, news journalism or record production, where ordinary people often cannot contribute in a valuable way.

On the contrary, speech is one of the forms of communication that is truly democratic and inclusive. But the media have historically cultivated professional, normalized speech of the type that can be called 'recital' and 'role play', and which is not very personal. However, with the emergence of the mobile phone and all kinds of reality shows on television since the 1990s, there has been a rhetorical turn towards ordinary talk and behaviour on radio also. This tolerance for ordinary communication is much stronger than, for example, in the 1960s, when the phone had no particular role at all in radio programmes, and everything had to be spoken according to received pronunciation.

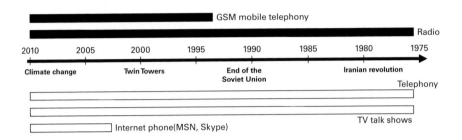

Figure 5.1 Timeline of talk media.

There are reality shows and singing contests, and quiz shows where anybody can sign up. For at least ten years the general public has been trained in singing, dancing, eating, arguing and displaying all kinds of (traditionally) private behaviour in public. Radio has a modest role in this huge endeavour, but none the less a vital one (see Scannell 1991). Radio has mobilized ordinary people, predominantly on the mobile phone, which gives a particularly direct and intimate contact between the private and the public. The sheer volume of talk radio is amazing. There are hundreds of dedicated talk radio stations scattered locally around in the USA and Europe. Phone-ins are among the cheapest forms of programme production, since there is no costly reporting and editing and no expensive traveling for the crew.

Figure 5.1 shows how stable the media involved in talk radio have been during the last thirty to forty years. The programmes are distributed either on AM/FM, DAB or satellite radio (see chapter 4), which I conceive of in general terms in this chapter as 'radio'. For the radio industry the only significant change in the context of talk radio is the introduction of the mobile phone among ordinary people.

Under the timeline I have listed three media set-ups that also convey lots of talk. Of course talk shows on television have existed so long that they influence conversations all across the nation, and the telephone medium is so obviously a part of our lives that we don't even think about it as a medium. The final category is internet phone, which involve networks of voice communication provided by companies such as Skype and MSN. Callers can congregate in a number of ways; for example, they can make conference calls, send chat messages, or go to one-on-one mode and talk in private.

It is important to notice that the mobile phone is a personal medium in comparison with the house telephone, which is a shared domestic medium. The mobile phone has been studied extensively in latter years (see, for example, Katz and Aakhus 2002; Ling 2004; Mercer 2006; Katz 2006). There is much greater room for privacy and intimacy from a speaking device that people carry with them at all times and only hesitantly lend to anybody. In less than twenty years the mobile telephone has gone from being rare, and an expensive piece of equipment used by the business elite, to a pervasive, low-cost personal item. In many households the individual phone has completely replaced the traditional landline telephone.

There was little or no talk radio in the strict sense before the 1970s, and then mainly in the USA. But there was an upsurge in the USA after the repeal of the 'fairness doctrine' in 1987. This doctrine was enforced by the Federal Communications Commission and required that stations provide free air time for responses to any controversial opinions that were broadcast, and the repeal provided the opportunity for partisan programming that had not previously existed (Douglas 2002: 491). Talk radio in the USA gained ground after this time, and in many other countries there is also a strong tradition of tabloid as well as political talk radio (see, for example, Ross 2004; O'Sullivan 2005; Tolson 2006). If we look all the way back to the 1950s, radio was not telephone-driven at all. In the golden age of radio there were lots of radio personalities, but they were all professional and had rehearsed every second of their performance in advance. It was all more formal, more exclusive, and more marked by role play.

The lively sound of voices

The first case study is a morning talk show on LBC. Nick Ferrari's morning show is a staple of the station's weekday schedule. There is no music, only talk, jingles, commercials and news at the top of the hour. At the start of this particular programme Ferrari asked what the listeners thought about the erection of mobile phone masts in their neighbourhoods. First we hear a jingle in which a woman praises Nick Ferrari in no uncertain terms and leaves the impression that the host is something of a flirt. The voices of the two speakers are cheerful and energetic, and seem perfectly suited to the start of yet another busy day in London. Their everyday voices are full of pitch changes and lively intonations. This form of talk sounds nothing like radio did in the golden age.

Track 17: LBC London: Nick Ferrari with Rosemary, 2004 (3:05).

- Rosemary's in Kew. Hello Rosemary.
- Hello.
- Morning.
- Morning.
- How are we today?
- I've got a crick in my neck today.
- We need you to jump up and down if England win.
- What?
- You weren't listening, were you?
- No.

–You know, have you ever heard of John in Bellingham, one of the callers?
– Yes.
– He's out of the prison now, which is good. And he has this rather unhealthy obsession that, if England win tonight, he wants to imagine you jumping up and down with glee.
– He needn't bother, cause I don't watch that bloody football!
–You didn't let me finish. Jumping up and down with glee, naked as the day you were born!
– I should think so!
– Ha ha ha.
– I wouldn't like the sight myself.
– Ha ha ha. Bless you Rose, ohh, you are lovely. Now, what's wrong with you and phone masts?
–Well, we've had one put up the top of our road.
– Seven sevens, Rosemary.
– Pardon.
– Seven sevens. Come on.
– I don't know.
– I'm trying to keep your brain sharp [snapping his fingers].
– Don't do this to me in the morning!
– Ha. It's forty-nine. You wrote them out in a little handbook a few months back.
– I know, but I haven't got it here.
– All right. Keep going. I'll just occasionally throw questions at you. Sorry, go on.
–We've had one put up the top our road, which faces the high road, and our road was …
– Capital of Spain?
– Madrid.
–Yea. That's good. Just to keep your brain active. It's like an NHS sponsored scheme I'm doing for you. Go on.
–Anyway this thing went up, they closed up the road and the blessed crane came. And I always take the local papers and read the notices, public notices, so I know …
–Three pounds seventy-five in old money?
–What?
–Three pounds seventy-five in old money?
– Oh do leave off!

And so it continues. Nick Ferrari is the master of ceremonies, and one of his specialities is to play tricks on his callers. He seems to be free of all expressive regimes, and just going wherever his next whim takes him. In contrast, Rosemary from Kew doesn't know the tricks of Ferrari's show very well. She is nonplussed by his playful, whimsical behaviour, and during the conversation we can hear how there is a tuning up of the relationship between the professional and amateur personalities, so that in the end they are on the same level.

Rosemary did not call in to Ferrari's show to play games, she called following his invitation to talk about mobile masts. It turns out that she campaigned successfully against a mast near her local school, and the telecom company actually had to tear it down. But Ferrari is not really interested in phone masts, he is more interested in confusion among the callers. It is enjoyable for listeners to hear people who are nonplussed, and in this sense Rosemary is the perfect caller. But she has a quick mind, and as she warms up we can hear how she begins to handle the situation better. This is especially noticeable when Ferrari asks her to jump (naked) up and down with glee if England wins, and she says 'I wouldn't like the sight myself'. If she calls the show again, she will be better prepared.

Phone radio was a new genre in the 1990s. There is still a learning process in the general public about how to act in the public sphere when you are in the safety of your own home. Really inexperienced speakers who are suddenly cast on air will have a challenging job aligning their manner of being to the manner of the programme. More skilled and streetwise speakers will project a personality that they have used successfully before and that they can also use in media settings. The cult of listeners who regularly participate in phone-in programmes will have a more coherent stock of behavioural characteristics in reserve. They are familiar with the host's typical manner of being and can readily adopt his favoured caller attitude. They have learnt the right technique for talking on the radio in the capacity of just another ordinary person.

Rosemary is an inexperienced phone personality. It is tempting to argue that this makes her more natural-sounding than Ferrari; at least she displays fewer mannerisms of role play and a more spontaneous reactions than he does. Along with other radio amateurs she might spontaneously laugh at something, regardless of whether it is socially acceptable to do so, and she may not even realize that this laughter has a public impact.

In everyday life the characteristic verbal behaviour is more clear-cut. Basically, verbal behaviour is not performed to a microphone or camera, although it is of course experienced by other humans, and can be full of tactics and hidden agendas. But still there is no intentional role play for the public sphere. There is something special about recorded and transmitted behaviour, since it reaches the ears of thousands, perhaps millions, and can be repeated and analysed as long as anybody cares to do so.

Professionals sound natural on radio because audiences are used to the way in which they project themselves; they are just as familiar with the presentation as they are with news and factual information. There has been a historical development here. Anders Johansen (1999: 167) points out that during the history of broadcasting there has been a blurring of distinctions between the speaker and the topic of the speech, between the personality and the social role. Radio communicates more by psychological symptoms than by clear messages (like news bulletins), and these psychological symptoms create new conditions for the communication of credibility. The subtly suggestive is favoured at the expense of what is demonstratively told. John Langer (1981: 361) points out another aspect of this: 'Simply put, what is important is not so much what you actually say, but the fact that you can be seen saying *for yourself*. The very act of speaking for oneself is a type of disclosure. Talking for yourself and being "caught" and recorded doing so individuates you, makes you a personality whether you are the Prime Minister or last week's national lottery winner.' Erving Goffman's (1981: 296) notion of *self-reporting* also touches on the psychological dimension of radio speakers. Many people make frequent reference to their own passing thoughts and feelings while talking about any given topic. The speaker is meant to be heard as an expressive field on which the symptoms of attitudes, emotions and fancies play out spontaneously.

Shouting and having fun

Personality journalism relies quite heavily on the sounds of raw human energy. The vocal chords of hosts and guests alike are often red-hot, and in addition there is a constant trickle of sound effects (ticking clocks, gongs, fanfares, etc.) and bits of pop and rock music. Personality journalism thrives on semi-chaotic social situations in the studio and between interlocutors on the phone. There are studio shows where the host and his guests quarrel, shout and scream, and regularly slam the studio door. If the host makes a technical mistake he is likely to talk about it in order to make it natural. What used to be off stage has now become a great attraction on radio.

The goal for the editors is to create a sense of noisy, youthful energy, and the host is the main vehicle for the noise. In the USA the term 'shock jock' is used for hosts that are particularly rowdy and crazy, and who often talk more with their co-hosts and studio guests than with the callers. Andrew Tolson (2006: 120) also refers to the 'zoo aesthetic' of much talk radio.

The breakfast show on BBC's Radio 1 from six to nine in the morning has a long tradition of shock jocks and zoo aesthetics (Tolson 2006: 113–16). The next case study is from the Sara Cox Breakfast Show in 2001. In contrast to Nick Ferrari's show, this programme plays pop music all the time, and the audio is heavily compressed to give it a rough sound. Quizzes are a standard element of phone radio, and Sara Cox's show is no exception. There is a daily segment called 'Mate or break', where Cox speaks to two people on the phone. Notice that I have transcribed only parts of the dialogue.

Track 18: BBC Radio One: Sara Cox with Nicola and Rachel, 2001 (3:50).

> – Nicola, have you any idea of the sort of forfeit that you might make Rachel do if she messes up this morning?
> – Yes, I do. Quite a while ago Rachel went to a pyjama party at a local nightclub, and she got pulled over by the police on the way home, wearing

her pyjamas, and they asked her to step out. So I think that I should make her wear her pyjamas all day, around the town and on a night out with me.
– Yeah, we like that one. Send us the pictures! I'll try to get a dozen polaroids out of this. Right then, ladies, are you ready?
– Yeah.
– Okey dokey. I'll just remind you, Nicola, just to really make Rachel's nerves worse. Basically Rachel has got to answer five questions correctly. She's got forty seconds in which to do it. And if she gets one wrong then you don't win the back catalogue, and you don't win the gig tickets to the Charlatans.
– Right!
– You know what I mean. So it's time to get pretty angry just in case Rachel messes up.
In case, yes.
– Are you all right, Rachel?
– No, I'm nervous.
– No pressure at all, but your friendship is on the line here.
– Alright. OK.

And then the quiz begins: Name one of the three number one albums by the Charlatans. What was the result in last night's game between Manchester United and Olympiakos? Whose album out this week is called *Wheel of Life*? What's the name of the Charlatans' guitarist? Rachel answers only the last question correctly, and she will have to wear her pyjamas on the forthcoming weekend.

How do the speakers come across on air? The two girls Nicola and Rachel giggle and chuckle like most teenage girls. They both make sounds typical of insecure speakers, such as hesitation, moaning and stuttering. Their behaviour on air resonates quite realistically with the everyday life of most listeners, who presumably would be just as nervous if they were to participate. Sara Cox is folksy and enthusiastic and tries not to be condescending towards Rachel. She talks in a carefree manner and has a hoarse, deliberately inarticulate style, sounding as if she was out partying hard the previous night. She is a deft master of ceremonies, and balances the role of confidante with that of the authoritative quiz host.

As suggested, personality journalism feeds on a rough and rowdy style of speaking. This also means that callers are sometimes put in a tough spot by the host. Ian Hutchby (1991: 74–5) argues that hosts can pursue controversy, find something to argue about in what the caller is saying, and adopt a stance of professional scepticism. Stations can attract big audiences based on confrontational talk, and many programme hosts quite consciously offend their listeners. But civil society has limits to the behaviour that a radio programme can cross. In 2007 the American talk show personality Don Imus referred to a team of female basketball players as 'nappy-headed ho's', which is a highly derogatory term for African-American women. His mother station CBS Radio sacked him within a week of this statement, but later the same year he was hired by WABC (Radio World 2007). This story goes to show that, at the same time as the zoo aesthetic and its breaching of social norms is sanctioned, it can also increase the market value to radio stations of the personality in question.

Confessing the blues

Confessional programmes can convey great intimacy because radio communicates in sound alone. There is often a fear of embarrassment in direct visual confrontation, for example if people are challenged to take part in a theatre play or invited to appear on television. Since radio is completely non-visual this embarrassment is avoided, and there is greater room for projecting your usual personality.

Phone radio has long invited the listener to 'work through' big and small private problems that they are facing (Ellis 1999). Their private lifeworld will in a sense be thematized in public. The process of working through is typically considered a positive activity, and stations can address almost any private psychological, sexual or political question without getting into trouble with their listeners.

The next case study is from the morning psychiatry show 'Dr Joy' at the AM station 710WOR, which is located in New York but syndicated to stations all over the USA. There is only talk and no music in the format, but of course there are jingles, commercials and top of the hour news. But first a welcoming promo: 'Thinking about fooling around with that girl at the office? Your husband drives you nuts? Dr Joy Browne is here to help solve all your personal problems at 800–544–7070.'

Track 19: WOR New York: Dr Joy Browne with Barney, 2002 (3:41).

    – Barney, you're on the air on Dr Joy Browne. Hi!
    – Hi! Can you hear me OK? I'm on a cell phone.
    – So far, so good.
    – I'm sitting in my house, so. OK. I'll just start with a question. I don't know if I should leave my wife or not.
    – Dear, how long have you guys been married?
    – Almost ten years.
    – What's making you so unhappy?
    – Well, um, a little over a month ago she started having this affair with this woman, who, which she's worked with.
    – When you say affair, what do you mean?
    – Well, it's kind of complicated, um … my wife has anxiety attacks.
    – OK. That's interesting but irrelevant at this moment. Can we go back to … I said what do you mean by affair?

Figure 5.2 Barney on Saturday night.

    – OK. She started going out with this woman friend …
    – No, no. Just tell me. Do you think she is having sex with another person?
    – Well she, what they told me when I confronted them was, I don't know
how to put it, but, my wife would, er, finger this other woman. OK? And
they told me that's all that happened, and it only happened a couple of times.

The conversation continues on the CD, but the transcription ends here. Barney
uses the opportunity to link up to the wider world, and discloses a problematic feature of his life to Dr Joy and the listeners. It so happens that his wife is
involved in a lesbian relationship, and he now wants a divorce. Barney does not
present himself in the same way as Dr Joy. He is not an entertainer; he exposes
a problem in his life as best he can.

    Although Barney sounds sad and miserable, he does not sound ashamed
about being so candid about his problems in public. He does not appear to be
a cynic or a victim; rather, he seems to have a pragmatic attitude to his life crisis. Barney does not really talk to the public; he talks sincerely to Dr Joy in
order to formulate and hopefully understand his own problem better. And
Dr Joy is even more pragmatic than he is. She is problem-oriented, down to
earth and businesslike, and tries to focus on the things that would make a difference in Barney's life. Three minutes is all he gets. This is an efficient piece of
emotional counselling that would have taken much longer at the doctor's office.

    As a personality journalist, Dr Joy Browne makes it her task to lure the caller
to be open and confessional. John Langer describes the regime of acting naturally

in the context of television shows. The talk show creates a carefully orchestrated illusion of casualness, and there is a leisurely pace about everything: 'The host and guest engage in "chat". During the course of this chat, with suitable questions and tactful encouragement from the host, the guest is predictably "drawn in" to making certain "personal" disclosures, revealing aspects of what may be generally regarded as the private self' (Langer 1981: 360). This strategy is as old as television, if not older.

Margaret Bruzelius (2001: 192) calls the USA 'a nation ready to talk'. Psychiatry shows attract great audiences with their unsentimental approach to personal relationships. In addition to Dr Joy there is, for example, 'Dr Laura' on the US satellite station XM Radio. Such shows make the most of listeners' readiness to ventilate their personal relationships in public. Along with the increase in phone radio, reality shows and other user-generated content, it seems that people do not consider the public arena to be distant and inaccessible; on the contrary, it is almost too easy to hook up with it, especially since people bring their mobile phone with them on their bodies. Andrew Crisell (1994: 194) suggests that the therapeutic aspect is fundamental to the genre of of phone-ins: 'It is possible to regard not only confessional but all types of phone-in as therapeutic in their effects.'

There is potential for serious division in the psychiatry type of programme. The host is the expert and authority on interpersonal behaviour, regardless of whether she is a trained psychiatrist; and the caller is a subordinate, troubled person regardless of his education and wisdom. But if the listener suspects that the host is insincere – a cynical businesswoman making easy money off of people's misery and lack of self-confidence – then the mood can go sour. To the unwilling listener Joy Browne sounds condescending, and it appears that she uses a routine voice for friendliness that she uses on the frustrated callers. It sounds like a tone of voice she would take on if she were to talk to a small child. In general, the personality journalist risks being heard as only apparently friendly, and this may become so sickeningly obvious to the unwilling listeners that they change station and never return.

The phone radio medium, 2008

Phone radio obviously relies on two separate public platforms, those of broadcasting and telephony. This mix of a mass medium and a personal medium makes programming more symmetrical in strictly technical terms. Here I will attend to the way that the mobile phone is technologically coupled with radio. Radio's technological basis is also analysed in chapter 2 (web radio and podcasting) and chapter 4 (terrestrial and satellite transmission).

Figure 5.3 shows that radio production is completely computerized. The studio microphone and mixing boards are hooked up to a computer system with software for launching jingles and commercials, and for manipulating the live feed before it goes on the air. From the studio computer the signal is sent

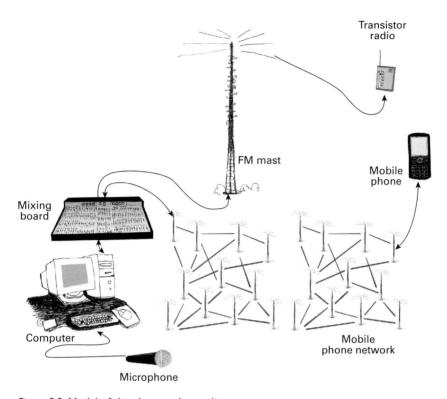

Figure 5.3 Model of the phone radio medium.

to the transmission tower (or streamed on web radio or sent to a satellite). Listeners receive the signals on small portable receivers as described before. In addition to this transmission platform the station can feed mobile or landline calls into the studio, and this feature in principle allows any listener to become a caller. The wireless phone network allows the listener to call the station from any location and any social situation.

As figure 5.3 suggests, now that the mobile network is hooked up to the radio medium, there is an enormous hinterland of potential speakers on radio. In practice all the world's phones could be connected through the telecom companies' infrastructures and subscription services. In principle any caller can reach any person in the world who has a phone number. The terminal will be connected to the central switchboard through a line (landline or wireless), where it will be hooked up automatically with the number requested. The phone company can monitor and record all conversations that take place in the network.

Like ground broadcasting, which I discussed in chapter 4, mobile telephony signals go through the air in a line-of-sight manner. Signalling takes place in a grid of transmission stations placed closely together, with reflectors that support the signal and make it reach nooks and crannies in the landscape. The stations are positioned so that they create an overlapping pattern of access zones, so that in practice the user can roam about freely and without caring about where they are (Ling 2004: 9).

In contrast to broadcasting, the telephone networks are common carriers for private messages; that is, they are constructed for one-to-one personal contact, and not for mass distribution of public messages (Mercer 2006). This implies that telecom networks do not necessarily have the editorial institutions and journalistic competence of radio and television stations. Although people can access broadcast signals on their phone, this is typically a completely separate functionality from that which the telecom operators cater to. There is no radio programming through the telephone networks, but there could have been.

The coupling of phone and radio seems to take place the other way around, by radio embedding phone conversations in its programming. This venture is based on commercial collaboration, where the phone networks supply the infrastructure to route messages to the broadcasting stations' internal systems, and the station takes care of all editorial procedures involved in the communication with callers. Callers can contact the radio station in three ways: by calling on speakerphone, by sending SMS messages, or by sending pictures. Along with these limited opportunities, where the speakerphone is by far the most versatile, new journalistic genres have arisen.

This brings us into the studio environment. In most stations there are only two or three people working on a phone programme. The producer has overall administrative responsibility and must make sure both that all elements of the programme are ready in due time and that callers and studio guests are ready to speak at the right moment. Again, depending on the scale of the operation, there may be one or several moderators, who take calls from the listeners and screen them all to decide who is suitable to be put on the air. The moderator may take note of vital information about the participant, so that the host has something to start from (Rosemary lives in Kew, and Ferrari has learnt this before she comes on air).

These shows must by definition be live, since they rely on callers to respond to the invitations made at the beginning of the show. However, American stations in particular have emergency plans because of the social risk-taking involved in talk radio, especially regarding the uttering of swear words and sexual profanity. Most shows have a time delay which allows the producer to switch to a recorded element if the station's moral regime is breached. Typically, a jingle or commercial element is launched, and during those ten to thirty seconds a new caller has been prepped and is ready to go on air (Boyd 1988: 240–1). If this social control by recording were impossible, American talk stations would probably allow far less participation from laypersons on the air.

The public switchboard

The purpose of phone-in programmes is to create a conversational flow, but not to create a dialogue. Editors and journalists are the bosses, and the callers are at the editors' mercy. Talk shows rarely allow callers freedom to tell the whole story or to follow their argument to a natural conclusion. In the radio industry the caller is basically one item among all the others needed to create an attractive and enjoyable programme. The host relies on a producer to monitor and select callers for the show, but the host is nevertheless the public switchboard who maintains the connection between callers and listeners live on the air.

The host must speak on two communicative levels simultaneously, but must primarily address the public of listeners. For decades it has been standard journalistic behaviour to talk *with* and not *to* the listener. This presumably draws the listener into the mood of the programme in a better way than a more formal address would do (McLeish 1999: 65). Secondly, the host must talk with the caller about the topic at hand, and also guide them through the procedures of a quiz or calm them down during a heated debate. If there is a problem, the relationship with the listeners is always the number one priority, and the conversation with the caller will be unsentimentally terminated.

The journalist's job is essentially to convince the callers and listeners that they are companions, and maintain this conviction indefinitely. A returning listener has discovered something attractive in the host's personality that makes it worthwhile to keep on listening. For decades the talk station's strategy has been to create trademark personalities for the different shows. The longer a certain personality has been kept in charge, the more credible it becomes for the regular listeners, at least as long as there are no scandals to corrupt the situation. The personality can be built over the whole lifetime of a radio performer, as in the case of Howard Stern and Don Imus, and there can be great bargaining value in having a strong public identity as a radio personality.

In regard to personality building, it should be noted that electronic media rely fundamentally on the repetition of the same type of performance. The repetition soon becomes a familiar, often comforting ritual (Carey 1989). Repetitive journalistic procedures have always been a prerequisite for loose and 'natural' talk on the part of radio personalities. The host will always perform in the same well-known acoustic space, in the same tone of voice, talking about more or less the same topics year after year, speaking the same kinds of formulaic sentences over and over again. Within the safety of a given set of procedures it is quite easy to create improvised and spontaneous behaviour.

Let me connect to history on this score. The rhetorical construction of companionship is as old as broadcasting itself. All radio and television programmes project some kind of social or personal mood, even news bulletins. This is because broadcasters have long since learnt that listeners easily develop a personal identification with the performers in radio and television. 'A host of notions of "being genuine" and "being yourself" dominate the legitimating rhetoric of broadcasters', Espen Ytreberg claims (2002: 492–3). Not surprisingly, textbooks can routinely point out that 'radio is, for many of its audiences, a life-long friend and constant companion' (Shingler and Wieringa 1998: 110). In the context of television Joshua Meyrowitz argues that personalities can become friends. 'Viewers come to feel they "know" the people they "meet" on television in the same way that they know their friends and associates. In fact, many viewers begin to believe that they know and understand a performer better than all the other viewers do. Paradoxically, the para-social performer is able to establish "intimacy with millions"' (1985: 119). Paddy Scannell (2000) argues that broadcasting addresses 'anyone as someone'. His point is that, even though everybody in the audience receives the same message, it is formulated in quite intimate terms, so that each listener will feel that it is addressed to them in particular.

Caller initiative

'Do you know the answer? Dial this number', the host pleads. 'Do *you* have a problem you want to discuss on air? Call us right now.' This insistent appeal suggests that in the 2000s there is a big demand for callers. Any listener may become a caller; it depends only on his initiative. Since transistor radios can be taken anywhere the opportunity to listen is ever-present, and since the mobile phone is of course also a constant companion, listeners can turn into callers at any time.

The caller has shown initiative in calling the station, and this is important. There is a big difference between making and receiving a call (Hutchby 2001: 111; Ling 2004: 132). If you make a call you know who you are calling, you know what you want to talk about, and you have chosen a time that suits you. If you receive a call you may not know who the caller is (although mobile phones can display both name and number), you may not like the reason for the call, and it may not be at a good time for you to talk.

Despite showing strong initiative by calling in, the caller has to go along with the programme's procedures, such as the rules of 'Mate or Break' on BBC Radio 1. As long as the caller follows the rules he is in control of his appearance in relation to the host and other participants. This allows the caller not to get too hung-up about his public performance; and he can focus better on the task at hand. My point is that procedures increase the likelihood that the caller will come across as a relaxed and credible person.

Radio is more welcoming than television when it comes to letting one's guard down and acting without too much caution. As suggested, the absence of visual mediation is important for relaxed behaviour, but another important reason is that the phone mouthpiece is so familiar to the caller that it further lowers the threshold for participation. The caller's contribution is to behave exactly how they always do. Buck Owens comments ironically on the communication skills required by mass media in the song 'Act Naturally' (1963), which was also covered by the Beatles. 'We'll make a film about a man that's sad and lonely, and all I have to do is act naturally', he sings. This rule of behaviour works well not just in the medium of film, but also in radio and television. The best way to take part in the media is to seek out the situations in which your personality is suitable, and proceed to act naturally. If you are sad, make a call to a sad radio programme. Clearly the threshold for being accepted in phone radio is not very high, as Owens with feigned self-irony points out: 'I hope you come and see me in the movie. Then I know that you will plainly see the biggest fool that ever hit the big time. I'll play the part but I won't need rehearsing, since all I have to do is act naturally.' However, the rule of 'act naturally' is symptomatic of very intelligent public communication which should not be underestimated.

The listening zone

Finally I will turn to the listener's perspective. Compared to a face-to-face relationship, that between the listener and the radio speaker is rather superficial. 'The person on the radio is a person with whom one can be close without having to tolerate all of the disadvantages of closeness' (Fornatale and Mills 1980: xix). The social relationship is amputated, and this is often the main attraction. If the radio is on for many hours, the voices may provide more of a humanoid mood than a direct encounter with other people.

To the extent that the listeners are attentive, they will relate differently to the two different types of speakers – the host and the callers. The host is the centrepiece of the programme, and in most cases listeners already know the personality well. The callers come and go through the programme, and since they are a dime a dozen they can be treated with less patience by the listener. However, listeners may still identify more passionately with callers than with the radio personality, since callers are ordinary people just like the listeners, and may talk about life experiences that are quite recognizable.

There is another reason why listeners may bond quite strongly with callers, which I have already touched upon from the caller's perspective. The mobile phone has a characteristic sound, with a narrow bandwidth, and it gives off bursts of noise when somebody speaks too loudly or the connection breaks up. The bad sound of mobile phones on air will be recognized by listeners from their own mobile phone conversations, and it invites them to recognize their own communication environments and their everyday phone conversations. Because of this, the listeners can feel closer to the callers on radio than they might otherwise do.

What about the listening zone? People often listen to talk radio in the deepest recesses of the home, for example in the bedroom late at night. This is a zone completely outside the public realm, and it is the scene of uncensored emotions, including loneliness and desperation. The listener knows that the programme is for 'anyone as someone' (Scannell 2000), and that it is only a para-social relationship (Horton and Wohl [1956] 1979), but he listens all the same. My point here is that the listeners need not take up a *citizen's* attitude. There is no need to relate the programme's output to the larger public sphere in order to have a valuable sociable experience. On the contrary, the listener is likely to become more entangled in his own life involvements and his own current mood.

Here is the core of personality journalism on radio. The purpose is to accompany the listener's life with the right moods at the right time, and in this sense always to charge or energize them and help them along in their lives. In this sense there is a positive influence of radio for listeners. Andrew Crisell (1994: 212) points out that, 'because we continue with our lives *while* we are listening, its content is, as it were, transplanted into our own existence and adapted to our own purposes.'

But the listeners do not only bond with the programme in a positive way through enthusiasm and endearment with the host. Identification feeds just as well on antagonistic emotions. Erving Goffman (1981: 247) points out that there are always angry ears out there. He suggests that audiences are not only easily offended by faults or remarks, but that they actively seek out faults that might be offensive. People's annoyance may blind them to the fact that the host plays out a contrived personality, and what annoys them may be exactly those personality traits that are put on as role play. The hostile engagement may go on for years without the listener switching to another station. On the contrary, the unwilling listener may build up a sophisticated private dislike of the personality. This is the freedom of the listener in a nutshell; you don't have to change station, you can just dislike radio personalities over time. For radio stations it is a win–win situation: if people really like the show they will keep listening, and if they really dislike the show they will keep listening.

Chapter 6

Loudspeaker living

Pop music is everywhere

People enliven their day with loudspeaker music, and they share it enthusiastically with friends, colleagues and family – inside their homes, in the car and at all kinds of public events from discos to sports venues. And there is a whole industry that caters to this penchant for musical timbres.

This chapter starts from the presumption that, whether people like it or not, Western media cultures are now quite saturated with *recorded pop music*. Music is disseminated in social situations in an industrial way by commercial companies and individuals alike. I have chosen four media configurations for closer scrutiny: 1) muzak in commercial locations such as shopping malls; 2) music radio in semi-public and private locations, such as the hairdressers and taxis and commercial vehicles; 3) internet jukeboxes involving a high level of personal choice in music, for instance Pandora and Last FM; 4) disc jockeying in clubs, pubs, cafés, etc., with limited attendance. This chapter has no sound examples. If you like, it is an oasis of silence in an otherwise noisy book.

The music media landscape

I am tapping into a rich cultural field when focusing on music in public settings. It has always been important to socialize and have fun with music, for example at the fairground, where the lively atmospherics of violins, accordions, singers and music boxes was integral to the experience (Lanza 2004). When it comes to music, relaxing moods have always been sought by ordinary people and serviced by professionals. Music is often peaceful, and music often allows you to take a break from the real world. Another way of saying this is that music can be *pacifying* in both good and bad senses of the word; it can be used for voluntary relaxation and for psychological manipulation (Riesman [1950] 1990; Mathieu 1991).

The soundscape of the twenty-first century is different from that of the nineteenth century. Now there are aeroplanes thundering overhead and the constant drone of traffic, which doesn't even cease at night. In the nineteenth century there was the clattering of horse-drawn wagons in the cities and shouting and screaming in the streets. Both societies are what Schafer call

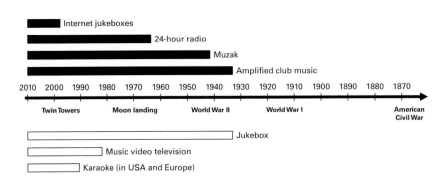

Figure 6.1 Timeline of music media.

low-fi soundscapes; there is a constant hum of different noises that drown out the characteristics of individual events. If somebody cries for help they may not be heard. In a hi-fi soundscape, on the other hand, every single event comes across more clearly. Schafer argues that 'the quiet ambience of the hi-fi sound-scape allows the listener to hear farther into the distance' ([1977] 1994: 43). There are still hi-fi soundscapes, for example natural surroundings such as high up in the mountains or out at sea in a sailing boat. Everything stands out, and the cry of a pelican a mile away is heard clearly against the background of relative silence.

Figure 6.1 shows the most common platforms for the dissemination of recorded music in the social and semi-public sphere in Western countries. Internet jukeboxes are a relatively new phenomenon, and were not widespread until streaming audio had been perfected in the late 1990s. While they appeared much later in many European countries, 24-hour radio services started to penetrate everyday life in the early 1960s in the USA. Notice that, in contrast to the previous timelines, figure 6.1 covers not just the contemporary period from 2010 back to 1975 but the entire historical span back to 1870. Recorded music played in clubs, bars and restaurants has been a normal thing since the 1930s, when sound could first be amplified in a commercial way. Analogous to these systems for public address are the speakers relaying propaganda in a country such as North Korea, which have the effect of a kind of acoustic brainwashing.

Below the arrow I have listed stand-alone jukeboxes, MTV and karaoke because they are related phenomena. Jukeboxes in cafés have spun hit records for customers for seventy years. MTV and other music video television stations are interesting because they are used socially by teenagers who demarcate their taste in artists and music. Since the rise of music video television in the early 1980s the concept of the video jockey has been popularized, and these figures have great influence on musical trends and charts. The idea of a dedicated video-based outlet for music meant that both artists and fans found a central location for music events, news and promotion (Millard 2005: 339).

Karaoke is interesting because of its intensely social character, where colleagues and friends drink and sing along at their favourite bar. To be more specific, karaoke, which spread from Japan to the United States and Europe in the 1990s, is a form of entertainment where amateur singers sing along to a well-known pop song using a microphone and a PA system. The voice of the original singer is removed or reduced in volume, and lyrics are usually displayed on a video screen along with a moving symbol that guides the singer (Wikipedia 2007, 'Karaoke').

Although MTV and other providers of music videos tend to dominate in the public eye, the sound media have an important independent function that goes further than that of audiovisual media. It is because they have no visual imagery, and no need for screens and monitors to be set up, that they can be even more deeply embedded in daily life, and supply a pure sensory experience of which listeners are often not consciously aware. Because of their versatility they contribute greatly to the creation of low-fi soundscapes in modern societies. And the tendency is clear: the Western media compete to saturate ever more aspects of people's social environments with music (and images). The forms of distribution and their musical timbres are so commonplace that the entire medium is often perceived more as a piece of furniture than real music (Lanza 2004; Barnett 2006).

Traditionally, listeners have been projected as active consumers, with a distinct taste in music that they enthusiastically pursue. An example of such a resourceful cultural figure would be Nick Hornby and the culture of record listening he describes in the novel *High Fidelity* (1995). His characters play records on the stereo to his liking, and project the moods and timbres that feel right for them. They are in command of their media environment, and proud of it too. I suspect that this attitude is not necessarily so widespread. On the contrary, I think that the industry (consisting of record companies, radio editors, club owners) projects this type of listener in a rhetorical way, because it is a flattering position for the consumer to be in. If you don't like the music you can always turn it off, the industry rhetoric implies. In this chapter I intend to show that things are not quite that simple.

Muzak at the mall

The word 'muzak' has broken free from its corporate parent and become a term for easy listening, middle of the road, or elevator music. Any type of repetitive music can be called muzak.

The Mall of America in Minneapolis/St Paul is the second largest shopping centre in the world and attracts millions of visitors every year. It has a highly sophisticated loudspeaker system, with closed-circuit systems for each individual store and a public address system for the entire mall (Sterne 1997; Connell and Gibson 2003). This is exactly the kind of public spaces to which companies such as Muzak and the 3M corporation sell their pre-recorded selections.

There can be many intentions behind music formatting, but it will always be the case that a company tries to inspire a certain shared mood among the shoppers. This mood can be organized so that it has a rising intensity of rhythm (and volume) over a certain period of time, followed by softer music and then a new rise of a slightly different intensity and duration (see Lanza 2004: 48ff.). Music can serve both as a welcoming mat and as a keep-out notice, Connell and Gibson (2003: 197) argue: 'In 1999 a suburban shopping centre in the Australian city of Wollongong began playing Bing Crosby music to stop teenagers hanging out there.' At the same time as Bing Crosby keeps teenagers out, he attracts the right kind of customers to the store, for example grandmothers buying Christmas gifts. Muzak corporations can play quite cleverly on various such types of simultaneous inclusion and exclusion based on recorded pop music.

Paddy Scannell has coined the term 'dailiness' to describe radio's formatting scheme, but it also fits muzak quite well. He refers to a service 'that fills each day, that runs right through the day, that appears as a continuous, uninterrupted, never-ending flow – through all the hours of the day, today, tomorrow and tomorrow and tomorrow' (1996: 149). Producers conform to the real-time progression of the larger society in which they operate, and exploit it to put the right kind of music into people's everyday settings at the right time. The public moods of Western societies vary with summer and winter; with workday and weekend; with morning, afternoon and evening. John Ellis argues that it is strategically important for media companies to understand the rhythms of the private sphere. Early on it 'became important to know when the various sections of the population awoke in the morning, took their meals, returned from work, went to bed' (Ellis 2000: 43).

I will go into the seasonal signature of muzak in some detail. The Muzak corporation has a service called Holiday, and customers can select from a long list of different religious and carnivalesque holidays – basically Western holidays respected in Europe, the USA and South America. The list goes like this: Christmas, Cinco de Mayo, Halloween, Independence Day, Mardi Gras, Oktoberfest, St Patrick's Day, Summer Fun and Valentine's Day (Wikipedia 2007, 'Muzak').

Let us select Christmas. At Christmas in the Mall of America, 'White Christmas' is a much played song, and it flows through the shopping mall in Bing Crosby's smooth crooning tones (listen to track 25 to hear his voice). The music has a set volume. It is part of the interior of the store, and there is no way that the listener can turn up the volume if he likes a particular song, or turn it down for that matter. The customer leaves the parking lot and goes into the Waldbaum supermarket. The management has chosen a solemn style of Christmas song: 'Silent Night', 'The Little Drummer Boy', 'Mary's Boy Child', 'Hark! The Herald Angels Sing', 'The Twelve Days of Christmas'. For a while

Figure 6.2 Christmas at the shopping mall.

the songs are quite comfortable, but if you start to get annoyed your only option is to leave. The Gap store next door plays a selection of funny Christmas songs: 'Rudolph the Red-Nosed Reindeer', 'Jingle Bells', 'I saw Mommy Kissing Santa Claus', 'All I Want for Christmas is my Two Front Teeth'. In the sports store they want you to buy skis, and you hear 'Frosty the Snowman', 'Winter Wonderland' and 'Let it Snow'. Christmas songs are now part of the West's low-fi background for two months a year, every year throughout our lives.

In the shopping centre listening is very often a *secondary activity*: the presentation is a background to other projects that receive the listener's full attention. It seems that the presentation is 'heard' rather than listened to. The sounds become part of the surroundings, like a piece of furniture or the wallpaper. According to Carin Åberg, the secondary listening process is mainly aesthetic and emotional. There is little knowledge gain and little interpersonal identification (Åberg 1999: 77–8). Many customers in the Mall of America walk around looking for bargains, and some are chatting with a friend on their cell phone.

But notice that this is by no means an unsophisticated or foolish way of attending to music. On the contrary, secondary listening in public and semi-public settings is actually a highly responsive way of relating to sound. In this type of listening the perceptual surface is more interesting than the symbolic or linguistic depths, and this surface can be called timbre. Timbre is not measurable by acoustic instruments in the way that pitch and volume are, it is an expressive quality that is experienced subjectively and according to the individual's skills of cultural perception. The repetitious relationship that people typically have with recorded music appeals more to a bodily engagement with rhythms and timbres than to any form of intellectual search for information or knowledge. You are more likely to hum along than reflect intellectually on the deeper meaning of the lyrics.

Music radio

In this section I will analyse the traditional FM music station and its way of saturating our lives with recorded music. Top 40 stations are both a barometer and an arbiter of musical taste, and radio airplay is one of the defining measures of success in the mainstream musical world (Hendy 2000: 141). First try to imagine the scale of these operations. A hit station that started a 24-hour service in 1975 will by 2010 have produced 306,000 hours of music, and in New York City alone there are a dozen stations that have aired since 1975. The maths soon become overwhelming.

For decades music radio stations have branded themselves differently from each other to attract niche audiences. The main strategy is to produce a signature sound, a kind of aural trademark that will be easy for the listeners to recognize. Furthermore, stations promote themselves through a constant trickle of jingles and promos that serve to establish their trademark. The running order of songs through the day is organized in playlists, and voices are compressed and filtered to fit into the timbres represented on the playlist. Everything is produced to fit into the overall sound signature of the station. Because of this very rigid structure, DJ's programmes have been called 'automated reality' (Hendy 2000: 112).

In the radio industry there is a large menu of formats to be taken up, and a company will analyse the market potential of the available niches at length before a station format is launched. The main formats are pop, classical, middle of the road, country, oldies, classic rock, easy listening, dance, urban (hip-hop and rhythm and blues), jazz and progressive rock (for a more detailed list, see Hendy 2000: 100).

Andrew Crisell (1994: 72) stresses that, although a radio format is full of bridges, changes, and indeed even pauses, there is no narrative development. The format logic conforms largely to the notion of flow, which Raymond Williams ([1975] 1990: 90) pointed out was about to overtake the notion of programming. Discrete programme units are no longer the main product of radio; rather, a complex web of sequences comes about. First, there is the flow or sequence of listed programmes within a particular day. Second, there is the flow or succession of items within and between the listed programmes. Third, there is the really detailed flow within this general movement, the succession and/or overdubbing of sound arrays in the individual jingle, reportage or commercial (ibid.: 96; Jensen 1995: 108ff.). David Hendy quotes a station manager who says: 'our programming is clinical and disciplined, and the way you do things in radio is actually more important than what you do.' Radio is a 'how medium' where 'style must come before content' (Hendy 2000: 98).

Music radio is more accessible and controllable for the listener than muzak. Firstly, you can have a transistor radio in any imaginable private situation; and there is a wide selection of music stations on offer in most cities in the West, so that there is a good chance you can listen to your preferred style of music too. Many people have the habit of listening to radio on their Walkman, and music has permeated the lives of such people to a far greater extent (Bull 2000). Sarah Vowell, in an experiment of listening to the radio all the time for one year, writes:

> The radio has become such a compulsive, constant companion that I've been home for around two hours, made three phone calls, cooked dinner, read a magazine cover to cover, and now, there's a grating guitar instrumental coming out of the speaker and I don't even remember turning the thing on.
>
> (Vowell 1997: 199)

This type of background listening is comfortable for everybody involved. Music radio is played in semi-public venues such as the hair salon, the taxi or bus, and the dentist's office. It masks less comfortable sounds, such as the noises of electrical appliances, street traffic and the chatter of people in the room. In many semi-public places the radio is always on, and the station has not been changed since 1985.

In contrast to muzak, radio (and internet) music allows the listener to adjust the volume, and there are many variations on who is in charge of the knobs. If you are wearing your iPod, you decide, whereas at home there can be disputes about both station choice and volume, and at the hairdresser's you can only ask politely. Notice also that music radio is used in many outdoor settings that fall between the various categories. For example, there can be teenagers playing basketball in a back alley with a boom box blasting out hip-hop music.

Radio listening is almost always a parallel activity, and I will explain this important concept in detail. When listening is a parallel activity the listener's attention shifts fluidly between the music presentation and some other ongoing project. Carin Åberg (1999: 77–8) says that parallel attention is likely to be both emotional and pragmatic. It is marked by short periods of sustained listening, sudden regaining of concentration after having been immersed in the project at hand, and a less premeditated situation of listening which could be considered more emotional, or mood-oriented as I would call it. Parallel listening is also widespread in the context of news and talk radio. Typically, you might arrange to do the dishes when a favourite programme is aired, but you may not be particularly attentive to the subjects that are discussed. Rather, you feel a social bond to the host and his voice, or the style of music that the station plays. You are taking part in a public mood that includes many more people than yourself, and this is a large part of the attraction.

I am stressing the function of music radio in social settings. One typical activity is to discuss the music, and argue about what is good and what is bad. At the hairdressers, if the station is changed, a discussion may erupt because someone gets annoyed: 'Hey, that's my favourite song you just interrupted!' Listeners discuss the difference between good and bad cover versions of a familiar song. They discuss and recommend grooves, beats, melodies, harmonies and, in a genre context, psychedelic sound, funk sound, bossa-nova sound. They are familiar with the West Coast sound the Philadelphia sound, the Liverpool sound, and with record label references such as the Motown sound, the Atlantic sound and the Phil Spector sound, with Bob Dylan's sound, Stevie Wonder's sound and Joni Mitchell's sound. The list could go on forever. The main point is that the concept of 'sound' is a vague and inclusive way of referring to music which modern music lovers know intimately.

The sentiments of parallel and secondary listening mean that artists cannot release their music without having reflected carefully on what kind of mood they will provide and what kinds of energy and attachments they want the listeners to feel. Although artists and companies cannot control the listeners' sentiments, they can safely assume that the 'sound' of their music will be influential in its own right. Paul Théberge says that individual 'sounds' have come to carry the same commercial and aesthetic weight as the melody, and argues that 'the "sound hook" begins to exert a force of its own, virtually demanding that any "authentic" rendition of the song be performed with the same or an equivalent sound' (Théberge 1997: 195).

Internet jukeboxes

The newest form of loudspeaker living takes place at the computer, and relates to music websites on the internet such as Pandora and Last FM. They rely on streaming audio, and really require a broadband connection for the listener to enjoy it fully. The use of internet jukeboxes is still limited mostly to the stationary computer in the office or the bedroom, and the lap-top if there is a wireless connection. Very often this kind of music is heard via headphones, and it therefore has a more private feel to it than muzak in shopping centres or music radio at the hairdressers.

There has been a rapid development in the internet jukebox industry. In the early 2000s companies such as Sonicbox and Spinner presented services that resembled music radio more than anything. In the graphical interface the listener could chose between roughly the same music formats as on radio stations (rock, country, rhythm and blues, etc.). The music is played back automatically from a central database, and there are randomizing algorithms of various kinds to reduce the risk of unwanted repetition of songs. Two things in particular make these services different from radio. When using internet jukeboxes the listeners can switch between formats without leaving the site, whereas on the radio this would imply that the listener was changing station. Furthermore, advanced jukeboxes such as Sonicbox have a huge database of music and provide a nuanced system of sub-genres within each format, so that one can choose between, for example, twelve types of rhythm and blues. Radio stations on offer in a given location, on the other hand, might not play R & B at all. Websites can exploit central databases to create highly interactive choices for the consumer, and traditional FM stations cannot do this.

People are using the internet mostly in private settings, and this type of listening is quite different from that of public venues such as the hairdressers. Private forms of listening can be more surface oriented than public music, since the private setting allows the listener to indulge himself more freely in his favourite timbres. Notice also that the listener here chooses the setting and the musical content entirely of his own accord, and also controls the volume. Compared to muzak at the mall, this is a good starting point for indulging in your favourite timbres.

Music jukeboxes such as Pandora have introduced a remarkable interface for catering to the individual's tastes in music. Basically, this site allows music lovers to create many different stations where they can select their favourite musical genres. Again, this software function is based on access to a tremendous backlog of popular music contained in centralized databases. Interestingly, in 2007 Pandora had to restrict its service to US audiences because of unresolved copyright issues.

Pandora is a kind of musical timbre analyser, and technically it is based on a categorization scheme developed by a group of music lovers in the USA. The company quite ambitiously calls the categorization work the 'Music Genome Project', playing on the Human Genome Project which analyses the entire human DNA structure. The implication is that Pandora attempts to capture all the different essential sounds of popular music so as to be able always to call up a song that suits the stated criteria. There are variables in the software that allow it to distinguish between different types of electrical guitar in Frank Zappa's catalogue or the different ways that Frank Sinatra, Dean Martin and Sammy Davis Jr sing standard love songs.

> We ended up assembling literally hundreds of musical attributes or 'genes' into a very large Music Genome. Taken together these genes capture the unique and magical musical identity of a song – everything from melody, harmony and rhythm, to instrumentation, orchestration, arrangement, lyrics, and of course the rich world of singing and vocal harmony. It's not about what a band looks like, or what genre they supposedly belong to, or about who buys their records – it's about what each individual song sounds like. This work continues each and every day as we endeavor to include all the great new stuff coming out of studios, clubs and garages around the world.
>
> (Westergren 2007)

Thanks to innovations such as Pandora's music genome software, the listeners have the world of music at their fingertips. They can create a station for disco, one for rock and another for hip-hop. The novelty is that the station presents songs according to the preferences that are continually put in, shown by accepting or rejecting the songs presented by the software. Let us say that you create a station called 'soul singing', and you start with Ray Charles's 'Hit the Road, Jack' to give the machine an idea of what you mean by soul singing. Every time Pandora puts on a song that you feel is outside the definition of 'soul singing' you reject it by clicking a 'thumbs down' button, and the software learns to reject similar-sounding songs in the future. You may not approve of contemporary singing like that of Beyoncé, and consequently you reject all songs with a contemporary, synthetic sound. According to the same logic, when Pandora puts on a song that you feel is right you give it the 'thumbs up'. I would, for example, have scored most of Otis Redding's songs very high on my soul singing station. This type of scoring can go on for as long as you like. If you get bored, and let the station continue to play songs without adjusting your preferences, it will go off on its own randomized trek through music history, and the soul may end up becoming folk.

Clubland

The fourth type of music consumption that I will discuss is listening to loud music in an enclosed public space, where the main occupations are often dancing, drinking, taking drugs and getting a break from everyday life. This is an intense way of sharing music with others, and it is in particulary strong contrast to personalized music jukeboxes such as Pandora and listening to a Walkman or an iPod.

The acoustic architecture of clubs is carefully made to project recorded music only. For example, many clubs do not have a big stage for musicians, only a DJ booth built into the wall next to the dance floor. This set-up, much like muzak technology, also imposes the sound on the listeners, but there are several important differences. A club presents a predictable musical scenario for the regular guest; they know in advance what kind of music they will get, be it hip-hop, techno, disco, rock, tango or country. People often have to pay admission to get into clubs, which attests to their attraction. Club-goers often act in the capacity of music lovers, and the timbres of the music are high on their agenda, whereas muzak is certainly not your main interest when you go shopping.

The setting of club music can be highly charged with media effects. Rave parties have been organized since the 1980s, and DJs play electronic dance music to the accompaniment of laser light shows, images projected on the walls, and artificial fog.

The DJ is crucial to this type of music consumption. The DJ's techniques in one sense resemble those of a radio host, but he can relate directly to the tastes of the crowd and is therefore far more flexible, and a good DJ will play along with a musical mood that is partly of his own making and partly based on the responses from the crowd. Since DJs are in such close contact with music lovers, they often pick up the new trends and promote them in the public sphere (for example, if they also have a radio DJ show), and they can also test out songs on the dance floor and see what kind of potential they have as dance hits (Connell and Gibson 2003: 182ff.). Club DJs rely on a smooth transition between songs and use a range of techniques to accomplish this. Typically, the DJ shifts between two turntables (or other platforms) and therefore always has the next song ready before the previous one is finished. He listens on headphones to prepare the next segue between songs, and often also speaks into a microphone to introduce songs.

When it comes to the club-goer's experience it is important to note that the act of listening is often a *primary activity*, which means that the music and its content – rhythm, melody and lyrics – is the main focus. It may also take place in parallel with other things, such as ordering drinks and chatting, but the music remains a crucial reference throughout. In primary listening the person will be concentrating through the duration of the sound; distractions will not be accepted, and there will be a substantial gain in pleasure and satisfaction (Åberg 1999: 77–8).

This is most evident on the dance floor, where club-goers are likely to give maximum attention to the music. This provides a more visceral and bodily experience than muzak and hit radio: imagine, for example, the bass drones of the subwoofer at a modern rave club. It is a very loud experience, and it hits you in the belly as much as in the ears. The loud volume is intended to shut out any type of speaking or communication except glances and touches between the people on the floor. 'Motion and escape is essential to rave and club culture', argue Connell and Gibson (2003: 205). Another setting where the combination of movement and music is particularly strong is the aerobics class at a gym, where the music can be almost as loud as at a nightclub (DeNora 2000: 90).

The club-goers clearly engage in what I call timbre enjoyment. Theodore Gracyk supplies a productive way of thinking about timbre enjoyment. He argues that what attracts listeners to recorded music is the familiarity bred by hundreds of repetitions, the possibility of getting to know the material surface of the music in a sensual way. 'We are free to savor and anticipate qualities and details that are simply too ephemeral to be relevant in live performance. When records are the medium, every aspect is available for our discrimination and thus for its interpretative potential' (Gracyk 1996: 55). Here we touch upon a fundamental feature of sound media to which I will return in later chapters. There is a repetition of sounds going on which is very influential. Listeners know in advance that they will be hearing well-known hit songs over and over again, and the expected repetition is the main attraction. They expect to be musically satisfied only *while they is listening*, not after having contemplated the musical structures in some kind of intellectual way. It is in any event quite difficult to remember the subtle timbres of modern pop music. No matter how well we know the structure of a recording, the immediacy of listening is the main thrill. As Gracyk (ibid.: 61) points out, pop music's precise quality is only known perceptually, while perceiving it.

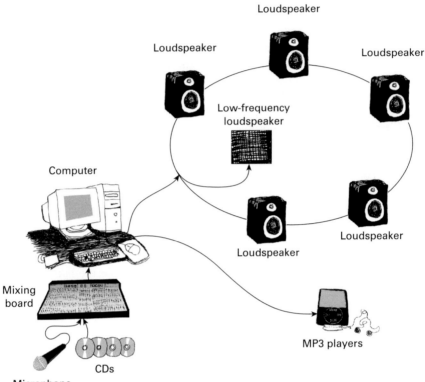

Figure 6.3 Model of the loudspeaker medium.

The loudspeaker medium, 2008

One thing in particular unites the otherwise disparate practices that I am describing in this chapter: the fact that the producers basically distribute music that was recorded by other producers. It is the art of recirculation, and it is equally true for muzak corporations, radio DJs, club DJs and internet jukebox programmers. Indeed, it can also be claimed to include the iPod user, who creates a private playlist and puts it on his iPod. The basic technique consists of creating a pleasurable and/or interesting loudspeaker experience for the listeners.

Figure 6.3 shows the structure of a closed-circuit system for sound amplification, and it essentially contains music recordings, a microphone for the DJ to speak and sing into and a computer through which the music is organized in playlists. Often there is a professional mixing board (or its computer equivalent) in order for the producer to play back music from several different sources in an efficient way, but this can also be done with the selector on a domestic amplifier. In really large loudspeaker systems, at a big nightclub in Ibiza or in the Mall of America, the music can be delivered by satellite or by dedicated broadband wires (Wikipedia 2007, 'Muzak'). There are many small loudspeaker operations, of which the old-fashioned jukebox in the café is the most typical.

The producers can project the sound according to two basic techniques that I introduced in chapter 1: loudspeaker placement and volume control. They decide which directions the sounds will go in, and can organize a sweet spot for a stereo system or 5.1 surround sound. They obviously also decide the volume at which the music is played. There are a variety of qualities in the reproduction of sound. Any ordinary loudspeaker contains bass and several treble elements, and reproduces the full range of musical sounds. It is also common to have subwoofers that reproduce the lowest part of the audio spectrum, and which are not often easy to hear but easier to feel. At the other end of the spectrum are megaphones, which have a muffled and narrow sound.

Loudspeaker systems can also be used to reinforce live public events in a specific locale or outdoor area, for example a political speech, an emergency message or a live concert. Public address systems have existed as long as there has been electrical amplification of sound (see Wurtzler 2007: 10–11). My interest in loudspeaker systems does not extend to these situations, not even such public events as a political rally or a live concert. These are often spectacular live events, with huge masses of people crowding together and reacting en masse. But they are localized in one unique place, and therefore are not really media phenomena in the way I conceive of them in this book. They do not rely on transporting the sound into other places (radio) or record it for later publication (music recording).

Earphone escape

The loudspeaker music media often have no documentary authority or transparency. Throughout this chapter I have stressed that the main experience for music listeners is to savour the surfaces and timbres of the sound, perhaps to dance and sing along as well – which is to say that the attention of the listener stops at the loudspeaker. The listener has no expectation that there is more than this, for example, that there are journalists, hosts or other responsible persons involved.

Earphones are the ultimate equipment for loudspeaker living. Notice that many interfaces for sound are designed to be handled by humans with their hands and eyes and ears in conjunction, but this is most emphatically not the case for earphones (or for loudspeakers in general). Loudspeakers are often almost invisible, since they may be embedded in restaurant walls, in car doors or in your ears if you wear earphones. Furthermore, loudspeakers typically stay in the same place for a long time, and become fixed objects in people's everyday surroundings.

This point is most clear in the case of earphones (or headphones, which are larger and worn outside the ears), which provide the same stable sound projection regardless of the movement of the wearer. If you walk away from a loudspeaker on the kitchen table, the sound appears weaker and its resonance changes, but this is obviously not the case with earphones.

Instead of just being channels for sounds, earphones can take on the character of presenting *keynote sounds* in the listener's everyday environment (Schafer [1977] 1994: 10). Consider a natural phenomenon such as a river running through a city. The water sounds are always there, and 'have imprinted themselves so deeply on the people hearing them that life without them would be sensed as a distinct impoverishment' (ibid.). In a completely mobile setting, the wearable music player creates a similar keynote sound. Recorded music in these cases becomes a fixture in a person's life.

From the beginning of the twentieth century, when people could play records as often as they liked, there developed a new and more inclusive way of engaging with music. The listeners would become more and more interested in comparing one recording with another (and live programmes with other live programmes), rather than comparing them with performances in a concert hall or other non-mediated settings. After more than hundred years of this process of internal reference, intricate ways of listening have emerged among people in general. People have learnt *not* to listen to sound to identify the causes of the sound events. They listen without considering that the experience lacks shape, colour or smell because they never expected it to have shape, colour or smell in the first place. Michel Chion (1994: 29) calls this kind of listening 'reduced listening'. Here it is the timbres of the sounds that are listened for, and not their reference back to some historical event. Arnheim ([1936] 1986: 35) says that minute discriminations in sound alone are desirable because they enrich 'the aural vocabulary by whose help the loudspeaker describes the world'.

Part II

Backwards history

Chapter 7

Tape control

A revolution in recorded music, 1970s–1950s

If the term 'revolution' is to be used at all in this book, it should describe the introduction of micro-electronics and magnetic tape in Europe and America. In the 1970s there was a wholesale uptake of synthesizers, tape effects and multi-track recording, and the musical soundscapes of the West were changed forever.

It is always dangerous to proclaim revolutions, but I will present three case studies that support my argument well. Firstly the Residents play a weird, tone-generated melody in 1974; secondly, Sly and the Family Stone play a densely produced funk track in 1973; and lastly the British rock experimentalists Traffic making psychedelia in 1968. All this music is heavily edited (cut up), and has nothing to do with the old 'live on tape' performances of the 1950s and before. The documentary realism of live recordings was marginalized in a matter of years. This change towards densely cut up and rearranged tape is the revolution I am talking about.

Backwards history

Now the backwards history will begin in earnest, and I anticipate a level of scepticism among some of my readers. But the move backwards from the present time to the past is quite simple; I jump from the digital media of our own time to the analogue media in their final configuration before they became obsolete. All the remaining chapters discuss analogue media in one way or another.

First I will sketch the general background atmosphere during the 1970s and 1960s. The period was highly advanced in technological terms, as the NASA moon landing in 1969 demonstrates. The Cold War was at its coldest, and the USA had strengthened its position with the Apollo programme (Hobsbawm 1994: 231ff.). On the cultural front grave old men had always dominated the public sphere, but now young people started making a claim to dominance. In the USA in the 1960s new rights were gained for women and racial minorities, and there was a more open and informal society, at least at the everyday level. It was a better time to live in both the USA and Europe for more people than ever before. Although bad things were happening, for example the Vietnam War, people's living standards went up in all countries of the West

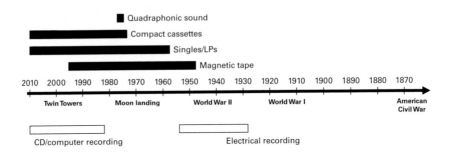

Figure 7.1 Timeline of magnetic recording media.

(see Marwick 1998 for a comprehensive study of the cultural revolutions of the 1960s). Consumer comfort eased the strain of living with the impending threat of nuclear annihilation, and the era was marked by cultural optimism.

In 1974 the media environment was very different from ours. There were no mobile phones, no personal computers and no internet. Computers were used only in banks, insurance companies and universities. But we should not underestimate the richness and attraction of this earlier media environment.

Figure 7.1 shows the platforms on which this chapter focuses in black. There were four essentially different platforms: magnetic tape, which was used mostly in professional production milieus; singles and LPs, used for the mass distribution of music; compact cassettes, used both for mass distribution and for personal recording of media sound; and the short-lived quadraphonic sound system. I will focus here on magnetic tape and the LP. Notice that LPs and cassettes are still available, although they are marginal compared to CDs and computer files such as mp3. The platforms that preceded and came after these analogue platforms are listed in figure 7.1 below the arrow. Computer recording is discussed in chapter 3, while electrical recording is treated in chapter 9.

However, there were several influential recording media in the mid-twentieth century. From the late 1920s sound film inspired creative developments in sound editing on celluloid film, and there was also advanced tape editing in radio plays and reportage quite early on. When television was introduced in the 1950s yet another platform for complex edited narratives came about (see Barnouw [1975] 1990; Winston 2005: 330ff.). Although these media worked independently of each other, there were many creative inspirations between them.

For the domestic media consumer in Europe and America there was colour television, and there was transatlantic telegraphy, telephony and telex (with its ticker tape to throw at the parade). There were 3D sound films from Hollywood, dozens of radio stations on AM, newspapers, magazines and books. As well as colour 35 mm stills film there were cheap, portable cameras for people to record their family history with.

Ordinary people in the West had acquired a very relaxed and natural attitude towards the mass media and the music industry. Young people would enjoy music on the stereo, blasting it out into the neighbourhood without any worries. Starting in the mid-1960s, recorded music entered a stage of explosive cultural activity, and artists such as Bob Dylan and the Beatles put their stamp on cultural history almost as forcefully as Shakespeare did four hundred years previously. Electronic media and their noisy pop cultures were slowly recognized as an important part of the cultural heritage, not only in the public eye but also among academics (for positive and negative perspectives, see Boorstin [1961] 1985; McLuhan [1964] 1994; Ellul 1964; Barthes [1972] 1993).

Musicians were increasingly technology savvy. If an artist had success, they would be allowed increasing creative control and high-tech recording equipment. This allowed them to break with traditional ways of doing things, and increased the potential for originality with the aid of high-quality sound, stereo and tape cutting and splicing. During the years of psychedelia and counter-culture there was an increasing popular acceptance of the expressive character of recording. Producers such as Phil Spector and George Martin became cultural icons in their own time (for studies of rock and popular music in this period, see Gracyk 1996; Jones 1992).

Not everyone liked the new production values. When Bob Dylan went electric in 1965 there was outrage among his fans in the folk song movement. Pete Seeger disliked the loud electrical sound so much that he said he wanted to pull out the electrical wiring system to stop the music (Shelton 1987: 302–3). This was an outcry against a certain type of *sound* just as much as against the commercial potential of Dylan's turnaround. It says something about the unnerving character of the electric guitar, bass and miked-up drums.

Recording signature, 1974

Now I will begin the analysis of music production with magnetic tape. Artists could choose between two production aesthetics: shaping sound in support of a live performance image, or shaping the recording as an artistic message in its own right. Along these lines William Moylan (1992: 77) argues that 'the recording process can capture reality, or it can create (through sound relationships) the illusion of a new world. Most recordists find themselves moving about the vast area that separates these two extremes.' Before the introduction of tape, artists had no choice but to support the live performance, and this seventy-year long state of affairs will be described in chapters 9 and 11.

The favoured style of music in the 1960s was a composite one which had the sound of something fragmented or cut up. The artists could choose the best of many partial performances during a prolonged recording process, and construct just one authoritative master that would be *exactly* as the producer wanted it to be; this is what I call the recording signature. Rock music production involved a complex repetitive process, tracks being assigned and filled with layer upon layer of sound elements, and small parts of performances would be redone regardless of whether the whole band was present. Like a literary text, the recording is aesthetically and rhetorically well organized.

Some rock groups pushed the new timbres and technologies to the limit. The first case study in this chapter is by the Residents, who used electronic tone-generators and rhythm boxes to create eerie melodies on the LP *Not Available* (1978). They played alternative synth and drum machine rock, and are still well known among lovers of alternative rock and art music. The album is among the best in the Residents' catalogue and was recorded four years before its release. I chose this track because it displays the equipment sound in a way that is parallel to the style of Autechre (track 11). Listeners in the 2000s may not find these sounds as eerie as listeners did in 1978.

In 1974 the production values of recorded music were very high, something that such contemporary artists as Steely Dan and Pink Floyd demonstrate. It was the peak of innovation in analogue technology, and the next step would be digital. Tape equipment had an aura of advancement, and it appeared in movies such as *The Conversation* (Francis Ford Coppola, 1974) and *Klute* (Alan J. Pakula, 1971). The Residents exposed the medium's potential for creating synthetic acoustics, a world that only exists because of electronic tone-generators. 'Never Known Questions' is a weird intonation of concerns, and the words are just as redundart as the melody, making the track sound like a kind of tribal incantation.

🔊 *Track 20: Residents: Never Known Questions, 1974 (1:20).*

> Falling guards and winking bards are just a need today.
> Falling guards and winking bards are just my needs. Okay?
> Okay. Okay. Okay. Okay.
> Okay. Okay. Okay. Okay.
> Okay. Okay. Okay. Okay.
> Okay. Okay. Okay. Okay. Okay.
> To show or to, to be shown is,
> A question never even not known,
> By many to exist,
> To show or to be shown,
> A question never, never known,
> not even by many to exist.

There are at least five instruments involved: piano, drums, synth/organ, horns, and a singing voice. The synths and voice all have the same wailing and hypnotizing sound, but the song after all conforms to traditional norms of melody, vocal performance and rhythm. This recording is not as extreme as the Residents' album *Eskimo* (1979), which departs completely from recognizable chord progressions. In the 1980s groups such as Tuxedomoon and the Cure would have success with sounds similar to 'Never Known Questions'.

It is not easy to hear what techniques the musicians have used. Even the most well-informed of listeners would be at pains to find out what was done in the studio just by listening to the album. We need the stories of people attending the recording sessions, we need a studio log and, most importantly, we need to know what equipment was used. Music lovers would increasingly attempt to disclose the techniques that were used in the recording studio and make sense out of all the different types of strange sounds. At the artistic end, mixing consoles and multitrack recording have become instruments in their own right. More to the point: this equipment has become an instrument in its own right. The medium of recording no longer just produces a good reproduction of musical events: 'The technical equipment is seen not as an external aid to reproduction but as a characteristic of the musical original, employed as part of the artistic conception' (Middleton 1990: 69).

The Residents and other artsy rock bands of the 1960s and 1970s, such as Frank Zappa and the Mothers of Invention, learnt brand new musical techniques (Watson 1993). Paul Théberge (1997: 220) argues that, in order to work creatively in the studio, 'musicians and engineers had to acquire both a basic theoretical and a practical knowledge of acoustics, microphone characteristics, electronic signal processing, and a variety of other technical processes.' Listeners responded favourably to the new sound. Simon Frith (1998: 244–5) claims that 'we now hear (and value) music as layered; we are aware of the contingency of the decision that put this sound here, brought this instrument forward there. It's as if we always listen to the music being assembled.' The process of modification was now an integral part of the aesthectic product, and the recording equipment was becoming as important as the musicians and their instruments. Remember that this structure of experience has now been in place for about forty years, and it difficult for us to imagine it as an untried thing. Nevertheless this is what I am attempting to do in this chapter.

As musicians and producers came to learn new techniques of producing sound, listeners came to learn more sophisticated ways of listening to that sound. Simon Frith describes the distinctly *hermeneutical* attitude that was taken towards these montages in order to be able to hear them as recognizably real.

> I listen to records in the full knowledge that what I hear is something that never existed, that never could exist, as a 'performance', something happening in a single time and space; nevertheless, it is now happening, in a single time and space: it is thus a performance and I hear it as one.
>
> (Frith 1998: 211)

From the early 1970s there were few expectations of documentary realism among popular-music listeners. However, the act of listening became more complex, and now had room for new uncertainties that could create a sense that the value of musical performance as such had been weakened. But in the end the techniques of multitrack sound became so widespread and so influential that it came close to being perceived as a neutral feature, appearing to be the 'natural way' of doing things, and seeming to be exclusively a matter of social appropriation rather than of material determination.

Continuity realism, 1973

One expectation in particular is almost ineradicable among listeners. This is the expectation that a song has a straightforward verse and chorus, bridges, harmonies and solos, and that it lasts approximately three minutes. Technology meant that live performance was no longer required, but the concert scene had a conservative influence in this regard, and a groove or beat that is not too extreme in aesthetic terms is also required for dancing. Both disco and funk in the 1970s demonstrate the need for straight continuity very well.

My point is that the traditional organization of songs was required for cultural reasons, just as it had always been. At the great festivals of the 1960s, such as Woodstock, the music from the LPs was played live. Audiences expected to hear the songs they loved more or less as they sounded on the stereo LP, but with extended solos and other embellishments. However, there was a subtle change going on in this regard.

It has something to do with the fact that multitrack recordings didn't need to convey a continuous event. The resulting recording could end up like the McLuhan LP, where all kinds of sounds were mounted on top of each other in a flow that bears little resemblance to traditional performances of speech or song. Hearing multitrack music, the public could not as easily relate the qualities of the finished piece to traditional musical qualities, such as good improvisation skills, a good mood in the band and other human aspects always associated with live performance. Among musicians there was an increased tolerance towards experiments on the part of the engineers, original editing and mixing decisions, and all kinds of experimentation with pitch, echo, reverberation, and so on. In short, the band might not be able to pull off a good live performance even if they wanted to. They had become good at something other than being a tight combo. In 1966 the Beatles stopped touring, and one of the reasons given was that it was impossible to produce live performances of the songs on *Revolver* (1966) and later *Sgt Pepper's Lonely Hearts Club Band* (1967).

The obvious way to avoid this dilemma was to use post-production techniques to create an extra rich and varied continuity recording. The next case demonstrates this strategy well. Sly Stone was an African-American vocalist and bandleader well known to lovers of funk and rhythm and blues. One of his best LPs is *Fresh* (1973). Here Sly and the Family have created a series of densely layered songs which are nevertheless quite straightforward sounding, and comfortable to listen to. The album was recorded on eight- or sixteen-track stereo tape.

Track 21: Sly and the Family Stone: If You Want Me To Stay, 1973 (1:26).

If you want me to stay
I'll be around today
To be available for you to see
I'm about to go
And then you'll know
For me to stay here I've got to be me
You'll never be in doubt
That's what it's all about
You can't take me for granted and smile
Count the days I'm gone
Forget reaching me by phone
Because I promise I'll be gone for a while
When you see me again
I hope that you have been
The kind of person that you really are now
You got to get it straight
How could I ever be late
When you're my woman takin' up my time
How could you ever allow
I guess I wonder how
How could you get out of pocket for fun
When you know that you're never number two
Number one gonna be number one
I'll be good
I wish I could
Get this message over to you now

The Family Stone was a large band, with at least ten different instruments and almost as many musicians. There is a trumpet, several saxophones, drums, bass, electric organ, electric guitar and piano, plus of course Sly's singing voice. The lyrics are easy to sing along with, in contrast to the Residents' track. The group of musicians is expressive and energetic, typical of early funk (Danielsen 2006).

Sly Stone is at this point in his career on a downward spiral of drug use and other standard rock-star behaviour, but this has not weakened his performance. He has a powerful and characteristic voice, which flexes and flows along with the dense accompaniment. Sly sings quite cynically about male–female relationships, and avoids political topics of his day such as the Vietnam War, the liberation African Americans and women, etc.

My main reason for presenting 'If You Want Me to Stay' is that it is a good example of continuity realism. Like most musicians Sly was economically dependent on going on tour to promote his records and earn money. As suggested, the live concert scene required a kind of conventional performance of the kind Sly's funk song is fully capable, while still exploiting the new production techniques to the full. In contrast, Stevie Wonder, on *Innervisions* (1973), camouflaged the extreme discontinuity of the recording process. He actually plays all the instruments on the track 'Jesus Children of America', and also sings all vocal parts and has arranged and produced the album himself, but it sounds like a full band of musicians playing enthusiastically together. This all goes to show that complex production can be arranged so that it becomes inaudible, and the unsuspecting listener would never hear it as the cut-and-paste production of a one-man band.

The strategy of continuity realism involves a tacit understanding between the producer and the listeners: the more the producers camouflage the multitrack characteristics of the recording, the more the listeners will acknowledge the musical qualities as authentic and skilful. This is *inaudible recording*: it tries to hide the discontinuity of multitrack production techniques and to pose as old-fashioned 'live on tape' recording.

Flaunting the montage, 1968

Psychedelic music displays well another approach to the magnetic tape medium. As I have stated, it had so many opportunities for *post-production* that continuity realism no longer had to apply. This feature was of course willingly exploited, for example in an extreme way by the Beatles on 'Revolution no. 9' (1968), and in a beautiful way by the Beach Boys on 'Good Vibrations' (1966). However, in purist milieus such as classical and folk music there was considerable consternation over the new production methods. They were considered radical and destructive.

Traffic was a rock group from England, and it is still well known to fans of 1960s music. The next case study is rather obscure, although it can be found on Traffic's breakthrough album *Mr Fantasy*, issued in 1967, the summer of love and psychedelic music. The British invasion was over, although several bands – the Beatles, Cream, the Who and Steve Winwood's Traffic – survived the change in music trends.

 Track 22: Traffic: Giving to You, 1967 (1:15).

> Listen baby, do you see this town … baby someday this can all be yours. Hey, Sweetheart … I mean … you know … I mean … it's like … you know … it's jazz man … I dig jazz … it's got … its like … it's jazz … is … is … you know … where it's at … you know where I'm at … I mean jazz.

The group only has three members, who play all the instruments and contribute all the vocals. It sounds as if there are three different voices, electrical guitar, bass, drums, electric organ and flute. It is difficult to say how many instruments there are, since of course one musician could be playing several different instruments on the completed recording.

The piece begins with a soft electric guitar that is drowned out by the montage of simultaneous bits of speech and scatting. The babbling is mixed up loud, but an up-tempo beat with an organ lies underneath and rises slowly as the recommendation of jazz progresses. With an electronic beep the 'jazz' takes over, and three minutes of polished jazz flute follows. My excerpt fades out after a minute, but at the end of the piece the dense babbling comes back, and suggests that the element of continuity realism during the jazz proper is really dependent on the new multitrack regime.

The first part of 'Giving to You' is an exemplary piece of multitrack tape music from the mid-twentieth century; it resembles track 1.1 with Marshall McLuhan, and is archetypal of early multitrack productions. This piece is primarily a *texture* of sound, and only secondarily is it a reference to a set of external events. The kind of voice manipulation used became more normal in the wake of Elvis Presley's early recordings: 'Elvis Presley's recorded voice was so doctored up with echoes that he sounded as though he were going to shake apart' (Chanan 1995: 107). In sum the listener is presented with a highly realistic impression of something impossible, what Evan Eisenberg (1987: 109) calls a 'composite photograph of a minotaur'.

But, in contrast to the Residents' track, it is quite easy to hear that the musicians are cutting up and splicing tape at full tilt. The so-called *cut-and-splice technique* which is used at the beginning of Traffic's 'Giving to You' was more widespread in film production and radio reportage. Such techniques lay the sound signal bare in a way that the gramophone could never accomplish. The reels and tape and wiring opened up recorded sound so that it could be touched and handled at length.

The magnetic recording medium

I will now discuss the technological basis of the new music culture. At one level there was nothing new. The magnetic recording medium was completely asymmetrical, just as the gramophone medium had been. Of course it inherited the structure of the industry, with professional distribution of music to dispersed listeners.

Figure 7.2 displays the main interfaces, platforms and signal carriers of the set-up I am investigating in this chapter. The recording studios were more complex than before, and there could be several multitrack tape recorders and mixing boards. The studio involved not just singers and musicians playing into a microphone, but also analogue synthesizers such as the Moog. The complexity of the medium is further shown by the fact that three different recording platforms were involved in the communication between producers and listeners: the professional tape system in the studio, plus the industrially copied singles and LPs and the industrially copied cassette tapes. The domestic stereo set with two rather big loudspeakers, a turntable and an amplifier was to dominate music consumption for twenty years, from the 1960s to the 1980s. The cassette

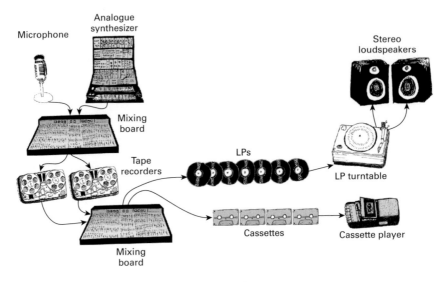

Figure 7.2 Model of the magnetic recording medium.

player was often in mono only, and was typically not used for high-quality listening experiences, but it was portable and offered a far more versatile way of listening to music than the LP stereo set.

All the platforms required electrical amplification. This meant that the LPs and singles were unplayable on the mechanical gramophones from the 1950s and before, and these playback devices quickly became obsolete. As the gramophone recording industry adapted to the magnetic production platform, there arose a distinct difference between the production equipment, with its enormous creative scope, and the domestic equipment, with its limited possibilities but high-fidelity experience. This was a process of professionalization, with a difference arising between the technical skills of producers and musicians on the one hand and the enjoyments of music lovers on the other.

The analogue signal carrier is a crucial feature of this medium. In contrast to the chapters of part I in this book, part II deals only with analogue recording, and this concept must be explained. To say that a signal is analogue means that the electro-mechanical movements for storing the signal are continuous with the vibratory movements at the microphone. The duration of the recording is physically proportional to the distance along the groove or tape band, and if the speed is not kept the same during playback as it was during recording the analogy will be lost. Analogue sound is also *degenerative*, meaning that it cannot be stored for a long time without deterioration, or copied to new discs or tapes without noise being added.

It is worth mentioning that magnetic tape is a very tactile material, and engineers worked with a hand–ear coordination that bypassed vision. The tape has other interesting qualities. While one second of sound on a 78 rpm record was contained in a little less than one lap along the circular groove (77 per cent of one lap, to be exact), one second of tape at 7.5 inches per second (ips) was contained in a straight strip the length of a grown man's hand from wrist to fingertip (Gelatt 1977: 299). While the 77 per cent of a lap on the turntable was virtually untouchable, the 7.5 inches of tape could be pulled out from the reel, cut free from the rest and *stand alone* as a tangible container of that second of sound. Consequently, the producer had no problem handling elements as short as one-tenth of a second. This kind of manipulation was impossible with the gramophone, where, as Roland Gelatt (1977: 299) points out, any splitting up of the recording would result in its destruction.

Gelatt sums up the developments in tape by comparing it with the older gramophone disc cutter, which had dominated the recording business up to that point: 'A compact, lightweight reel of tape would play uninterruptedly for half an hour; a bulky and heavy record for four minutes. Tape did not wear out; records showed evidence of real deterioration after thirty or so playings. A broken tape could be spliced quickly and easily by anyone; a broken record could be tossed into the trash basket' (Gelatt 1977: 288). And he points out that the maximum frequency response of a sound recording had been extended to a range of 20 to 20.000 Hz (ibid.: 299). It seems that the electromagnetic analogue could contain more of everything that was valuable – longer performances, more frequencies and more loudness – and in addition it became less degenerative.

By the late 1950s the tape machine had been improved from one track to two track, and this separation of tracks along the length of the tape made it possible to introduce stereo to the mass market (in combination with stereo pickups and new amplifiers). The two strands of sound had to be kept separate all through the mediation process, starting with two microphones routed through two channels on the mixing console to two separate tracks on a tape recorder. For playback the listeners needed an LP with two separate signals engraved and picked up by two pickups and amplified to two loudspeakers.

Michael Chanan (1995: 144) describes how frequently the electronics industry launched new versions of the tape technology. Indeed, it resembles the way in which that computer software is regularly updated. Companies such as Nagra and Ampex introduced multitrack recorders, first with two tracks, then with three and four, before 1960. During the 1960s eight- and sixteen-track machines became industry standard. For each track there had to be a dedicated play- and recording-head, and on the tape itself there had to be guard bands to prevent sound from spilling over from one track to another. Furthermore, each play-head had to function independently from the others, so that, for example, one could record the drums and bass on two tracks without recording anything on the other two, and later record on the latter without recording on the former.

The functionalities of tape were convincing as far as the music industry in the USA was concerned. From 1947 there was a landslide towards tape in the radio industry, and magnetic recording soon became a standard tool for producing documentaries, for delaying the airing of programmes, and for storing sound in archives. 'The old disc recording instruments previously used for broadcast transcriptions were unsentimentally abandoned. In a short and significant contest, tape had prevailed decisively' (Gelatt 1977: 288). The same dramatic replacement soon took place in the music recording industry, at least in the USA. 'Tape's invasion of the recording studio, begun early in 1949, proceeded so implacably that within a year the old method of direct recording on wax or acetate blanks was almost completely superseded' (ibid.: 298–9).

Proliferation of techniques

The most striking new technique was that of the producer star. From the time of Thomas Edison the sound engineer had been an equal partner with the performers, meaning that sound quality had just as great an influence as musical quality on how things were to be done in the studio. Engineering was not recognized in a positive, creative way until the advent of advanced recording processes in the 1960s. Before then, the engineer spent all his time improving the signal chain instead of aiding the artist to take advantage of creative potentials at the interface.

By now album sleeves referred to engineering as the craft of securing the best possible sound quality, while production was the craft of making aesthetic decisions about mixing and editing processes. And, increasingly, the musicians were their own producers. Steve Jones describes the double achievement: 'The evolution of recording equipment moved … toward [both] greater accuracy in the preservation of the space and time of the event and greater flexibility in subsequent manipulation of that event' (Jones 1992: 47–8). The creative artists were at the helm of this two-pronged innovation.

Editing is a very important new technique. As I have described, tape could be recorded on, rewound and played back immediately without noticeable detriment to sound quality. Such immediate playback was crucial to the art of multitrack recording, as it allowed the recording to be built up using layers of overdubs. 'On the horizontal, one moment of sound could be followed by another that did not follow it in real time; on the vertical, any sound might be overdubbed with another that was recorded at a different time' (Gracyk 1996: 51). In order to edit a single track without destroying the signal on the other tracks the technique of 'dub editing' or 'punching in' or 'flying start' became the norm (Chanan 1995: 144). For example, if two seconds of drumming had to be redone, but the guitar and vocal tracks were to be untouched, the tape would be wound to the right position, the faulty performance would be erased, and the new drum part would be punched in.

There were also new techniques for musicians. Studio musicians and band members would know in advance that their contribution was only partial, and that it would probably be used in a different way on the finished master. A guitarist might have a three-second contribution to a given song. Paul Théberge (1997: 216) says that 'individual performances became less important than the manipulation of individual strands of recorded sound material.' Studio musicians first supplied the raw material for the recording, and subsequently the producers did the job of making it all fit together. In many cases the musicians were reduced to the role of manual workers in a production controlled by one person, for example in the case of Roger Waters and Pink Floyd or Frank Zappa and the Mothers of Invention.

The techniques of balancing or mixing the sound also gained a new complexity. In the studio the microphones were placed in optimal relation to the sound source, and the signal was routed into the mixing console in the control room. Here the mixing engineer would monitor all sounds and adjust parameters such as frequency response, reverberation and volume. This set-up had basically been in place since the late 1920s, but now each microphone (or electronic source) could also be assigned to a separate track on the multitrack tape machine. Mixing would generally refer to the later stages of recording, where the basic tracks were calibrated in relation to each other on each pertinent parameter, and when everything was just right it would be recorded on a master stereo tape. In the gramophone era there was no such thing as the 'later stages' of recording.

Home stereo

On the domestic end of the medium there was a significant change of equipment, and increased interest in the technologies of sound. The LP was ushered in on the market in the late 1950s, and it could contain up to twenty minutes of music on each side. This was in itself a striking improvement, especially for lovers of classical music, who could now hear much longer stretches of a symphony without interruption (Millard 2005: 204ff.).

In the 1970s young adults bought their own stereo systems, and they had more powerful amplifiers and better loudspeakers than before. The term hi-fi freak denotes people who are obsessively concerned with their technical set-up and often less concerned about the music. People could play their good sound very loudly, and gather with friends to enjoy the music. Stereo sound soon became a popular new fixture of the home (Chanan 1995: 94).

Stereo means that two different tracks are separated through the recording and playback process, and different sound sources (instruments and vocals) can be placed in the different channels. I will return to Traffic (track 22) from 1968 to demonstrate the point. Traffic placed some instruments entirely in the right

Figure 7.3 Music lover with stereo system.

and others entirely in the left channel; for example the flute is in the left channel. This seemingly crude mixing is a symptom of how new stereo was. The musicians and producers had not really found a good way of using stereo, so they separated everything fifty–fifty in the two channels. Early Beatles recordings, for example *Help* (1965), also had very crude stereo effects.

In the 1960s stereo records were often played on simple mono equipment, and none of the stereo effects could be heard. Those who actually owned a stereo system with two speakers would notice that the music was more powerful and impressive *in the room*. 'Essentially', Roland Gelatt argues, 'stereo aimed at reproducing the spaciousness, clarity, and realism of two-eared listening' (1977: 313). 'Because the sonic image emitted by each speaker differed in slight but vital degree, an effect was re-created akin to the minutely divergent "points of view" of our own two ears' (ibid.: 314). He goes on to say that that no one hearing stereo tape recordings for the first time could fail to be impressed by 'their sense of spaciousness, by the buoyant airiness and "lift" of the sound as it swirled freely around the listening room'.

In chapter 3 I discussed the analytic attitude of the music lover in the 2000s, when the synthetic sounds of computers had supplied new variables to listen to. In the 1960s it was stereo that supplied new variables. The listener could now balance two signal outputs to his own liking, steering the sound towards a sweet spot by loudspeaker placement as well as electronic balancing on the amplifier. This allowed people to listen to music in a new way, 'savoring its

breadth and depth as well as its melodic outlines and harmonic textures'
(Gelatt 1977: 314–15). If the listeners were seated in a fixed position in their
living room, the sweet spot, they could locate different sound sources in the
recording on a horizontal line between the left- and right-hand side of the
stereo system.

Stereo created an image of better sound also in the commercial sense of the
word. The record company rhetoric continued to be one of superlative recommendation of a new sound experience, just as with electrical recording in the
1930s and with CDs in the 1980s. In 1960 RCA Victor stated that what they
called 'Living Stereo' creates a 'more natural' and 'more dimensional' sound: 'For
the first time, your ears will be able to distinguish where each instrument and
voice comes from – left, right or center. In short, enveloped in solid sound, you
will hear music in truer perspective.' In the 1970s Quadraphonic surround sound,
which relied on four separate channels throughout the recording and reproduction process, was also introduced. For various reasons this initiative failed to enter
the mainstream markets (see Harley 1998: 290).

Stereo loudspeakers could be seen as a way of making recorded sound even
more realistic than before, since it resembles human bidirectional hearing.
But in perceptual terms this notion was problematic. The problem had long
been encountered in movie production. In 1930 a film sound technician, frustrated by the spatial signature resulting from the use of multiple microphones,
described the blend of sources as creating a listener construct 'with five or six
very long ears, said ears extending in various directions' (Altman 1992b: 49).
Instead of realism, what was added was a bigger and more impressive spatiality,
noticeable in the greater precision of sound placement and the greater dynam-
ics of volume. But there was no increase in the documentary realism of sound.
Evan Eisenberg points out:

> That many listeners are still uncomfortable with stereo is evident from
> the way they place their speakers: pointlessly close together, or else on
> opposite walls. The latter arrangement is even more comfortable than
> monophony, as it creates no focus of attention, so no illusion of human
> presence, so no disillusionment.
>
> (Eisenberg 1987: 65)

From being relatively true to the central perspective of sitting in the best seat
in the concert hall, recordings were increasingly catering to a subjectively
pleasing experience for listeners. The aesthetics of recording turned away from
the ideal of perfect reproduction of performances at the microphone, and further towards an ideal of perfect balance of sound at the loudspeaker.

There is an interesting environmental dimension to stereo sound. Glenn
Gould, writing in 1966, argued that domestic 'dial twiddling' 'transforms that
work, and his relation to it, from an artistic to an environmental experience'. 'The
listeners' encounter with music that is electronically transmitted is not within the

public domain', Gould claims. 'The listener is able to indulge preferences and, through the electronic modifications with which he endows the listening experience, impose his own personality upon the work' (Gould 1984: 347). He elaborates on the sense of intimacy that high-quality recording gives: 'The more intimate terms of our experience with recordings have since suggested to us an acoustic with a direct and impartial presence, one with which we can live in our homes on rather casual terms' (ibid.: 333).

Chapter 8

The acoustic nation

Live journalism, 1960s–1930s

If there is such a thing as an enlightened public, in the mid-twentieth century it was informed more by sound than by light. Television was not established, and radio was a paternalist voice in the life of the West. This was the golden age of sound radio, and it could reach 50 to 60 million people in countries such as the UK, France and Germany, and even more in the USA. In 1969, Americans owned 268 million radios (Schafer [1977] 1994: 91).

I will tell the story of radio's auditory rhetoric by providing case studies of dominant broadcasters over a time span of thirty-eight years and going into the production procedures of NASA, NBC, the BBC, CBS and Swedish Public Radio. All had a conservative production culture that focused on live programming. This was easy to exploit for nationalistic purposes, and every nation of the world did so.

Backwards history

The ideological setting for broadcasters was challenging. Graham Murdock (2005: 219) argues that European governments were fearful of popular insurrections in the 1920s and 1930s, and in response they set out to make the nation the primary source of social identity. The BBC and other national broadcasters played a particular role in this symbolic nationalization. Looking at the world stage from the 1970s and backwards, there was a constant state of conflict – in the post-war era between the free world and the communist world, and before that between the Allies and the Axis during World War II. Broadcasting had been used as a large-scale propaganda tool also before the war, in Germany in particular, where Adolf Hitler had the dark genius of Joseph Goebbels to guide him. There was a constant war of words in sound radio (Briggs and Burke 2002: 217).

During the war the public mood in European countries and North America was very tense, ranging from fear and hatred to self-confidence and pity. In Europe at least, citizens had to endure a blackout every night for close on six years. The desire for safety and comfort within the home was strong. Radio had a double function in this regard. It was an imposing presence that could bring

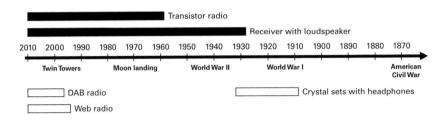

Figure 8.1 Timeline of analogue radio.

bad news – for people in Europe there was a great chance that such news would affect them directly (being enlisted in the army, having to flee from imminent bombing, more death and no end in sight) – but it was also a comforting presence bringing music, entertainment and the good mood that broadcasters tried to spread among the population. There are many studies of radio's role during the war; see, for example, Barnow 1968; Briggs 1970; and Bergmeier and Lotz 1997.

As the black boxes in figure 8.1 indicate, this chapter deals with a remarkably stable period in broadcasting history. From the mid-1920s all the way up to the 2000s people listened to analogue radio with loudspeaker receivers, represented either by big cabinets placed in the living room or by portable transistor radios. Essentially, people didn't have to buy new receivers unless they broke, although FM radio was introduced in the 1960s and induced many people to buy new equipment. Notice that the crystal set is placed under the arrow, because it really belongs to the pioneering age, and not to the mature radio medium that this chapter will describe.

During this long period radio was firmly established as a popular medium in Western countries. These forty years of development in media also spawned television, telex, sound film and radio. After the war there was a great increase in the production and purchase of consumer electronics, because parts of the huge production capacity that had been developed to fight the war was redirected to the needs of civil society (Chanan 1995: 92).

If we go all the way back to the pioneer days in the 1920s, when the BBC and other early broadcasters were established, not even radio was a proper media environment. There was less of it in time per day, and therefore it was a scarcer communicative resource. More importantly, listening techniques were less rooted in the cultural and domestic environment than they are today. The whole form of communication was less ordinary and more serious than it is now. Although there were great advances in every direction, this impression of radio as a spectacular new medium lived on until television took over from it in the 1960s.

During this period it dawned on the industries of culture that wireless was becoming a new profession alongside the old ones, such as newspaper journalism and movie making, and this meant that it was more attractive to culture workers. As employees in the new medium gained experience and self-confidence they continued to perfect the new craft with a sensitivity and common direction lacking before. From this early approach there emerged a skill with an expressive identity of its own: radio journalism.

Sounds from the moon, 1969

Before going into the national sounds of radio, I will present a case of global broadcasting. In the 1960s it became normal for broadcasts to have several hundred million people listening or watching, a good example being the transmission from John F. Kennedy's funeral in 1963 (Dayan and Katz 1992: 126). The USA showed its superiority in both technology and mass mediation with the NASA moon landing in 1969. It was called 'the greatest show in the history of television', and was watched by 125 million Americans and 723 million other people around the world (Briggs and Burke 2002: 253). The historic relay from the Mare tranquillitatis to Houston, Texas, was arranged by American technologists and astronauts in July 1969 and demonstrates well the great reach of broadcast media. This giant leap of electronic mediation had been facilitated by almost a hundred years of innovation, and the step onto the moon was the final proof of the unnatural capacities of these innovations. As suggested, most people watched and heard the moon landing on television. Radio had been marginalized by television as the main national arena for big events such as this.

If Marshall McLuhan's notion of the global village was ever pertinent, it was during the hours of this transmission, when millions of people were tuned in to the same sounds and images, their movement concerted into shared attention to their receiving apparatus, and a lifetime of memories was set in motion for many different people based on the same sounds and images. The lunar transmission demonstrates perfectly the documentary realism that live broadcasting facilitates – the sense of getting perceptual access to a world somewhere else through technology.

Track 23: NASA: Neil Armstrong on the Moon, 1969 (1:19).

[Heavy electronic noise throughout. Bursts of distortion.]
– Buzz, this is Houston. F2 one-one-sixtieth seconds for shadow photography on the sequence camera.
– OK.
– I'm at the foot of the ladder. The LEM footbeds are only depressed in the surface about one or two inches. Although the surface appears to be

very, very fine grained as you get close to it. It's almost like a powder.
[long pause]
– I'm gonna step off the LEM now.
[long pause]
– It's one small step for man, one giant leap for mankind.

There is an interesting acoustic architecture to these sounds. Initially, the words were formulated inside a helmet with rather poor acoustics. Since there are no sounds in the vacuum of outer space there is no acoustic space to reproduce and represent. Indeed, the sounds from the moon came exclusively from within Neil Armstrong's helmet, and were facilitated by microphones and amplifiers brought to the moon by the astronauts.

The audio signals were beamed back to earth across the approximately 240,000 miles of empty space, picked up by satellites orbiting over the Atlantic and the Pacific Oceans, and relayed to the primary reception station at Mission Control in Houston (Goodwin 1999). From Texas they were further relayed to national stations all over the globe, and finally the connections into living-room receivers were made from aerials on mountain tops or tall buildings. This complex process made it possible for Armstrong's words to be heard in millions of homes. In listening locales the ambience was further determined by the quality of the listeners' equipment and the individual room acoustics. These details suffice to show that the moon transfer was obviously a *non-local event* (Aarseth 1993: 24) entirely lacking in geographical limitations.

What about the temporal dimension? This event was live at the point of transmission, but since it was sent from the moon its temporality was if possible even more confused than its ambience. Admittedly, there was an unbroken contact between the events on the moon and the perception of them on planet earth, so in a strictly physical sense one could say that the Armstrong quote took place on the moon and all over the world at the same time. But since for all practical purposes there is no 'moon time', the event had to be planned for a suitable 'earth time', and since the Americans controlled the presentation they arranged it for US prime time on the evening of 20 July. In Norway it was an early morning event on 21 July, while in some other parts of the world it was a lunchtime or afternoon event (Bastiansen 1994). The crackling sounds from the live broadcast naturally lent the quality of immediate disappearance, relaying a contingent event that could only be experienced right then, by the people living and listening in on that quite memorable Sunday/Monday.

I will also comment on the soundbite rhetoric of Armstrong's statement (Scheuer 2001). The sounds and images from the lunar event were of course recorded on tape, or else we would not be able to hear them now. The transmission was recorded for documentary purposes, centrally by NASA, nationally by hundreds of radio and television stations, and privately by thousands of listeners. News services all over the world repeated the soundbite 'A small step for man, a giant leap for mankind'. But Armstrong pronounced it wrong. He

Figure 8.2 Neil Armstrong on the moon.

should have said: 'A small step for a man, a giant leap for mankind', which would have brought out the difference between himself as a mortal individual and the larger society of humans that he represents. Armstrong later claimed that this phrase was something he came up with of his own accord, but the phrase is so appropriate to the occasion that it would probably have been chosen regardless of who actually stepped down first. NASA is the real producer of these words, while Armstrong is a replaceable actor-astronaut.

This NASA case illustrates a critical point made by Murray Schafer ([1977] 1994: 77), namely that a man with a loudspeaker is more imperialistic than one without. Schafer is concerned with the dominance that can be gained by sheer media volume, and there is no doubt that the NASA transmission was a form of imperialism also at the level of sound. The rocket noises and flames and smoke of the huge technological set-up infused the event with extra credibility and authenticity. The machine hum, microphone noises and the other scrambling, crackling, hissing, fluttering disturbances added on the long transport through space made it abundantly clear to audiences across the world that there was an unprecedented technological feat taking place. This means that the poor technical fidelity of the NASA sound feed gave listeners good reason to acknowledge this as a transfer from the moon, and here is a subtle form of noise imperialism. Notice that there are many conspiracy theories about the moon landing in 1969, and there is much evidence and counter-evidence regarding it (Phillips 2001).

The national radio public

The next case takes us back to earth, and helps to clarify radio's status in the 1960s. At that time listeners could take several features absolutely for granted. There would be a constant offer of programmes from multiple stations, and some stations even ran for twenty-four hours a day. And they would serve up a sound quality of little or no distortion, so that the soundscapes were very comfortable in the home.

Radio journalism consisted, for example, of national sporting events, Saturday night programmes, and news events on a regional and national level. This was a public sphere that people could not choose; they lived in the midst of it whether they liked it or not. Radio's national public is at the heart of this chapter. It was already on the wane in the 1960s because the pressure from television meant that both listeners and producers were looking for something new, and radio stations started airing pop music and other forms of lighter, more commercial content that would not involve the same collective spirit.

Remember that the BBC had been defining British home communications since the 1920s (Briggs [1961] 2000, 1965, 1970). Traditionally, radio was at the centre of the home, and the programmes were solemn and serious. Another way of putting it is that public service broadcasting was dominated by a coercive or authoritative address. In contrast, commercial broadcasting in the USA and on the European mainland was dominated by a more inviting or agreeable presentation. In 1967 the BBC changed its overall stance and adopted a more informal delivery than before. Radio was under pressure from television, and in a move to counteract this the BBC reorganized its output into four channels. Radio 1 was the real novelty, because it broadcast nothing but pop music; it was to become the teenage pop music station, and stop the audience leakage to Radio Luxembourg and pirate stations such as Radio Caroline (Crisell 1997: 140; Briggs and Burke 2002: 227; Hendy 2007).

The next case study is a jingle or promo from the very first day of BBC's Radio 1, with Robin Scott and Tony Blackburn in the studio (Brand and Scannell 1991). It exhibits a cheerful mood, and several musical styles are mixed together with sound effects on top. It demonstrates well the new sound of an old medium.

Track 24: BBC Radio One: Promo, 1967 (0:27).

[American style choir] The voice of Radio 1
just for fun

music [altered]
too much
– And good morning everyone, welcome to the exiting new sound of
Radio 1.
[Up-tempo beat, trumpets, dog barks]

Notice that the jingle is produced in the style that I discussed in chapter 7 as
'flaunting the montage'. This is supposed to sound advanced, playful and
slightly reckless. The live show was fast-paced and entertaining, and used all
kinds of verbal effects that were really invented by American radio DJs. It had
been taken up by Radio Luxembourg and pirate music stations of various
types, and now it was also taken up by the BBC.

The sound of this jingle signifies a dramatic shift in the style of radio. During
the 1950s and 1960s there were two crucial changes in the media infrastructure of domestic life that meant radio programmes came to be regarded as
background noise. As I have already pointed out, television pushed listening
habits out of the evening prime time and into the morning and afternoon.
Second, the cheap, lightweight transistor radios that had come on the market
in the 1950s meant that radio programmes could be listened to in many more
everyday situations than before, so that it would not be a big deal to have radio
sets in the kitchen, the living room, the bathroom, the bedroom, the car and
the office. The fact that, in 1979, 95 per cent of all cars on the road in the USA
had radios (Fornatale and Mills 1980: 20) suggests the level of penetration.

Formatted programmes meant that radio was even was more predictable
than before. Scheduling consists of making the flow of programming predictable on a hourly basis (Ellis 2000), and stations followed their fixed schedules and seasonal events slavishly. Commercial stations in the USA perfected
this strategy long before the monopoly stations in Europe. During prime-time
hours, schedules tended to be split into fifteen- or twenty-minute segments,
with four of five musical and spoken numbers in each segment (Barnouw
1966: 127), and commercial stations would insert commercial messages
between each song. Typically, there was an alternation of vocal and instrumental numbers, which brought some variety to the broadcast output. In this way
both variation and predictability were accomplished.

Radio was in a sense becoming less important and more available at the
same time. This gave station strategists good reason to orient programming
towards a less attentive form of listening. In the USA this strategy is shown
clearly in the 'formula radio' that was first established in the late 1940s, and
mainly played Top 40 pop music (Fornatale and Mills 1980: 13). This is the first
inkling of what is generally called 'format radio', or 'wallpaper radio', and that
generally refers to the industrial production of social surfaces in sound. This
was a careful construction of inconspicuous programming, and it was all
planned so that it would not be reflected on; it engaged the listener by semi-
conscious invigoration and *moods* rather than by explicit attention to content.

Kraft Music Hall, 1943

Entertainment was a staple of radio in the early period, and it required quite specific techniques. By the 1930s every programme was expertly staged for sound alone, and the listeners were becoming used to this specialized expressive form. There was no need for imaginative supplements to something that was lacking in the broadcast. Rudolf Arnheim ([1936] 1986: 135) states categorically that nothing is lacking in good radio: 'For the essence of broadcasting consists just in the fact that it alone offers unity by aural means.' If a programme demanded supplementation by visual imagination it did not properly utilize the medium's own resources.

The bigger setting of live orchestras, entertainment shows and theatrical performance can be called *the resounding studio*. Live music was needed at all hours, and small combos, duets, trios and quartets came through the studios by the hour. There were station orchestras of various sizes depending on the size of the studio, often up to twenty musicians (Briggs [1961] 2000: 253). The biggest studios could have an audience present during the show, something that would lend it a live eventfulness lacking in the smaller studios. Foley artistry was an important part of the resounding radio studio. Although the concept comes from the movie industry, it generally refers to the creation of sound effects live in the studio (Mott 1990). Foley artistry was part of many genres, for example episodes, skits, situation comedy, radio drama and dramatized news reports. It had both humoristic and serious potential. In terms of acoustic architecture, the resounding studio shows invariably enacted what Edward Hall (1969) calls the 'social distance', and not the 'intimate distance'.

The next case study takes us back to World War II, just before Christmas 1943. The performer is the great radio star Bing Crosby, with his big-budget production and high-quality sound. He was a successful performer who made films in Hollywood and had shows on national radio, and now he had enrolled as an ideologist in the war effort, with the task of entertaining people. The grandeur of the resounding studio is well demonstrated with this excerpt from NBC's Kraft Music Hall in 1943. This was a very popular Saturday night show with several million regular listeners, and it was aired from 1933 to 1949 (Wikipedia 2007, 'Kraft Music Hall'). During December 1943 the war had turned in the favour of the Allies, and there was more optimism than before. Bing Crosby could sing 'Happy Holiday' with enormous resonance in the home.

🔊 *Track 25: NBC: The Kraft Music Hall with Bing Crosby, 1943 (1:46).*

The Kraft Music Hall with Bing Crosby, Trudy Erwin, John Scott Trotter and his orchestra, the music maids and Lee, Yoki, the charioteers, and Bing's guest for this evening, Paramount star of the Technicolor musical *Riding High*, Ms Cass Daley. And here's Bing Crosby:

Happy holiday, happy holiday,
While the merry bells keep ringing
May your ev'ry wish come true.
Happy holiday, happy holiday,
May the calendar keep bringing
Happy holidays to you.
If you're burdened down with trouble
If your nerves are wearing thin
Pack your load down the road
And come to Holiday Inn.
If the traffic noise affects you
Like a squeaky violin
Kick your cares down the stairs
And come to Holiday Inn.
If you can't find someone who
Will set your heart a–whirl
Take a little business to
The home of boy meets girl.
If you're laid-up with a breakdown
Throw away your vitamin
Don't get worse, grab your nurse
And come to Holiday Inn.
[Repeat chorus]

We hear a big orchestra which is miked-up very carefully. There are vocals, whistling, a choir, trumpets, guitars, violins, a piano, and not least the wonderful applause of the audience. The melody is fast-paced with snappy lyrics, and the sound of the orchestra is lush and inviting.

The grand, reverberant sound was the signature of entertainment. The studio audience was important both for inspiring the artists to perform naturally and for creating a lively atmosphere in the home. Cantril and Allport point out that the hosts needed the audience in order to settle into the public mood of radio, as was for example the case with comedians: 'Since radio comedians almost invariably have stage training, they know how to take cues from the audience whose responses they can both see and hear.' But radio permits of no such feedback, and therefore the social basis of laughter is destroyed and humour itself is put at risk, they argue. This is why the studio audience is so important. It 'restores to the comedian some of the advantages lost when he forsook the stage for the studio. Nowadays few radio comedians dare work without a studio audience' (Cantril and Allport [1935] 1986: 222).

Consequently, audience responses were considered an essential part of the studio atmosphere, and microphones were used to build up the laughter and applause. Barnouw (1968: 99) describes how there was typically a warm-up session by one of the comedians so that the audience could be drilled to give the appropriate response. 'Come folks, I can't hear you! You can do better than that!' He held up the sign: "APPLAUSE!" [...] Echoing with the roar of laughing crowds, these theatres gave the impression of a continuing vaudeville tradition.'

Bing Crosby comes across as a cheerful singer, fully in command of his art and his orchestra. But in a sense it was the live studio audience, represented by the applause after the performance, who were the main protagonists in this type of show. Cantril and Allport's listening survey from 1935 suggests that the laughter and applause made the programme more enjoyable for listeners. They felt less foolish when joining in a gaiety already established in the studio, and were 'drawn still further into the atmosphere of merriment' (Cantril and Allport [1935] 1986: 223). It is quite clear that the studio audience was important for inspiring the domestic listeners to go along with the show and have fun. Overall, it seems that the reverberant acoustics of the studio influenced the listeners' reactions in a 'deep-lying and for the time being quite unconscious' way (ibid.).

Radio personalities

The next case study is also an entertainment programme, but it is quite unlike The Kraft Music Hall. The show was called 'The Brains Trust', and it consisted of a lively dialogue between studio speakers based on questions sent in to the BBC by the listeners. The Britons had been bombed by the Germans for some time, and programmes such as 'The Brains Trust' were a wonderful pastime during this ordeal. During the years many speakers appeared, but the core team was the philosopher C. E. M. Joad, the biologist Julian Huxley and the retired naval officer A. B. Campbell. The host was Donald McCullough. We hear them discussing the question 'What's the difference between fresh air and a draught?'

Track 26: BBC: The Brains Trust, 1943 (1:06).

> – Next question, I'm afraid the last one, from Miss Moore of Southgate. What is the difference between fresh air and a draught? [mild laughter] Are we going to get at this from a philosophical, a medical, a scientific or a physical point of view? Medical? Doctor, could you give us an idea do you think? Fresh air and a draught?
> – I think that what is meant ... what is behind this question er is ... [laughter] ... a prejudice. In other words the person really feels that the draught is an evil thing, but a draught really is only a small instalment of fresh air.
> – Your idea?
> – Surely a draught is fresh air coming through a little hole and impinging upon a little bit of yourself, that's to say it's not affecting you equally [mild laughter].
> – Gould?

– Surely the distinction is this: It is fresh air when you put the … window down yourself and it is a draught when the person [the words drown in laughter].

– Yes, I think we'll close on that heavy blend of sociology, philosophy and psychology.

There are four men around the table, and they all carry themselves very consciously in relation to the microphone. There is also a small studio audience that laughs softly at times. The speakers engage in a quite sophisticated verbal artistry, and, although it is produced with the same resounding acoustics as Bing Crosby's entertainment show, there is little resemblance in the overall mood. The task for each speaker is to sound interesting and smart and funny, and in short to be a radio personality.

Although the conversation must have been rehearsed before going live on the air, the panelists succeeded in creating a good-natured and seemingly spontaneous conversation. They challenge each other with their wit, and create subtle verbal points in the typically English style of understatement. There is lots of sloppy articulation and instability in the pitch and volume of the speakers' voices, and the conversation is constantly interrupted. This form of talk bears little resemblance to contemporary radio genres such as news reading or lectures, but it certainly resembles everyday speech, and is eminently suited to inspire a sense of sociability among listeners.

The programme's semi-professional speakers simulate the mood of a dinner party and its enthusiastic conversation. Programmes in this genre would typically have a well-known host and guests of public renown would appear regularly, for example artists, writers, academics, lawyers and doctors. The point is that they became more and more well trained as radio speakers, and could handle verbal and social challenges in public. Such clever speakers could, for example, sound angry or frustrated in just the right way, and increase the entertainment value of the show.

As suggested, 'The Brains Trust' provides an example of the emerging radio personality. In 1935 the psychologists Cantril and Allport pointed to the listeners' tendency to relate to radio speakers as fully comprehensible personalities.

> Voices have a way of provoking curiosity, of arousing a train of imagination that will conjure up a substantial and congruent personality to support and harmonize with the disembodied voice. Often the listener goes no further than deciding half-consciously that he either likes or dislikes the voice, but sometimes he gives more definite judgments, a 'character reading' of the speaker, as it were, based upon voice alone.
>
> (Cantril and Allport [1935] 1986: 109)

Indeed, listeners identified strongly with the persons behind the voices. Rudolf Arnheim ([1936] 1986: 145) argues that voices familiar from radio intercourse will simply be tansformed into *familiar people* to the listener, not remain familiar voices of unfamiliar people. In this regard the radio personality was quite unlike the star of Hollywood.

The basic technique of the radio personality was to make himself feel at ease in front of the microphone, and convey this ease to the listeners. But this is a difficult thing to do, Arnheim argues:

> Such an atmosphere is most difficult to achieve in broadcasting, and certainly never by means of big things, always by little ones. 'Stimmung' (atmosphere) is not got so much by jokes and showing off, not by strenuous efforts to gratify, but far rather by the genial affability of the host who serves his guest in a friendly way without making much fuss.
>
> (Arnheim [1936] 1986: 75)

Arnheim goes on to describe a popular speaker from Berlin radio who spoke about legal matters: 'He spoke, obviously with a cigar-end in his mouth, without manuscript or notes.' 'He stuttered, groped for words which immediately occurred to him, generally inspired ones.' 'Law and public-speaking were second nature to him, and it was not in his line to treat them with ceremony. The world became a cozy parlour were he sat and spoke at the microphone.' Informal ways of speaking were attractive for listeners, and this strategy is at the heart of radio's sociability to this day.

In 1938 the *Radio Times* concluded that 'When all is said and done, broadcasting, with all its elaborate mechanisms, is based on and aimed at, the home' (quoted in Scannell and Cardiff 1991: 374). And during the 1930s broadcasting indeed gained a remarkable presence in the home. Raymond Williams ([1975] 1990: 26ff.) has made a classic statement about the influence of radio in the home. He argues that the transformation from wireless telegraphy to broadcasting led to what he calls a 'mobile privatization'. On the one hand people gained an easy, almost non-geographic access to the marketplace of ideas, where the difference between centre and periphery was quite irrelevant. On the other hand the *family home* became an important centre of cultural attention, and public matters could more readily be cultivated in a private setting. Cheap receivers were a significant index of this modern condition with its novel social identifications.

A novel cultural technique can be observed among domestic listeners. They were acquiring the conventions of a documentary realism especially created for the family home. It was supposed to be a collective experience where the listeners could not expect their most individualistic interests or desires to be fulfilled. Cantril and Allport ([1935] 1986: 22–3) pointed out that: 'If I am to enjoy my radio, I must adjust my personal taste to the program that most nearly approximates it.' The listeners had to adapt their personal interests to one of the common social moulds that radio offered. 'If I insist on remaining an individualist, I shall dislike nearly all radio programs', Cantril and Allport argued.

Figure 8.3 Home sweet home.

Nervous news reading, 1941

The serious journalist's voice from a news studio could carry great weight in the public, especially in times of political tension and war. Most often the journalist read from the script, and the stations favoured medium-pitched male speakers with good diction and high stress tolerance. There were new techniques to be learnt for the news readers.

Clearly, the voice had to be able to convey a sense of authority. 'I have a job *if* my *voice* is all right', the journalist William L. Shirer wrote in 1937. 'Who ever heard of an adult with no pretenses to being a singer or any other kind of artist being dependent for a good, interesting job on his *voice*?' (quoted in Barnouw 1968: 77). Arnheim ([1936] 1986: 92) complains about people who are too loud for broadcasting, and who make themselves 'spatially noticeable' by moving about in the studio or turning their head away from the microphone while speaking. This points to the professional importance of voice control, combining an ability to become transparent with a sonorous, authoritative and physiologically attractive voice. No real affect display, no happiness, anger, sadness or interest were allowed. Erik Barnouw (1968: 150) says that even while uttering words that involved the death of thousands the newsreader should only 'display a tenth of the emotion that a broadcaster does when describing a prizefight'. In the late 1930s the BBC selected three journalists from the newsroom as presenters to build up experience in the specialized task of reading the news.

'Without going into personalities, it had become obvious that some announcers were temperamentally very much better suited to tackling news at a moment of crisis than others' (Scannell and Cardiff 1991: 131).

It was soon acknowledged that the speakers should not sound too detached. A news event was easier to grasp if there was a sense that the speaker reacted to it in a natural way, or reacted like the listener imagined they might do. These emotions would, however, be discernible only through very modest inflections of the voice, and not through dramatic effect. Very little emotion was needed before the listener noticed it.

The next case study is from the tense period during which the USA entered World War II (see Johnson 1999: 778ff. for the full story). On 7 December, 1941 the entire US population listened to the dramatic news on network radio. Hour by hour the drama unfolded, as reports about the US response to the Japanese attacks on Pearl Harbor were read out. At the Washington desk of CBS Albert Warner analysed the White House reactions to the bombings (Douglas 1999: 188). As the news keeps pouring in, presumably on telex, the news team continuously updates the script. Here is a portion of the breaking news from that fateful day.

Track 27: CBS: Breaking News, 1941 (1:34).

> – Although officials in Washington are silent on what would be the definite consequences of a Japanese attack on Hawaii or an attack on Thailand, there are indications of … what … is being considered … and the steps which may be taken this very afternoon. The first would be a severance of diplomatic relations with Tokyo. An immediate naval blockade, in which the American navy would take a leading part along with British units, is the other probability. Both these steps could be taken by the president on his own executive authority, but an effective naval blockade of course could not continue long without hostilities. As a matter of fact, according to the president's announcement those hostilities are already under way with the Japanese attack on Pearl Harbor. And just now comes the word … from the president's office that a second air attack has been reported on amy and navy bases in Manila. … Thus we have official announcements from the White House that Japanese airplanes have attacked … Pearl Harbor in Hawaii and have now attacked army and navy bases in Manila. [pause] We return you now to New York and will give you later information as it comes along from the White House. Return you now to New York.

Warner is audibly stressed. He returns us to New York for much the same reason that the 1010 WINS anchor went live to CNN during the terror attacks on the Twin Towers (chapter 4). At that point it is impossible for him to talk coherently. Warner was already a little shaken before the reports about another air attack reached the studio. He continues reading as before, but we can hear how his voice trembles, and how he struggles to continue reading his script in a normal way as he attends to the new information. He discloses the new developments in bursts of words, with short strained pauses in between.

My point is that Warner's staccato speech did not ruin the informational function of the bulletin; on the contrary, it reinforced it because in effect it carried an emotion that the listeners were likely to feel themselves. Albert Warner demonstrates that loss of control may inspire a stronger sense of credibility than ordinarily, as the dialogues from 1010 WINS also demonstrate. Had Warner let his voice tremble on purpose, and had it been done by all the news readers as a regular trick, there would have been less intensity to the performance. The excerpt shows that, in radio, tiny deviations from the norms of speech may induce heightened feelings of trustworthiness.

The identity of newsreaders and public speakers in general was felt to be important for the credibility of the messages. The invasion of Norway in 1940 forced Norwegian broadcasting to take place on short wave from the BBC in London. After a period of using British-Norwegian speakers, a Norwegian politician argued that 'a familiar Norwegian voice would improve the broadcasts both qualitatively and psychologically' (quoted in Dahl 1999b: 124). At the outbreak of the war the BBC instructed bulletin readers to identify themselves by name before reading the news (Schlesinger 1992: 30). Rather than being anonymous voices, they were to become individual persons.

The international conflicts made national identification more important than before. The major division was between the Allies and the Axis powers, that is, the 'Big Three' – the USA, Great Britain and the Soviet Union – versus Germany, Italy and Japan. During the 1930s and 1940s the news bulletins that filled the air on short and medium wave would be highly contradictory. The national broadcasting stations were part of an ideological struggle, and were used instrumentally for various political purposes. For example, the Reichsrundfunk in Germany and the BBC in Great Britain had strikingly different strategies and often contradictory claims about factual matters. The listener's sense of truth and relevance would be influenced by their national sympathies and antipathies. Clearly the American subject would be more likely to believe the American stations than the Japanese broadcasts in English. Consequently, the news was likely to be felt as trustworthy if there was consensus among the station and the individual listener, and likely to be felt as in doubt or simply false if there was no such consensus.

Bulletins and reports were typically presented in an attitude of self-confidence and trustworthiness, and if the listeners were inclined to identify with this attitude they would of course hear the news as credible and truthful. This is indirectly touched upon by John Peters (2001: 710), who argues that witnessing presumes a discrepancy between the ignorance of one person and the knowledge of another. The listener acknowledges that the broadcast speaker has a factual outlook that he himself lacks. Therefore there is a coercive appeal in the very act of reading the news or describing events: it is supposed to imply that *this is the truth.* If the listener didn't have good reason to think otherwise, they would simply trust that the station conveyed matters of war and conflict and government in a correct way.

Especially before World War II there was great public trust in radio, but this ended brutally with the propaganda excesses of the war. The domestic sense of witnessing real events on the world stage seems to have been great in the 1930s. If a domestic discussion arose, anyone with information picked up on the radio would settle the matter, 'because nobody doubts that what is said on the radio is the pure and clean truth' (Dymling 1934: 33). In 1939 *Fortune* magazine surveyed the American people's sentiments towards the press. If presented with conflicting versions of the same story in the two media, 40 per cent believed the radio and 27 per cent believed the newspaper (Stott 1991: 241). In some circles radio was felt to have become too influential. There was public concern that people were depending more and more on broadcasting for their knowledge of world affairs. In 1938 the *Weekly Review* said: 'They are becoming too passive and being passive they will be more easily led. Where they will be led depends on the viewpoint of those who control the channels of information' (quoted in Gumpert and Cathcart 1979: 12).

There is a classic example of how strong the authority of news reading was in the USA in the 1930s, namely Orson Welles's fictional play *War of the Worlds* (1938). It was particularly scary for the listeners because Welles exploited the sound and diction of the news bulletin. Some listeners who tuned in after the play had begun actually believed the Martian invasion to be true, because they heard a plausible news reader describing panic in the streets as the invasion progressed. They were simply fooled by a way of speaking. The Welles radio play has become a symbol of radio's influence on people's sense of reality in the 1930s (Sterling and Kittross 1991: 252–3). In my interpretation it demonstrates the power of this way of speaking to make listeners feel that they had direct access to the world.

Outside locations, 1931

We are now at the very beginning of radio's function as a public medium. In the pioneer years live reportage was an important rhetorical technique. In acoustic terms *the outside location* was established in the early 1920s, and typically the broadcasters used a telephone line from the location to the transmitter. Public speeches government figures and Sunday church services would often be relayed in this way. More generally it would be used for spectacular 'live at the scene' effects, one of the first of which was a running commentary from the Derby races in 1921 (Briggs [1961] 2000: 52). It pointed towards the techniques of 'eyewitnessing' which were to become such a staple of sports programming, live news shows, documentaries and all kinds of factual material. William Stott (1991: 248–9) argues that the ambient sounds made the listener feel 'the pressure of reality on the speaker, endless and incommunicable.

All that the speaker left unspoken – found unspeakable – testified to the reality of his experience.'

One new journalistic profession was particularly tailored to the radio medium, namely that of the sports reporter. In 1931 live commentary had become a professional skill, praised by the public. Referring to the very broadcast that is presented below, a Swedish newspaper wrote that listeners 'would probably agree that it is hardly possible to improve on the technical perfection and journalistic performance of a radio reportage of this type than what was accomplished this Sunday' (quoted in Dahlén 1999: 120). In Sweden the reporter Sven Jerring was greatly admired for the domestic enjoyment he was able to create. In 1927 a listener noted that '[t]he man is simply made for the microphone. He has a unique ability to find the right words, a fast-working mind and a good-humored manner than is invigorating' (quoted ibid.: 80).

The final case study for this chapter is a sports broadcast from Swedish Radio, with the Swedes and the Finns engaging in an inter-nation athletics competition. Sports were hugely popular, and radio had very early learnt to exploit this popularity. Notice that the Swedes had historically been the stronger country, and Finland had previously been a Swedish protectorate, and this added to the tension of the competition. We will hear the live commentary for the 400 metre run.

Track 28: Swedish Radio (SR): Sports Commentary, 1931 (1:05).

> – The starting shot. It was an even start. Through the curve the four are keeping the same distance as at the start. But Aki Järvinen and Strandvall are closing in on Erikson and Vattenfelt. At the far end of the field Järvinen and Strandvall are in the lead. Järvinen closes up on Strandvall and Vattenfelt. Erikson runs upright but with a long and wonderful pace. Now he reduces the distance between him and Järvinen. They are side by side on the curve, the last curve. As the runners reach the final length Erikson is in the lead by a hair's breadth. And there is a good fight between Vattenfeld and the Finn. Still even; completely even. Järvinen fights his way ahead powerfully ... and Strandvall ... Erikson gives up ... he has no more to give ... and the Finns get ahead of Vattenfeld ... the Swedes last.

Both the Finns and the Swedes would be biting their nails in excitement during the 400 metre run. The Swedish runner Erikson is in the lead almost to the finishing line, but ends up last. He had nothing more to give, and the outcome was very disappointing to the Swedes. We can hear how the mood of the sports supporters is subdued as they see the outcome. Since the Swedes came last, there was nothing to cheer about; the supporters turn quiet and so does the radio commentator. Although the Finns must have been thrilled, they weren't around to make themselves heard.

Sven Jerring had fully embodied the microphone as an extension of his ability to express himself. There is even a photograph of him wearing a microphone on a support around his neck. The transmission was of course live, and the acoustics lively and engaging. The ambient sound adds to the impression of witnessing the event as it proceeds, and it invites a sense of presence at the sports stadium.

This excerpt demonstrates microphone behaviour that would never occur outside the radio medium. The reporter talks about the events under the presumption that his interlocutors cannot see anything of what is going on; and furthermore he does so in a low voice that would not be heard by anybody present at the stadium. He addresses himself wholly to the absent listeners. In my interpretation this is an example of microphone behaviour having become naturalized, and it demonstrates the speaker's conformity to the broadcast setting in a striking way. It would be hard to find evaluation criteria for this behaviour outside radio.

The radio medium

It is time to define the medium of radio in technical detail. During the golden age of the 1940s and 1950s it had become highly asymmetrical. In the increasingly tense political climate of the early 1930s Bertolt Brecht had recommended that radio broadcasting should be turned into a two-way voice medium. He had in mind a quite symmetrical medium, where a network of amateurs could transmit from their personal equipment and speak to a public sphere that would have greater political impact the more people in society used it: 'Radio is one sided when it should be two. It is purely an apparatus for distribution, for mere sharing out. So here is a positive suggestion: change this apparatus over from distribution to communication. The radio would be the finest possible communication apparatus in public life, a vast network of pipes' (Brecht [1932] 2001).

Radio in Germany did not develop in the way Brecht wanted. On the contrary, the Nazi regime in Germany under the direction of Joseph Goebbels controlled everything that went on air on the Reichsrundfunk. In other countries the same tendency towards monopolization and control was clear, even though it was often based on a sounder moral base than was Nazi propaganda. The BBC with its public service ideals about informing, educating and entertaining is an example of a benign regime.

Figure 8.4 displays the main interfaces, platforms and signal carriers of the set-up I am investigating in this chapter. Notice that the microphone and the mixing board were the crucial interfaces for producers, while gramophone recorders were employed for archive purposes, and tape decks were increasingly used for recorded reportage. On the receiving end there were radio cabinets and transistor receivers, both with loudspeakers.

First I will describe the basic transmission platform and its signal carrier in some detail. A short-wave tower would be around 100 metres tall, a medium-wave tower somewhat larger, and a long-wave tower could (and can) be over 500 metres tall, being held to the ground by thick steel wires.

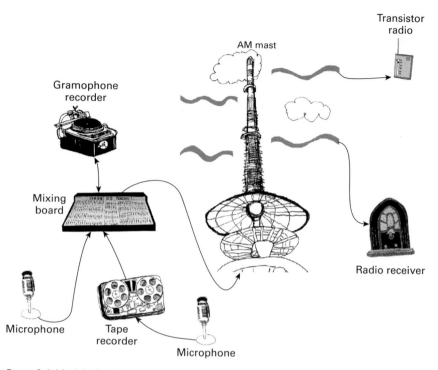

Figure 8.4 Model of analogue radio.

Radio transmission exploited the natural environment in a spectacular way, as the signal is carried through the air between the antennas. In this period stations transmitted with what was called ground waves and sky waves. The waves that were propagated along the surface of the earth through soil and water conductivity were called ground waves. They could travel far beyond the horizon, but the reach varied with variations in conductivity and the dampness of the lower regions of the atmosphere (Head *et al.* 1996: 80). In the medium-wave band, which was used by stations across Europe and the USA, distribution took place via ground waves. Ground waves spread better in the daytime than at night, because at night there would be disturbances from sky waves.

Sky waves introduced even more earthly variables. The waves that went straight up into the air were first presumed to disappear into outer space, but in actual fact they bounced off a region of the upper atmosphere. To illustrate the dimensions, notice that the Atlantic Ocean is a mountain of water 100 miles high between Britain and Canada (Douglas 1987: 54), and sky waves could scale it in a fraction of a second. Short-wave radio could utilize sky waves with great efficiency and accuracy from the mid-1920s. Refraction from the sky was particularly strong after sunset, because of changed qualities in the ionosphere. The waves travelled across the earth in a wide-angled and floating movement that relied on a dozen other variables relating to time of day, weather conditions, time of year, magnetic fields, electrical machine interferences and other things. The magnetic layer of the upper atmosphere that was named the ionosphere was not experimentally verified until 1925 (Winston 1998: 272).

At night the clear reception area for sky waves increased dramatically, so listeners could receive signals from far away, especially during long cold autumn and winter nights (Pegg 1983: 19). Depending on the quality of the receiving apparatus, especially antenna construction, an avid amateur could pick up signals from several continents during the night. The peculiarities of wave propagation demonstrate that global dimensions were very quickly thought of as inherent to wireless, and this internationalism made a striking contrast to the tangible, small-scale machinery of gramophone repetition and the precise private contact established by the cable telephone.

At the broadcasting houses there were studios and control rooms where the creative and technical staff worked. The microphone was a strange interface to work with for performers who were used to the theatre stage, but in radio the microphone often replaced the vibrant and immediate reactions of a live audience, since studio audiences would only be gathered for bigger events. Speakers had to be able to face the microphone all on their own. The singer was used to continuous feedback on good or bad elements of the performance, but now this would be absent, and performers would be uncertain about the quality of their acts. There is ample evidence that artists were plagued by anxieties, whether or not this resulted from 'the new techniques of wireless being mentally overwhelming, or the lack of routine among participants giving the debutants little calm' (Dahl 1999a: 77). And it did not relieve the performer's embarrassment to be warned about the awful noises that could be caused by such innocent acts as handling the script, clearing one's throat and coughing. Erik Barnouw (1966: 136) writes that some stations disguised the microphone as a floor lamp to avert anxieties, but this practice had disappeared by the mid-1920s. 'Perhaps talking to a lampshade seemed no more natural than talking to a microphone', he adds dryly. Nervousness was a feature of first encounters, and it was reduced with training and increasing professional experience.

I should mention the awareness of acoustic architecture in radio. It was soon understood that good acoustics would be indispensable to expression in wireless, and before long the studio set-up of recording companies was adopted (see chapter 11 for more details). In 1920 KDKA in the USA, which is often considered the first regular radio station, used a tent to shield the microphone from extraneous noises (see Barnouw 1966: 71). 'It is evident to me', a British station manager said in 1922, 'that we have to face immediately several problems requiring solution by acoustical rather than electrical experts' (quoted in Briggs

[1961] 2000: 73). When broadcasting houses were built they had carefully planned internal architecture, with performances taking place in draped and acoustically protected studios, and the work of signal processing and transmission taking place in control rooms.

Everything went directly on air, but there were several pre-production processes taking place in the control room. The final balance was created on the mixing board. By the 1930s there was a fader for each microphone, facilitating rapid fade in and out, cross-fades and balancing of foreground and background effects (Barnouw 1966: 192). The studios were routinely equipped with multiple microphones. Erik Barnouw (1966: 192) reports that in 1927 eight or more microphones were used on the stage, with lights to show which of them were in operation. There would be a microphone for every important source of sound, and the work of balancing the output to the air took on great creative importance. The participating artists would not just rehearse their performances for artistic perfection; they would also be monitored during the live performance. Typically there was talkback communication between the studio and the control room, and studio assistants would coach the host, the artists and the musicians about proper distance to the microphone.

The *voice alone acoustics* was acknowledged very early. In 1936 Rudolf Arnheim wrote about the acoustic architecture of wireless. He pointed out that close-up microphone speech sounds intimate because it seems to move the voice distinctly into the listener's room. In contrast, more distance between the performer and the microphone makes the whole space of the performance resonate and creates a greater sense of roominess. In general he emphasized the importance of making proper use of the difference between near and far (Arnheim [1936] 1986: 67), and to remember that every distance has its own expressive value. He also suggested that, since the volume can be turned up and down by electrical means, this feature should be used actively to enrich the expressivity of distance illusions (ibid.: 70).

I will now stress the combination of real-time transmission and the broadcasters' strategies for liveness effects. All the programmes discussed above went live on air – with a possible exception of the Bing Crosby performance. The real-time characteristics of radio had been cultivated for several decades, and were centre stage in the production setting. But by being absolutely live the radio also ran parallel to national clock time, and all the public and private events with which people were occupied.

Timeliness on the radio was therefore obviously related to clock time. Shaun Moores argues that radio brought precise temporal measurement into the private sphere, and helped to domesticate standard national time. He quotes a writer from 1933 who marvels at the 'broadcasting of time', which is, 'rightly considered, one of the strangest of the new things that the harnessing of the ether has brought us'. Moores adds that there were of course clocks in many households before wireless telephone arrived, 'but only with the development of broadcasting did synchronised, nationwide signals get relayed directly and simultaneously into millions of living rooms' (Moores 2000: 55). In 1924 a newspaper columnist comments on the impact of this simultaneity: 'The boom of Big Ben, which is rung in London and heard by us in Derby almost any night we care to listen, is one of the wireless stunts which creates an impression' (quoted in Pegg 1983: 147).

Loudspeaker living

When the new superheterodyne receivers became household items in the late 1920s and early 1930s, the social relationship with radio changed dramatically. The change from headphones to loudspeakers meant that there was an instant socialization of radio programmes. There is no way to overestimate the importance of the domestic setting for radio programmes. Briggs and Burke (2002: 179) argue that 'cinema took people out of the home, and the gramophone kept people in it.' But clearly, the medium that really brought people home was the loudspeaker radio. The domestic orientation is a fundamental requirement for radio's becoming part of the everyday living environment.

Crystal sets did not run on electricity, but used what little power the transmitting signal had. Consequently they gave off a very weak signal that was hard to amplify into a locale, and people were inclined to listen on headphones (Scannell and Cardiff 1991: 356). Listeners had constantly to follow up the signal as it moved across the dial, and tap the 'cat's whisker' with its aimless reception attempts. In 1924 the BBC encouraged people actually to listen, and not be overpreoccupied with the receiving equipment. John Reith suggested that 'our minds are obsessed and distracted by the agency, and the music has not had a fair chance' (quoted ibid.: 360). When the crystal set was moved into the living room the pater familias typically sat isolated and immersed in his own experience, his wife and children watching and waiting for their go. Keeping silent was a household chore, and the listening experience in a sense became even more isolationist (Moores 2000: 46). My point is that when headphones were used radio listening was a solitary activity. People sat alone, feeling an 'electronic kinship with an invisible scattered audience', and yet they also felt 'the incredible distances involved in this form of communication that ultimately reaffirmed the individual listener's anonymity and isolation' (Sconce 2000: 62).

As I have said, during the 1920s the expensive superheterodyne receiver was introduced to the mass market. Because of its cost, it remained a luxury item far into the 1930s. But it was greatly superior to the crystal set. It had a whole series of electron tubes that filtered and amplified the electromagnetic signal before reproducing it in a moving coil speaker. With this equipment the first really good sound experience was introduced into the home. When placed in the living room or the kitchen, a loudspeaker filled the space with a new, acoustically immersive version of broadcasting. This became the default experience of radio.

It is important to remember that static, interference and fading could still make listening a very frustrating experience. But it seems that listeners had the ability to disregard the problems of sound quality and focus on the programmes. Cantril and Allport ([1935] 1986: 119–20) expressed wonder at people's ability to overcome the blur of transmission: 'Adaptation to the change in the quality which a voice undergoes in such transmission seems to be remarkably rapid and thoroughgoing. Even the subtlest inflections may be successfully analyzed out from all the extraneous sounds.'

With the new acoustics there could be a more active use of radio to create eventfulness in the living room, something which was reflected by the popularity of genres such as dance music, exercise programmes and quiz shows aspiring to involve the whole family. It would have been hard to engage properly with the rhetorical intent of such programmes by the use of headphones. The most important aspect of this domestic acoustic was the rise of *the listener family*. The listening experience could now be shared by everyone in the home, and not just with an imaginary community in the ether. The programmes acquired the status of an inclusive group activity or a 'public hearth'. In 1935 the *Radio Times* in Britain described this mood:

> To close the door behind you, with the curtains drawn against the rain, and the fire glowing in the hearth – that is one of the real pleasures of life. And it is when you are settled by your own fireside that you most appreciate the entertainment that broadcasting can bring.
>
> (quoted in Moores 1988: 34)

The loudspeaker made it more comfortable to stay tuned for long periods of time. In the 1930s the increased quality of reception on the new receivers reduced the annoying noises of the atmosphere to a whisper, and the human sounds came more forcefully to the fore. For the first time listeners could leave the apparatus to its own devices, lie back in the armchair and simply listen.

Chapter 9

Microphone moods
Music recording, 1940s–1930s

Pop music is characterized by an intimacy with singers that runs so deep in our auditory perception that we almost never think about it. This intimacy has much to do with the microphone, which was developed for music recording in the 1920s. The modern recording industry was the result of a convergence of two great industries: that of acoustics and that of electricity (Briggs and Burke 2002: 145), where the electrical microphone was the big new thing.

I will illustrate the story of the microphone in music by going into case studies of three different recording artists. Edith Piaf in 1940 comforted the French people with her soaring 'L'Accordéoniste', which became a big hit. The Swedish artist Harry Brandelius in 1938 released 'The Troubadour', a hymn to all the dead people at whose funerals he had performed. He seems to sing it more to himself than to the listener. Finally, the French classical vocalist Charles Panzéra sings 'Chanson triste' with little sense of personal sadness, since performers of art song are not expected actually to live through the emotions of the character (love, melancholy, hatred, etc.). All these real and imagined moods of the singer became audible with the microphone and electrical recording, and new cultural techniques emerged at both ends of the medium.

Backwards history

Politically the 1930s was a tense period in Europe and the USA alike. The countries of the West were in a deep economic depression that started in 1929, and furthermore the Nazi party was on the rise in Germany and the communist party was gaining ground in Europe. Many countries were ruled by oppressive dictatorial regimes – either fascist or communist. The idea of 'mass society' was dominant (Hobsbawm 1994: 108ff.), and its morality is aptly captured by Charlie Chaplin in his film *Modern Times* (1936). The tramp works at a highly mechanized factory where he is caught up in the wheels of the machine, and where he is bereft of his individuality. Strong ideologies presented the individual person as a small, dispensable wheel in a big machinery, while the dictator himself would speak at huge rallies, with a dozen big, imposing microphones in front of him to show his importance.

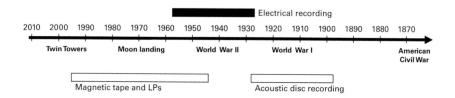

Figure 9.1 Timeline of the electrical recording medium.

The mass media had a double role in this political climate. They were tools for the power elites to govern their people, exemplified by Franklin D. Roosevelt's 'Fireside Chats', which famously made him very popular, and the use of entertainment on film, music records and radio during the war gave people something else to think about. The other aspect of the mass media in the 1930s is that they helped to cultivate greater intimacy. Indeed, the 'Fireside Chats' were a symptom of how the media now addressed people in their homes (Barnouw [1975] 1990: 72). And there was really a more lively home sound-scape – with recorded music and verbal intelligence making a difference in the everyday life of people – which was greatly appreciated.

The 1930s and 1940s were undoubtedly a period rich in electronic media, with radio, telephone, telex, sound films and telegraph, and the small beginnings of micro-electronics could be seen, for example, in advanced radio receivers and movie equipment (for a thorough presentation of this era, see Briggs and Burke 2002: 106ff.).

Figure 9.1 shows that electric recording had approximately twenty-five years' dominance in media history, which is not a long time compared to that of the magnetic tape and LPs discussed in chapter 7 and the acoustic recording media discussed in chapter 11. When electrical recording was introduced in the mid-1920s, acoustic recording disappeared very quickly because the microphone and electrical pickup were indisputably superior to the acoustic horn.

During this period the music business had its worst crisis ever. It began at the same time as the depression of 1929 and continued far into the 1930s. The depression caused poverty among an increasing number of people, and they could no longer afford to buy gramophones and records. In addition, radio emerged as a potent medium of music and entertainment, providing programmes that were free of charge. Record companies such as Columbia and Victor struggled in the USA, and His Majesty's Voice struggled in the British Empire. The microphone and the new, intimate qualities of popular music helped the music industry to overcome the crisis (this story is well told, for example, by Millard 2005: 162ff.).

The new intimacy with performers could also be experienced in the sound film. There was, for example, a differentiation of languages and voices and sound effects that gave the movies new creative directions (Briggs and Burke 2002: 172). Imagine the wealth of experience that emerged in the movie theatre when all the sounds in the world could add to the communication.

Before the introduction of electrical recording around 1925, no musicians would perform with a microphone unless they played the radio circuit. During the fifty years after Edison's invention they sang into an acoustic horn, without batteries or electric circuitry, and it was the sheer pressure of their voice that moved the stylus. The only experience ordinary people had had with microphones before that time was the carbon mouthpiece of the telephone, which did not have much to do with music.

The passionate crooner, 1940

Edith Piaf was a great microphone communicator. She recorded 'L'Accordéoniste' during a particularly bleak period at the beginning of World War II. German military forces invaded northern France and pushed millions of refugees southwards, and in particular towards Paris. Tensions were high, and in this setting Piaf used her musical talents to make a subtle political point. We can imagine that during the day people would listen nervously to the radio news, while at night they would try to relax by enjoying good music on the radio and the record turntable. There is no actuality in a recording, no danger of receiving unpleasant news, but there can be good stories that put things in perspective.

Edith Piaf sings a chanson in the classical French style, where there is always an intense human story of some kind (Frith 1998: 170). 'L'Accordéoniste' has left for the front, and the desperate prostitute who was in love with him and his music becomes more desperate than ever.

Track 29: Edith Piaf: L'Accordéoniste, 1940 (1:09).

> The prostitute is alone on the street corner down there,
> Men don't want girls who look unhappy,
> And too bad if she dies, her man will not come back any more.
> Goodbye all the beautiful dreams, her life is ruined.
> Nevertheless her sad legs lead her to a dive
> Where there's another artist who plays all night.
> She listens to the java, she hears the java,
> She closes her eyes, the dry spirited fingers,
> It goes right through her skin from bottom to top.
> She wants to yell out, it's physical,
> Then to forget she begins to dance,
> To turn to the sound of the music.
> Stop! Stop the music!

We hear an orchestra with seven or eight musicians. There is the female lead singer, the accordionist, the pianist, guitars, drums and perhaps two or three violins. There is a strong dynamic contrast between the soft and gentle beginning of the verse and the crescendo at the end. Several microphones are placed around the studio to pick up every instrument at its best, and the sound is recorded live on disc.

Edith Piaf's performance is emotionally charged, endearing and intense. The lyrics may tell a tearful and somewhat clichéd story, but the sound of Piaf's voice and the orchestra that supports her emotional outpouring so exquisitely would be very attractive to music lovers of the time. She was not alone in using this style of singing – artists such as Marlene Dietrich and Vera Lynn were also immensely popular. They all sounded heartfelt and sincere as communicators of sad stories about the war and its suffering. And there is something about the contemporary situation in France that makes it almost meaningless to say that Piaf plays a role completely detached from herself. She is also threatened by the German invasion, and she can identify strongly with the hard urban life of the prostitute described in the lyrics. The local French audience would also readily associate Piaf with Parisian nightlife. The story of the song becomes attached to the personality of Edith Piaf regardless of the facts, and this has everything to do with Piaf's intimate vocal timbres (see Frith 1998: 170–1 for a good description of her qualities as a singer).

If we cross the Atlantic we find Frank Sinatra's style as the signature sound of the first microphone generation. His great success as a crooner shows that the personal qualities of the voice gained a commercial potential that would have been very hard to accomplish during the acoustic recording era. Roy Shuker (2001: 53) argues that the early crooning experiments laid the foundations for the distinctive vocalization of later pop and rock music. Imagine Sinatra at his smoothest, with strings and the whole orchestra supporting the soft and mellow mood of the melody. In both lyrics and performance such songs are tailor-made to charm the female fans with 'trembling emotion'. Michael Chanan (1995: 68) argues that vocalists knew how to treat the microphone as an instrument in its own right, not just as a passive means of capturing sound. Crooning became a singing style where the performer would be 'sliding up to notes rather than hitting them square, and with a sensual, ululating tone that comes from deep in the throat'.

The public voice had become private. 'At first there was something almost scandalous about this closeness. Singers had started to express an intimate bodily quality that violated common decency' (Johansen 2002: 177). The microphone had opened up the mediation of 'emotional spaces belonging to really intimate situations: Singers can sigh, whine, moan, whisper, mumble – as if they were alone, or only together with one person' (ibid.: 178–9). In the context of 1930s and 1940s American radio entertainment, crooning became widespread as a way of addressing the home in a relaxed, inviting manner.

Figure 9.2 Music lover in Paris, 1940.

In chapter 8 I analysed Bing Crosby's 'Happy Holliday' (1943), which is a good example of crooning in a resounding studio environment.

But what was really new here? Since recording was still completely dependent on live disc-cutting, the bias towards documentary realism was not significantly altered. The crucial difference was that the new components relied on artificial energy supplied by an electron tube amplifier and freed the singer from always having to sing very loudly. Instead of being driven by the sheer acoustical energy of performances, the process of engraving was now done electrically. Since it was no longer necessary to reproduce the volume directly from the grooves, the equipment could be optimized for signal accuracy instead of volume accuracy (Watkinson 1998: 5).

The new skills of Frank Sinatra, Bing Crosby and other American artists in the 1930s were cultivated specially to make the listeners feel that the contact was *personal and intimate*. Again, an advertisement on a Victor record sleeve in 1931 is telling: 'Victor Records (on the Victor Radio Electrola) reproduce for you not only the voice or instrument of the musician, but his very self and the surroundings in which he sings or plays.'

Realism consisted of feeling that the singer's 'very self' was conveyed in the recording. The microphone was sensitive enough to convey a loud and clear voice without any particular effort by the performer. It was receptive to sound instead of resistant to it, as acoustic recording had been. In a sense the microphone was built to human proportions. The singer could embrace its stand, hold it in their hands and touch it with their lips. Among artists there was a tendency to treat the microphone as a confidant or an accomplice. Any instrument could in principle be played in this close-up and intimate way, as exemplified in the 1950s by the trumpeter Miles Davis on the album *Kind of Blue* (1958).

Quiet documentation, 1938

It would be erroneous to argue that intimate singing came as a *result* of the microphone. There could of course be intimate effects in popular song regardless of the existence of recording equipment. In this section I will point to the way in which the microphone became part of a long-standing ideal of quiet solo singing. As in the Hollywood film, the ideal was that there should be no traces of the production machinery in the completed product. This was in reality a quite conservative ideal that was especially suitable for the recording and documentation of folk and traditional songs.

The next case study is a folk ballad sung by Harry Brandelius in 1938, and it is probably performed without any conscious cultivation of microphone effects. Brandelius, a Swedish singer who had his breakthrough that same year with a cheerful song about the sailor's life, was twenty-eight years old when he sang this song. He became so well-liked in Sweden that he was later voted the country's most popular artist of the century (Wikipedia 2007, 'Harry Brandelius'). He even toured the USA and played for Scandinavian emigrants.

Track 30: Harry Brandelius: Spelmannen, 1938 (0:59).

> I don't want to dig the earth, I don't want to chop any wood,
> I want to dream through the weekends till the sun has gone down,
> And in the evening's red fire I will rise up with my fiddle,
> And play until your dead shine bright like the evening sun.
> I will play when you bury your dear ones in the earth,
> I will play all the sorrow in a song without words,
> And the blackness that is death and greeted you by your bed,
> It will flow like a stream of sorrow from my strings.

Brandelius sings a Nordic blues, about a troubadour who has intense existential struggles and a gloomy and sad outlook on life. The song is an assessment of his own worth in society. Brandelius strikes a fine balance, since he is actually a singer by trade, albeit a more successful one with fewer worries. This is role play on his part, for at that time he was a successful singer with big hits in Sweden, but he portrays the character convincingly.

There is a quiet determination to Brandelius's singing style. Although he sounds sad, he does not sound defeated, although at the end of the song his mood seems to become more desperate. He projects here the age-old attitude of the troubadour, where a lonesome man wanders the countryside trying to earn money by singing and playing. In the USA Robert Johnson is a good example, while Bob Dylan before 1964 was also convincing this role. Recordings of 1930s blues and folk singers always sound as if they were recorded for archival purposes more than for the public – a kind of social anthropology, if you like.

My point is to demonstrate that the folk and blues tradition had a natural affinity with quiet performance. Evan Eisenberg (1987: 156) says that recordings by such artists often give the impression that they are singing and playing for their own gratification, something that they would presumably also do in settings without a microphone. But Brandelius could not have sung his ballad in such a low voice to an audience in a concert setting; they simply would not have heard him. The volume of his voice is tailored to the microphone after all, and although he may not consider the microphone a confidant, à la Frank Sinatra, at least Brandelius goes along with its requirements.

Rudolf Arnheim ([1936] 1986: 80) suggests that this form of quietness heightens what could be called the *emotional realism* of the performance. The loud voices of concert singing do not appeal to Arnheim, who thinks there is something unnatural about the maximum display of lungpower in art song. Most importantly, he acknowledges the possibility of producing much greater feeling through the microphone: 'the quiet voice trembling with inner emotion, the suppressed outburst, the note of real feeling that needs no blustering to make one aware of it' (ibid.: 82). In a moderate way this is what the Brandelius excerpt demonstrates.

Arnheim ([1936] 1986: 78) also suggests that electrical recording created a 'spiritual and atmospheric nearness' of performer and listener that fostered a 'special art of intimate singing and playing for the microphone'. This quality would resemble that of singing in private, face-to-face situations, and would be likely to inspire a sense of trust and intimacy between the listener and the singer. Eisenberg (1987: 155) suggests that musicians could now try to fascinate listeners by *inwardness*: 'Instead of leaping out at the listener this sort of artist seems to ignore him, and thereby draws him in.' In the jazz tradition the non-communicative soloist was to become very influential.

In the 1930s the influence of the microphone extended beyond the studio and into the expressive fabric of the musical artist as such. Stage appearances had to be bolstered by public address systems, for without amplification 'the crooning Mills brothers and Miss Poop-poop-a-do could not have been heard beyond the third row' (Chanan 1995: 69). Electrical amplification made the listening experience very different from natural perception. While a speaker would previously have had to shout to be heard at the back of an arena, amplification

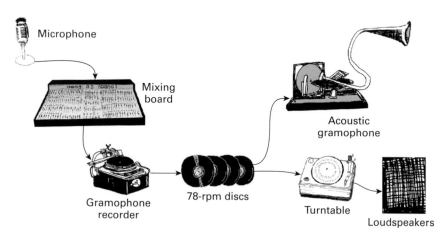

Figure 9.3 Model of the electrical recording medium.

made it possible for them to whisper and still be heard loud and clear hundreds of metres away. After amplification became commonplace, a power cut during a performance would mean that a singer would lose their personal intensity and be reduced to shouting.

The electrical recording medium

The electrical recording medium was completely asymmetrical. Music production was highly professional, whereas listeners could only play their records over and over again. But this technique had been in place from the introduction of acoustic recording, and it was the great sensitivity of microphone and amplification that struck everyone as the novelty. After fifty years of the quite primitive techniques of the gramophone and its acoustic horns, electrical recording was a remarkable improvement.

Figure 9.3 displays the main interfaces, platforms and signal carriers of the set-up I am investigating in this chapter. Notice that the microphone and mixing board were brand new interfaces for the artists, and in the 2000s they seem so basic that it is difficult to imagine that there has ever been music recording without them. Notice also that on the receiving end there are two different platforms for the same signal carrier. The 78 rpm disc could be played both on the old mechanical gramophone and the new equipment, which consisted of amplified pickup with a loudspeaker.

It is important to understand how a microphone works. The telephone and radio broadcasting were electro-mechanical media, and had exploited microphones from the beginning. But until the development of broadcast studios in the early 1920s microphones were little more than telephone mouthpieces (Chanan 1995: 56), and it was notoriously difficult to amplify the weak electric signals enough for them to be cut on a disc. Perhaps just as importantly, during the 1920s the industries of broadcasting and gramophone were in competition, and the record business baulked at coming under the influence of the techniques, aesthetics and politics of broadcasting (Morton 2000: 26). But in the late 1920s acoustical recording was discarded across the board, forever. In 1927 Lindsay Buick describes the basic interface of the new electrical platform with great enthusiasm.

> This delicate electrical instrument is set up in the midst of a comfortable room, furnished with all the appurtenances of the art. Before it the singer stands and sings as naturally as though it were his audience. Behind him again is grouped the orchestra free from the restraint of undue crowding. The notes given out by the performers create a series of sound waves which are caught up by the sensitive coil operating in a strong magnetic field within the microphone. These waves are in turn transferred to wires which carry them on to the recording machine, perhaps miles away, where they operate upon the cutting tool, which obediently traces upon the wax 'blank' every vibration of the air as it goes throbbing from the musicians.
>
> (Buick 1927: 103)

In the 1920s the microphone stood in the studio with the authority of an all-perceiving ear. For some years the microphone was unprotected. This means that it lacked every form of dampening, and therefore picked up every sound whether or not these also created distortion, and it distorted all sounds slightly whether or not they were loud. Often circuit breakers and electron tubes would simply blow out and completely destroy the recording. The microphone's hypersensitivity made the restrictions on the performers' movements much stricter than before. A recording engineer recollects: 'If he hums while he plays, he must stop it; and if he breathes through his nose, he must open his mouth a little so that he may avoid what can sound like a consumptive intrusion on the finished product' (quoted in Morton 2000: 27). If the musician played too close to the mike, or the mike was touched, it would create noises on the recording, and it could completely overpower the musical performance. The shuffling of feet, coughing or the crackling of paper would get the same unwanted prominence.

The sound signal was carried on the 78 rpm disc. It was a mono system, and this means that there was no realistic reproduction of human bidirectional hearing and also that there was very poor reproduction of the spaciousness of the sounds. As Rudolf Arnheim comments, 'A realistic spatial distribution of sources of sound in the transmitting-room does not attain its specific effect on the listener – it is wasted trouble' (Arnheim [1936] 1986: 56). The producers wanted to create a more well-defined sound by rhetorical placement of the sound sources in the studio, but the breakthrough of such techniques would have to wait until stereo sound was introduced in the 1960s.

Along with the microphone came the mixing board. This control device allowed several sources to be blended and balanced according to the wishes of the producers. The mixing board is still a part of the basic interface of recording, and its used more or less universally in sound production, whether for live concerts, films, television or radio. Electrical recording introduced a series of new techniques relating to electronic signal processing, such as the use of mixing boards to balance the signal and the reliance on strict separation of the studio and the control room.

David Morton (2000) points out that studio techniques became more scientific with the electric recording medium. 'Already steeped in the methods of science, electrical engineers responded by creating instruments to measure audio "signals", and borrowed heavily from the methods and vocabulary of acoustics' (Morton 2000: 26). Since the electronic signal was only accessible through meters and calculations, this introduced the practice of measuring sound quality independently of listening and content quality. With time this technically embodied perspective on sound came to be referred to as 'audio', and the term denotes a completely objective dimension of the signal. In order to measure the audio quality of a voice the engineer need have no appreciation of what was performed, and no musical training.

The studio environment

The technical developments described above make it important to analyse the practices in the electrical studio environment. The producer was seated in the control room and gazed into the studio through double-glazed windows. He could regulate the volume coming through the microphone with faders, and also signal to the performers if they had to reposition their instruments (Goldsmith and Lescarboura 1930: 31). Technically, the qualities that could be listened for were the dynamic range of the mix, and its bass, mid-range and treble characteristics. In time musicians in the studio would start to wear headphones to monitor the sound of their performance *during* recording, and to take cues and communicate with the control room. With the widespread use of this electro-architectural interface it seems that the act of recording had moved into a space of its own making.

The sound-proof studio became a standard component of recording facilities, and also of radio stations. And as I am arguing here, a set of new strategies for keeping the signal under control were developing in this environment. The sound studio was built to be hermetically enclosed, since now the signal travelled via wires through the walls into the control room. By 1923 the BBC had built several sound-proof studios: 'On the walls and ceiling were wooden fences holding six layers of fabric spaced about an inch apart to damp reverberation. For the same reason there was a thick, heavy carpet on the floor' (Briggs [1961] 2000: 193). Briggs adds that it was not unnatural for artists to complain about having to force their tone to get through the silencing regime. There were sound-proof walls, ceilings and floors, and an authoritative distinction between normal action outside and the strict code of silence that typically reigned inside the studio. The habitat of musicians became hot and claustrophobic, reflecting their sole function as pickup spaces. In 1930 Goldsmith and Lescarboura describe this setting in broadcasting: 'A double set of doors marked the entrance to the studio, with conspicuous white lights to indicate that the studio was not on the air at the moment, or red lights to indicate that the studio was on the air and that SILENCE must be observed' (Goldsmith and Lescarboura 1930: 30).

The first electrical control rooms were built from the late 1920s. All signal processing took place in the control room, and this meant that the musicians were alone in the sound studio while producers, arrangers and engineers watched and monitored the performances from the outside. Since the electric signals were routed through the mixing console in the control room on its way to the disc-cutting machine, they could be electronically manipulated on the way. The practice of tapping sound from electric cables into the board and then feeding it back inspired increased research into the electronics of signal processing, a field of electronic engineering that had previously had no part in musical production (Morton 2000: 32). Technicians could now regulate the volume *internally*, that is, by adjusting the electrical power supply to increase or decrease the volume sent to the disc independently of the volume in the sound studio. Also the mixing board could be fitted with equalizers that emphasized or de-emphasized certain bands of frequencies, typically split into treble, mid-range and bass (ibid.: 32). Because the mixer could regulate several channels one could set up several microphones in the studio, and these could be dedicated to different instruments to enhance the clarity of each. Consequently, the style could be a compound of individual sound sources that no longer had to conform to the central perspective of the acoustic horn or the single microphone.

Editing was a rare technique in the studio environment. Live on disc recording was the absolute production norm. There would be a loss of quality if the sound was re-recorded from one disc to another – a deterioration of one generation, as it was soon called. But technically speaking the disc-cutter could be used to superimpose sound on sound. The noise reduction of electrical recording made it more realistic than before to undertake this kind of editing, and several popular artists made creative use of gramophone overdubbing in the 1930s. Les Paul is often mentioned as one of the most proficient. Notice the amount of work involved in this overdubbing technique.

> I would record a rhythm track on the first disc, then I would play along with the rhythm track and lay the needle down on the second disc which would simultaneously record me playing along to my rhythm track. The second disc would now contain two guitar parts. Going back to the first machine, I would put the needle down onto the disc and record, say, a bassline along with the music from the second disc. Then for other instrumentation, I would just repeat the process, *ad infinitum*.
>
> (quoted in Cunningham 1998: 26)

Les Paul pushed the technology to its limits: 'I would go down as many as thirty-seven generations before I finished a recording, but the quality would start to deteriorate' (quoted in Cunningham 1998: 27). It must be noted that the superimposition of sound on sound was still done in a way that made the resulting montage *final*, in contrast to later media such as tape and hard disc. Tape could be seamlessly modified until everyone was satisfied, and there was no need to re-record each modification live to a new disc in order for it to be preserved.

Although there was little exploration of weird sounds in popular music and radio, there was all the more experimentation among such modernist composers as F. T. Marinetti, John Cage and Pierre Schaeffer, who introduced the term *musique concrète* (Perloff 1997; McCaffery 1997; Kahn 1999: 110). They produced sonic art with variable speeds, distortion, and all kinds of environmental and electronic sounds that were mixed together on record. Sonic artists also used tone-generators to create sounds completely internal to the technology. But in pop music production the electric recording medium was not typically used to create strange and unnatural sounds. The main concern of the industry was to create better documentary realism than before.

High fidelity, 1931

Westerners first realized what good sound could be during the 1930s. Electrically amplified sound from sensitive microphones allowed for intimate behaviour from the musicians and singers, and this gave music lovers a more enjoyable experience, at home, at parties, in the pub or in the park during summer. Radio broadcasts were still typically ridden with atmospheric noise, and the telephone was as low-fi as ever. This suggests that the rise of high fidelity coincides with the rise of microphone recording.

Roland Gelatt suggests that the electrical improvements helped to revive the gramophone industry from the depression of the early 1930s, and the concept of 'high fidelity' was about to become an explicit consumer interest and new industry niche. He points out that the phrase did not come into general use in the USA until 1933 or 1934, but then it was 'exploited with a vengeance' (Gelatt 1977: 270).

High fidelity was inaugurated as a cultural phenomenon when music lovers started purchasing the electrific gramophone and its attendant loudspeaker. Notice that, since the sound was in mono, only one loudspeaker was needed. By this time radio reception had long since become a fixture of the living room, and equipment producers such as Philips and Victor had started to market the 'radio-phonograph'. This was a 78 rpm turntable with an amplified pickup and a radio receiver. The frequency range of this equipment was four times wider than that of the acoustic gramophone, and the control knobs on the front permitted domestic control over volume and tone (Chanan 1995: 56–7). RCA Victor promoted this new device aggressively on the sleeves of their record releases: 'The

World's Greatest Musical Instrument is Victor Radio with Electrola', its great achievement being 'Faithful reproduction, natural performance'. 'It is a proven scientific fact that your ears cannot tire of them, for the reason that one record differs from another exactly as two pieces of music differ; they have nothing in common except supreme beauty, realism and naturalness of the music they reproduce' (Victor Red Seal sleeve, 1931). To the pathos of such marketing strategies Gelatt laconically remarks: 'Would record buyers never tire of hearing that absolute perfection in phonograph reproduction had finally been achieved?' (1977: 270). I could say the same thing about the 2000s, especially regarding the never-ending perfection of high-end stereo equipment.

Audiences learnt a new way of attending to the loudspeaker. As I have stressed in this chapter, it was easier for the listeners to be aware of the nuances in the music and to get a sense of the locale in which the performances took place. Loudspeakers were greatly valued for improved intelligibility, volume and dynamic range. To the public ear the main improvement was therefore an increased documentary realism in the recordings, and in the home.

The final case study comes from France. The famous French vocalist Charles Panzéra sings a Lied in the art-song tradition, accompanied on piano. The composition is well known to classical music connoisseurs all over the world to this day. 'Chanson triste' was composed by Henri Duparc and the lyrics were written by Jean Lahor.

Track 31: Charles Panzéra: Chanson triste, 1931 (1:03).

> You will rest my poor head,
> Ah! sometimes on your lap,
> And recite to it a ballad
> That will seem to speak of us;
> And from your eyes full of sorrow,
> From your eyes I shall then drink
> So many kisses and so much love
> That perhaps I shall be healed.

Panzéra, who has a well-trained tenor voice, stands beside the piano, which is played by his wife. This music is made for the salons of Paris, and is parlour music in the most elevated sense. This is in all probability a single microphone recording. Since there are only two sources of sound, they could be balanced simply by the way in which they were located in relation to each other and the microphone. Since the volume is regulated electrically, Panzéra can relax, and his subtle timbres and inflections can be given more prominence. Although the new sensitivity would be used more creatively by popular singers than by classical performers such as Panzéra, one clearly hears that he sings more softly and subtly than performers on acoustic recordings. Listen for example to Ellen Gulbranson from 1914 (track 34), and the contrast is clear.

Panzéra sings to nobody in particular. His vocal melody is pure art, and he doesn't have to sound *triste* in order for the performance to be moving. Both melody and lyrics are marked by sadness and longing, but this mood does not extent to the singer. Panzéra recites the music in the way in which classical singers are supposed to do, and did not experiment with the tension between role play and personality in the manner of Edith Piaf and Harry Brandelius.

Panzéra is a familiar name in musical literature because of Roland Barthes's celebrated essay 'The Grain of the Voice' (1977). Barthes names Panzéra as a singer who embodies the mysterious grain. Without going into the complexities of what the grain really is, it seems clear that it could be recorded, and that we hear it on the recording presented above. Barthes suggests that Panzéra does not primarily attract the listener because of lung volume. 'All of Panzera's art, on the contrary, was in the letters, not in the bellows (simple technical feature: you never heard him *breathe* but only divide up the phrase)'. Barthes praises 'the purity – almost electronic, so much was its sound tightened, raised, exposed, held – of the most French of vowels, the *ü*', and also suggests that 'Panzera carried his *r*'s beyond the norms of the singer' (Barthes 1977: 183–4). It would be speculative to say that electrical recording inspired Panzéra to sing as he did, but it certainly made it easier for Barthes to hear what was sung.

My point is that there was better sound in the 1930s than ever before. Roland Gelatt (1977: 223) argues that the simulation of the 'atmosphere' of music played in the concert hall was a great new attraction. Gronow and Saunio (1998: 39) recount that 'sharp-eared music lovers could hear that something crucial had happened – at least by the time Columbia issued its recording of a 5000-strong choir singing *Adeste Fideles*, in June 1925. Recording a huge choir like this by the old method would have been impossible'. Interestingly, Lindsay Buick comments on the improvements in fidelity by referring to the same release: 'This record, though not faultless, had such wonderful power and definition that those who had previously regarded chorus records as the ugly ducklings of the gramophone library said at once: – "Here, indeed, is something new"' (1927: 101). But in 1936, almost ten years after the microphone was introduced in recording, Theodore Adorno refused any idea that recording was about to become a means of expression in arts and culture. 'Nowhere does there arise anything that resembles a form specific to the phonograph record – in the way that one was generated by photography in its early days' (Adorno [1934] 1990: 56). In light of the recordings by Edith Piaf, Harry Brandelius and Charles Panzéra that I have just analysed, it seems that Adorno was right. The radical development of a form specific to the phonograph record happened only with the introduction of multitrack recording in the 1960s.

Chapter 10

Atmospheric contact

Experiments in broadcasting, 1920s–1900s

The cry for help could fly through the air in wave form, from the *Titanic* to other ships in the Atlantic, and on to the American mainland. Voice transmission was a natural miracle in 1912, and had been so for six years. It was like a telephone connection where anybody on earth could listen in on the call. The wireless was absolutely live and inherently public. In the 2000s we live in the midst of this atmospheric contact whether we like it or not. It is a fully completed infrastructure on a level with railways, motorways and electricity, and has been so for the American and European citizen for around ninety years.

As I described in chapter 8, by the 1930s the soundscapes of radio had become a national experience. But if we go back to the 1920s and before, wireless was an international activity, and it only involved people with a particularly strong interest or motivation – often scientific, cultural and commercial. A certain part of the electromagnetic resource had been colonized and was being moulded into the public domain. This chapter deals with the period before there was any journalistic preparation of content or responsible editorial gate-keeping, and before there was an audience to whom such programmes might be distributed.

Backwards history

The period from the 1920s back to the 1900s saw its share of political conflicts on the world scene. World War I from 1914 to 1918 was the biggest and most technologically efficient war yet seen by mankind, with an Eastern and Western front stretching across Europe for four long years. In 1917 the USA entered the war, which ended with a decisive victory for the Western Allies, just as World War II (Hobsbawm 1994: 21ff.; Zinn 1980: 377ff.).

In this war radio had a marginal role as a public medium, but it was important for military communications. Telegraph had revolutionized military communications since the 1840s (Briggs and Burke 2002: 338), and now wireless transmission did so again. Movable units communicated with central command in secret codes, and there were also experiments with the walkie-talkie principle for sound communication. In this regard there was an enormous difference from

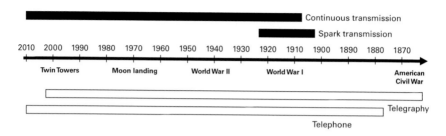

Figure 10.1 Timeline of the wireless medium.

what took place during World War II, when radio most definitely had an influence on public opinion. Electronic technologies for sound were not widespread except for the telephone system, but notice that Woodrow Wilson was among one of the first politicians to speak successfully through a PA system, at a political rally in 1919 (Schafer [1977] 1994: 114). Both before and after this period there was enthusiastic experimentation with all kinds of electronic technologies. The entrepreneurial drive of great inventors such as Guglielmo Marconi, Reginald Fessenden and Oliver Lodge was crucial to the new developments.

Figure 10.1 shows how remarkably stable the wireless media have been. The continuous transmission that was later to be known as AM and FM broadcasting was functional from the mid-1900s, and works according to essentially the same principles today. Notice that the spark transmission technology that Marconi invented could not compete with the superior technologies of the electron tube, and was gradually superseded. Below the arrow I have listed the telegraph and the telephone, which had both become elementary features of modern societies before 1910 (for studies of the telephone and telegraph, see Brooks 1975 and Pool 1977). The basic experience of instantaneous live signalling was well known from these two media long before wireless transmission came along, and this eased the task of finding a purpose for wireless transmission.

The media environment in the 1910s and 1920s was richer than we might think with hindsight. A relatively wealthy city-dweller in Europe and America would own a telephone, play recorded music on the phonograph, go to the movies to see 'silent films', and occasionally send a telegram. We should not forget the enormous influence of written forms, such as newspapers, magazines, books and letters between friends and business partners. This was the age of literacy, with English becoming more and more *the* language communication as emigration to the USA soared and millions of people acquired a new mother tongue.

The ocean liner *Titanic* struck an iceberg and sank on its maiden voyage in April 1912. It had been designed to provide a express service between Europe and the USA for the White Star Line. It sank in two hours and forty minutes, but the telegraph operator managed to send distress signals other ships, and to the mainland, where the news was relayed to the White House (Briggs and Burke 2002: 156). After this highly publicized event there was much stronger public awareness about the benefits of the wireless. As a direct consequence of the disaster, an international ice patrol was established to report on threatening icebergs, and foreign-going passenger ships had to be on radio alert twenty-four hours a day (Wikipedia 2007, 'Titanic').

Going backwards from 1912 the story of live media reaches its starting point, and it is becoming a history of disappearance: there are fewer and fewer users. The technology was less complex and more governed by natural forces, and then there was only theoretical knowledge about radio waves among physicists such as Heinrich Hertz and James Clerk Maxwell.

Clearing the channels, 1920s

Innovators and investors were in pursuit of *clear channel* for the new medium. In the early 1920s technical disturbance was a paramount issue for radio listeners; 75 per cent of the correspondence to the BBC complained about interference and other problems relating to reception (Pegg 1983: 40). The ambition of the BBC's chief engineer in 1924 was to 'enable the listener to forget about the technique of the service' (quoted in Briggs [1961] 2000: 184). There was so much extraneous noise during transmission that the signal could not be received clearly, and this hampered the public development of radio. During the 1910s and 1920s the research laboratories worked overtime to reduce the interference. The dream was a signal free of noise, which would have greater documentary realism and therefore be more responsive to nuances of expression. Until this problem was solved there could be no mass mediation of sound.

In the late 1920s radio was still noisy, but the act of listening had become a more comfortable experience. The focus was now more on public contact through the medium than the medium itself. The relaxed attitude is expressed by a listener in a newspaper in 1924. 'Of course, we have become so used to the wonder of wireless (when it is not playing tricks) that we are apt to say, "Oh, it is nothing; we often hear that". Ten years ago, if you had been told that such a thing would be possible in a million British homes, you would have been very hesitant to believe such scientific progress probable' (quoted in Pegg 1983: 147). Before the period of great public interest in radio, the main attraction was the atmospheric noises of the technology itself. But this was an attraction for the few – mainly military men, ship telegraph operators and interested amateurs. They attended to radio in raw form and took part in the social shaping of the new medium.

The case study for this chapter relates to the raw sounds of atmospheric contact. The term 'atmospherics' refers to disturbances of the signal produced by electrical phenomena such as lightning, though it can also refer to the electrical phenomena causing these disturbances. In the early years of broadcasting people would hear the following sounds in attics, garages and aboard ships, and they would always hear them via headphones.

Track 32: Tuning in the AM Spectrum (1:01).

The noises are a reminder of the powerful natural forces that had to be subdued before comfortable communication was possible. The less noisy the contact, the less it reminds us of the technological infrastructure in which it is made. There are two signal sources in this montage – a pulse from some electronic appliance and a Morse signal that waxes and wanes – and there are also indeterminable atmospheric timbres that echo oddly. They typically have a very rapid pulse: at times it is almost screaming, and it soars and sinks according to atmospheric conditions as well as the turning of the tuner knob. Its metallic white noise characteristics are decidedly uncomfortable when listened to for longer periods of time.

This is not a historical document of the atmospherics of early radio, simply a collage that I have made especially for the book, but it helps us to become aware of atmospheric sounds. Such noises were so noticeable that they infused the listening experience with a strange feeling of alienation. Rather than being put in contact with the world of cultural action, people heard the sounds of the technology and its natural surroundings, sounds that are essentially without meaning (like the sounds of the computer modem), but which had great allure for amateur radio operators, who took pleasure in searching the air waves and savouring the qualities of the atmosphere.

A natural public sphere

The live communication of wireless was a novel phenomenon with great impact on later mass media. What really distinguished transmission was the great and unbound range of signalling and its inherently open access. The spherical propagation of waves was a natural adjunct of radiation, and although the waves could be harnessed for transmission their signal would always be accessible to a third party with a crystal receiver. Signals could be picked up in several places simultaneously without anyone having control over where it happened or how to prevent it. Far into the 1910s the lack of privacy and confidentiality was considered the chief drawback of wireless. The telegraph communicated between two fixed points and could easily secure privacy for its customers. Broadcast signals, however, were free all to pick up. There was no business model for such a technological set-up. Raymond Williams ([1975] 1990: 24) wrote that broadcasting was a system 'primarily devised for transmission and reception as abstract processes, with little or no definition of preceding content'.

The development of broadcasting is therefore the story of breaking free from the abstract process of signalling back and forth through the air, and turning the nature of transmission into a positive feature. In order for this to happen there would have to be an explicit recognition of the public potential of transmission among station owners. As early as 1893 there was something resembling a broadcast station in Budapest, Hungary. This was *Telefon Hirmondo*, which sent regular programmes through a telephone network. At most they had 6,000 subscribers (Briggs and Burke 2002: 147–8).

But wireless transmission could do better than that. It could potentially reach any person who had a receiver set and was within reach of the transmission tower. Everything depended on inventors, who would acknowledge that this all-inclusive access could have economic potential, and also that it could become a leisure rather than a specialist activity. In 1907 the scientist and entrepreneur Oliver Lodge made an early proposition. 'It might be advantageous', he wrote, 'to "shout" the message, speaking broadcast to receivers in all directions, and for which the wireless system is well adapted.' He suggested that this shouting could be used 'for army manoeuvres, for reporting races and other sporting events, and generally for all important matters occurring beyond the range of the permanent lines' (quoted in Briggs [1961] 2000: 32–3). What Lodge talks about is a centralized system of propagation, and it could be called a medium prototype, since his idea was to broadcast to receivers in all directions at the same time, and therefore effectively create a public arena.

In a rudimentary sense there was already a public ethos to transmission. Hugh Aitken (1985: 190) describes how, in order to secure contact, amateurs had to attend to the weather forecast, the humidity and other variables. Among these aficionados there evolved a sense of shared fascination, a community based on a new and intriguing vocabulary with terms for the different noises encountered across the spectrum, and, as I have already noted, a great interest in the sounds of different kinds of resistance, wavelengths and degrees of clarity of signals. As the use of wireless apparatus became more widespread this conversation with and through the atmosphere became more and more varied, from the grassroots up. The development of the internet is a parallel in this regard (Naughton 1999: 11). In 1916 David Sarnoff made another early proposition for radio as a domestic medium, where he more or less takes for granted that there is public interest in it.

> I have in mind a plan of development which would make radio a 'household utility' in the same sense as the piano or phonograph ... The receiver can be designed in the form of a simple 'Radio Music Box' and arranged for several different wave lengths, which would be changeable with the throwing of a single switch or pressing of a single button. The 'Radio Music Box' can be supplied with amplifying tubes and a loudspeaking telephone, all of which can be neatly mounted in one box. The box can be placed in the parlor or living room, the switch set accordingly and the transmitted music received.
>
> (quoted in Barnouw 1966: 78)

Notice that Sarnoff was not talking about a headphone appliance like the crystal set, but one with electronic amplification and a loudspeaker. He was thinking about an inviting and inclusive soundscape that could be shared in the living room much like piano or gramophone music. This is a far cry from the technological timbres of the atmospheric contact at the time of Sarnoff's memo.

Susan Douglas (1999: 57) has pointed out that ordinary people learnt how to listen to wireless telephone at the same time as stations learnt to broadcast a decent product. Both producers and consumers had 'empty intentions' that had to be filled with something useful. In this period of pioneer auditory rhetoric during and after World War I it seems that wireless had a more transparent and symmetrical contact than in later years. The medium incorporated a greater sense of mutual innovation, a sense that both parties were in the process of finding out what ought to be the terms of contact. For example, a lot of hesitation, pauses, speech faults and other forms of off-stage expressions came on the air, and there was little concern that this was unsuitable behaviour. The social negotiation of behaviour in the new medium was a crucial part of developments for decades to come.

Marshall McLuhan ([1964] 1994: 8) observes that initially every new medium involves the essence of an old medium, and that innovation in the media progresses by looking in the 'rear view mirror'. His theoretical adversary Raymond Williams ([1975] 1990: 25) refers to the method of creating content in radio as 'parasitic'. Both song and speech performances sounded like they had always done, since it had become apparent to producers that 'the approval of listeners invariably increased in direct proportion to the familiarity of what was being sung or played' (Briggs [1961] 2000: 68). This conservative attitude meant that public speech styles were adopted from political, religious and educational speechmaking. Radio's approach to orchestra performances was adopted from the concert hall and the gramophone recording studio, the approach to dramatic plays was adapted from the theatre, and the approach to news bulletins about politics, state events and sports was adapted from the newspaper and telegraphy. The wireless was built by grafting familiar public performances on to the new medium and by appropriating already dominant ways of doing things for the mouthpiece.

This did not happen without protest, as one might imagine. The contemporary writer Lindsay Buick (1927: xvi) suggests that the live access to events through wireless broadcasting is an invasion of the domestic sphere. He argued that, although broadcasting will always fascinate some people, 'there are many to whom, for temperamental reasons, radio would never appeal – people who know what they want, and will not be satisfied merely with what they can get.' Wireless encourages capriciousness of attention, cultivates a curiosity without direction and teaches the listener to turn on the apparatus with no expectations. Buick displays a concern with the fact that the listener has no control over what he will end up engaging with, except that it happens *now* and is shared by all listeners. Instead he recommended the 'calmer culture' of the gramophone (ibid.).

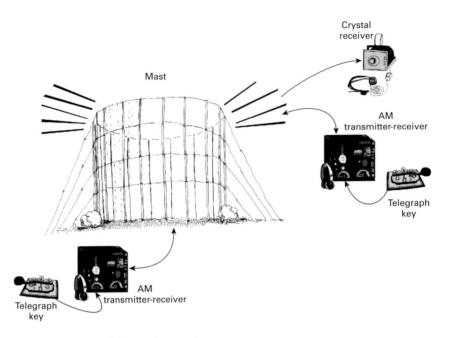

Figure 10.2 Model of the wireless medium.

The wireless medium

The first fully functional transmission platforms were connected in a symmetrical way, which means that there was no real difference between producers and listeners as we know it today.

Figure 10.2 displays the main interfaces, platforms and signal carriers of the early wireless medium. The telegraphic key was an important interface, and the Morse signals went into the amplifier and then to the antenna, where they were beamed out into the surroundings. The producers could also speak to other people on the air, but there were no proper microphones in use, only telephone mouthpieces with very poor sound quality. There were no dedicated sound studios with sound-proofing, and all transmissions that might resemble public progammes (with music, lectures, etc.) were strictly experimental. Notice that the huge mast in figure 10.2 would only be erected by professional organizations such as the military or commercial wireless telegraphy companies. Amateurs could receive the signals on crystal sets, which had headphones and were reception-only devices, though the more well equipped among them owned their own amplifier/transmitter with a mouthpiece and telegraphic key, and could send out their own signals. They would erect relatively big antennas, typically with wires strung on rooftops and between buildings, but they would not have anything resembling the huge mast depicted in figure 10.2.

As noted in the beginning of the chapter there were two different transmission platforms: that constructed by Fessenden (and others), which used electron tubes and sent out continuous signals, and Marconi's, which sent out digital signals based on electrical sparks. Both platforms could transmit with the same type of antenna, and the user interfaces also worked for both.

At the fundamental level, the technologies of transmission and reception make up a platform of *live* contact. This live contact was a consequence of the fact that atmospheric transportation takes place at the speed of light, and therefore there is practically no time between sending and receiving a message. In contrast to the gramophone, where the final product had a highly controlled signal composition and was distributed to record shops in the form of discs, transmission introduced an instantaneous mode of public communication.

As suggested before, Lindsay Buick (1927: xiv) was concerned with radio's absolutely live features. 'Wireless, as we know it today deals only with things of the moment, with things transitory; it preserves nothing to us. We listen to a broadcasted programme and when it is finished it remains only as a memory.' Rudolf Arnheim stated that the glory of wireless was that it cultivated the 'inspiration of the moment' ([1936] 1986: 127). More to the point, he also called wireless an 'apparatus whose technical peculiarity simply consists in enabling sounds made at a particular spot to be simultaneously reproduced in as many and as far removed places as one wishes by disrespectfully breaking through boundaries of class and country' (ibid.: 226).

In order to become communicative the new resource had to have a reliable signal carrier of some sort. Waves had to be focused at a certain frequency that both parties could access, and in this common 'place' a strong signal had to be available. The technically focused radiations were named *carrier waves*, and the successful maintenance of such a 'place' was called *syntony*. Hugh Aitken (1976: 34) argues that the development of syntony was crucial to the human colonization of the electromagnetic resource: 'Syntony, or what we call tuning, is what makes it possible to locate a radio transmitter or receiver at a particular frequency or wavelength in the radiofrequency spectrum and at no other. It is the concept that makes place and rights of occupancy possible.'

Inventors at first presumed that the carrier wave moved straight ahead until it met an obstacle and was then refracted. Under this presumption Marconi experimented with transmission in two ways: ever more transmitting power and ever larger aerials (Aitken 1976: 197). In 1901 he raised aerials several hundred feet high to accomplish his transatlantic crossing and also used kite-born aerials extended a thousand feet into the air (Winston 1998: 272). However, it soon turned out that the atmosphere was more complex than the notion of direct waves suggested. For example, experimenters noticed that the range of long waves was much greater at night than during daytime hours. The main reason for Marconi's success was not the height of his aerial, but the fact that the long waves that he used were carried along the curvature of the earth because of the electrical conductivity of soil and seawater (Inglis 1990: 36). Experimenters realized that different parts of the spectrum had different transportation properties, and because of Marconi's success with long waves this was where testing was concentrated. Long waves had the advantage of producing steady carrier waves, and were also easy to generate with the equipment available at the time (ibid.).

Speaking into the air, 1910s

As the account of the *Titanic* in 1912 tells us, at that point it was sensational and very useful to be able to hear a voice on the wireless, and not just atmospherics and Morse code. Here we stumble upon a clear case of technological determinism. It was only on account of the invention of the electron tube that the idea of wireless as a sound medium could begin to be realized in earnest during the 1910s. Without the continuous signalling that the electron tube permitted, no sounds could be conveyed through the air.

The most sensational early sound transmission was probably Fessenden's experiment on Christmas Eve 1906, when he used long waves to transmit music and speech from his experimental station at Brant Rock, Massachusetts. In preparation Fessenden had purchased a good phonograph and several records containing marches by Sousa, arias by Caruso, and violin solos (Douglas 1987: 156). Three days before the showcase, he had notified ships to listen in for his special public transmission. The writer A. F. Harlow describes the event:

> Early that evening wireless operators on ships within a radius of several hundred miles sprang to attention as they caught the call 'CQ CQ' in morse code. Was it a ship in distress? They listened eagerly, and to their amazement heard a human voice coming from their instruments – someone speaking! Then a woman's voice rose in sound. It was uncanny! ... Soon the wireless rooms were crowded. Next someone was heard reading a poem. Then there was a violin solo; then a man made a speech, and they could catch most of the words. Finally, everyone who had heard the programme was asked to write to R. A. Fessenden at Brant Rock, Massachusetts – and many of the operators did.
>
> (quoted in Briggs [1961] 2000: 25)

What must have been especially impressive as far as telegraph operators were concerned is that they could receive sound with crystal receivers made for telegraphy. Aitken (1985: 75) suggests that 'few if any of them can have heard a human voice through their headphones before.' Operators 'were utterly amazed to hear actual voices and musical tones in earphones that up to then had reproduced only static and the harsh *dits* and *dahs* of Morse code' (Head and Sterling 1978: 117). The Fessenden broadcast inaugurated a long period of experiments in sound transmission. Amateurs explored the new realm by reading poetry, playing musical numbers and presenting other types of verbal entertainment at their stations.

I am arguing that the electron tube is a very important material feature of the early sound media, and I will present my argument in detail. Before sound could fill the ether some method had to be found of producing waves that were continuous and consistent in form, and these were called continuous carrier waves. On such a platform it would be easy to superimpose sound as variations of the amplitude of the carrier wave, or more precisely to superimpose an analogue of an electrical signal from a telephonic mouthpiece. In the years from 1904 scientific and engineering work in this direction resulted in the invention and gradual improvement of the electron tube. It was capable of 'sensitive, rapid, subtle variations in accordance with the changing volume and pitch of speech' (Head *et al.* 1996: 21). The electron tube was variously described as 'the Cinderella of electrical science', 'the magic lamp of radio' and 'the truest "little giant" in all history', and was also considered the greatest invention since fire, the lever and the wheel (Briggs [1961] 2000: 26). Its prime inventor, Lee de Forest, exclaimed that it gave mankind the power to command 'electricity itself, not just its manifestations' (Head and Sterling 1978: 110).

There is good reason for referring to the electron tube as a revolution in wireless communications. As the electron tube was refined it turned out that, in addition to supporting voice analogues, the new platform was far more stable than Marconi's spark technology (Aitken 1985: 162ff.). Firstly, the electron tube carried the signals with very good syntony, and this made reception more reliable as well as reducing the problem of station interference, so that more stations could transmit in the same geographical area. Secondly, it amplified the signal in a much more 'internally' powerful way than spark technology, and this increased the range of the signals without need for greater electrical power. Thirdly, when electron tubes were used in receiving equipment it considerably improved the quality of the signal. However, it was very expensive to use tubes in receivers, and the improved reception platform did not become standard until the 1920s (Douglas 1987: 169ff.).

In 1906 the crystal detector was also introduced on the market. At the time the coherer was the only means of receiving signals. This was a very basic device which could only pick up digital signals (dots and dashes). Like the coherer, the crystal detector was purely mechanical, running only on the electricity extracted from the incoming signal. It did not have a good tuning system, and the operator had to hope for good atmospheric conditions in order to receive properly. But it could pick up the continuous waves and translate their energy into an electrical analogue that was audible as sound in headphones. This is an important juncture in broadcasting history, because the sound signals were recognizably human. The electron tube and the crystal receiver inaugurated the kind of mass mediation we know as 'sound broadcasting', and it can be dated to around 1906 (Douglas 1987: 196–7).

Interestingly, the crystal receiver was the first apparatus that was constructed for reception only. It was not only passive-attentive, it was without any means of control over when there would be signalling or what the signals would concern. The user of a gramophone could play a disc with the content imprinted on the label and do so at their leisure, and a user of a telephone could make outgoing calls as well as being notified of incoming signals. But the amateur operator at a crystal receiver would be utterly powerless to control the incoming message; they could only choose the time at which they wished to tune in. They was effectively put in a position of anonymous atmospheric voyeur listening in on other people's intermittent activities (Aitken 1985: 54–5).

Remember that in the 1900s there were no radio stations with professional content, and wireless was an activity for enthusiasts. Crystal listeners would therefore typically not be active in a social way, nor identify wireless as a stable acoustic medium for sustained conversation and music or concerning the events and trivialities of everyday life. To say that early reception was widespread would be misleading. The most that can be said is that it was an emerging social field, and work was ongoing to extend it towards other types of communication. Until the introduction of well-planned programmes in the 1920s, wireless would remain a homeless cultural experience.

Morse code communication, 1900s

In 1912 there were 1,224 licensed amateur stations in the USA (Head and Sterling 1978: 115), and in 1921 the total number of registered amateurs in Britain was 3,000 (Briggs [1961] 2000: 46). Two-way communication was an experience for experts, and the main users were telegraph and telephone operators, government agents, military personnel, scientists, experimenters, business opportunists and technology freaks. On account of the mess of components, the perceived danger of the electric sparks, and the need for absolute silence when monitoring the ether, most amateur operators dabbled in the barn, the basement or the garage.

Many operators preferred to listen to the Morse code on headphones instead of registering them on the inker – which punched out the Morse signal on strips of paper. The headphones were typically telephone earpieces put to new use, and they had very limited frequency response and poor volume. Operators had to be quite attentive to distinguish the faint Morse signals from the noisy atmospheric resistance that would invariably accompany the signal. When an inker was used for reception, the sending speed could not exceed twelve words per minute because of the mechanical sluggishness of the relay and the inker itself. But a good operator who used earphones could copy thirty-five words per minute, although this presumed that the other operators were able to encode at this speed (Aitken 1985: 190–1).

Operators tuned in patiently through the night, picking up and exchanging signals with people in faraway places, taking down new call numbers, keeping

Figure 10.3 Marconi at the spark transmitter.

an orderly log – even writing letters to persons who identified themselves sufficiently. These digital-acoustic deciphering skills were an important part of transmission for at least half a century.

The first spark of contact

I will go back to Marconi's first sparks at the turn of the nineteenth century. Since very few of the processes of transmission were either automated or well functioning, this early state of things gives a more ready access to the fundamental workings of the medium than later configurations.

Marconi invented digital broadcasting in the simple sense that he could only transmit short and long pulses that could be combined into digital codes such as Morse. This digital telegraphy relied on raw electromagnetic force to throw the signals into the air. A powerful electric generator drove current into a circuit that was connected to a Morse key and an aerial made of copper wire. When the Morse key was pushed a series of electrical sparks jumped across a small air gap separating the ends of two metal rods, and these sparks generated radio frequencies that radiated into space. Spark-induced signals thus consisted of a rapid series of separate carrier waves thrown into the air, which was very different from the continuous carrier waves generated by electron tube equipment.

Hugh Aitken (1985: 89) recounts that a spark transmitter placed in service on the American east coast in 1913 gave off 'a high-pitched, almost musical note, easily read through static, and up and down the eastern seaboard the distinctive note of the big rotary spark, first from Brant Rock and later from Arlington, became very familiar to naval and commercial operators.' By 1901 Marconi had constructed a 25 kilowatt spark transmitter that facilitated his famous first signals across the Atlantic. A contemporary journalist described the technology: 'When the operator pressed the telegraphic key, a spark a foot long and as thick as a man's wrist, the most powerful electric flash yet devised, sprang across the gap; the very ground nearby quivered and crackled with the energy' (quoted in Douglas 1987: 56).

The spark platform could not transmit messages in sound, as I have stressed. Hugh Aitken (1976: 11–12) recounts that 'many people tried to transmit the human voice by modulating the output of a spark transmitter. They all failed. Even at very high spark rates and with low dampening coefficients spark transmitters were too noisy to transmit speech without intolerable distortion.' As I pointed out above, the carrier wave could only be interrupted to form 'on' and 'off' signals.

In the first decade nobody had any means for determining where in the radio frequency spectrum a particular carrier wave was (Aitken 1976: 267). Each push of the telegraphic key would emit an explosive signal that would change in frequency as it travelled. Spark-induced waves therefore spread all over the spectrum, and made any one transmitter interfere with all others (Head and Sterling 1978: 108). This made it impossible for transmitters within range of each other to share the frequency spectrum, and the transmission was therefore a unique geographical event. In practice an act of transmission colonized the whole ether. In 1901 de Forest and Marconi both made public demonstrations of their technologies at a boat race in New York, completely ruining each other's signalling because of this lack of frequency specificity and time-sharing arrangements (Douglas 1987: 56). At that time the maximum reliable transmission distance was around 50 kilometers (Douglas 1987: 31). When transatlantic messaging was accomplished it was thought that only one station in England could transmit to America at a given time (Aitken 1976: 245).

Transmission is a miracle

In the late nineteenth century radio waves were considered a natural miracle. Theories about electromagnetism were put to the test in laboratories and workshops around the world, and slowly the innovators learnt to understand the nature of electromagnetic waves. In this way man gained control over yet another natural resource. In the 1900s and 1910s there was excitement about the harnessing of the raw electromagnetic forces for two-way communication. With pathos the inventor Lee de Forest wrote: 'I discovered an Invisible Empire of the Air, intangible, yet solid as granite' (quoted in Lewis 1991: 1). De Forest suggested that it was all there to begin with, and that the humans had only to learn to exploit the natural abilities of electromagnetic waves.

In the early decades the electromagnetic resource was typically referred to as 'the ether'. Literally this means 'the upper air', and it resonates with 'ethereal', which refers to a quality of unearthly lightness, like that of a spirit or fairy. The ether was a popular conceptual model for the wandering, boundless and fluid character of the carrier waves. There are contemporary descriptions of the atmospheric contact as a 'wailing of winds lost somewhere in the universe and very unhappy about it', 'celestial caterwauling' and 'noises that roar in the space between the worlds' (quoted in Peters 1999: 212). It is interesting to note that, at the same time as electromagnetic transmission was introduced to the general public, there was also a great interest in spiritualism. For a period in the 1910s and 1920s it was believed that contact could be made with the dead through the medium of the mysterious ether, and it was fashionable among the middle and upper classes to arrange séances (Sconce 2000; Peters 1999).

By the 1890s the strange waves were under empirical investigation by scientists and electrical engineers. Heinrich Hertz of Germany had demonstrated their nature, and he had also shown that they could be set in motion by certain devices and detected by other devices. The discovery of electromagnetic waves was in many ways analogous to the discovery of a new continent, Hugh Aitken suggests: 'To be sure, what was discovered was not territory in the geographic sense, and the resources made available for human use were suitable not for settlement, farming, or mining, but primarily for communication' (1976: 37). This emerging continent had no recognized boundaries, there was no clear understanding of how much room there was, and nobody knew how many 'places' could be colonized. Scientists had made the discovery, but engineers had to translate it into terms that businessmen, bureaucrats and communicators could actually deal with. During the 1900s researchers such as Marconi, Fessenden, de Forest and their teams worked to make a cultural resource out of something nobody had ever laid claim to before. Something utterly real was created out of thin air.

For the contemporary person in the 1890s it was intellectually challenging to be told that Morse code or speech could come out of an interface with no connective wires. While the gramophone produced its sound from a tangible rotating disc, and while the telegraph and the telephone at least had wiring throughout the distance between interlocutors, the contact of transmission involved invisible and fugitive qualities that stopped short of collective comprehension. The energy of the signal was radiated through empty space and registered without any sign of 'ponderable' matter (Aitken 1976: 134).

When the mechanical mind first encountered electric technology it exclaimed '*What greases the damned thing?*' (Marvin 1988: 19). The names coined for the technology demonstrated the need to associate the new devices with more familiar and tangible equipment. 'Wireless telegraph' and 'wireless telephone' suggest that transmission is like telegraphy or telephony, only without the wires. These retrospective names cut through the strangeness of the new field of contact, and attached transmission to interfaces that were more familiar.

The fact that radio waves could pass through solid objects was especially remarkable and thought-provoking. In 1892 the science writer Sir William Crookes was in a well-informed wonderment at this new world: 'Rays of light will not pierce through a wall, nor, as we know only too well, through a London fog. But the electrical vibrations of a yard or more in wave length … will easily pierce such mediums, which to them will be transparent' (quoted in Barnouw 1966: 9). In addition to acknowledging their existence Sir William expressed expectations that the waves would be utilized for communication, in particular he suggested that they would extend the abilities of the telegraph and telephone. 'This is no mere dream of a visionary philosopher. All the requisites needed to bring it within the grasp of daily life are well within the possibilities of discovery.' The firm grasp that modern science had on the facts of nature made it reasonable that such a platform for communication could emerge 'from the realms of speculation into those of sober fact' (ibid.).

The basic technological ambition was to be able to control this radiation as a means to certain ends. Even those who understood the scientific principles behind transmission could be amazed that such instantaneous transportation of signals through thin air was actually possible. J. A. Fleming was one of the inventors of transmission, but nevertheless he was amazed, and in 1911 he wrote:

> No familiarity with the subject removes the feeling of vague wonder with which one sees a telegraphic instrument, merely connected with a length of 150 feet of copper wire run up the side of a flagstaff, begin to draw its message out of space and print down in dot and dash on paper tape the intelligence ferried across thirty miles of water by the mysterious ether.
>
> (quoted in Briggs [1961] 2000: 27)

Fleming describes the experiential drama of actually accessing the new realm and making contact through it. Clearly, Fleming and his contemporaries could not conceive of this technology as an environment for news and entertainment among billions of humans. In the twenty-first century, almost a hundred years after Fleming expressed 'vague wonder' at the properties of the wireless, people use mobile phones, wireless internet and a host of other wireless communication technologies every day without wondering about them at all. They simply don't consider wireless transmission to be strange. As I pointed out in relation to the internet in chapter 2, for most people the incomprehensible settles into the habitual and its wonderful properties vanish. Alfred Schutz (1970: 247) writes: 'The miracle of all miracles is that the genuine miracles become to us an everyday occurrence.'

Chapter 11

The repeating machine
Music recording, 1920s–1870s

The gramophone allowed endless repetition of a sound event, and this was to become the most groundbreaking innovation in the history of sound. The machine did not discriminate according to language or musical style; it recorded everything in exactly the same way. It was like Alan Turing's 'universal machine', except that what was universalized was the repetition of sound events.

In this chapter I will describe the first fully successful ways of using the repeating machine for musical purposes. The case studies all demonstrate different aspects of the new art of recording. Bessie Smith was among the first African-American artists to gain a wide audience, singing 'St Louis Blues' in 1924 with Louis Armstrong accompanying her. A traditional Swedish folk song is performed by the operatic singer Ellen Gulbranson in 1914. And finally, the powerful presence of Enrico Caruso performing 'The Siciliana' in 1901 concludes the musical analyses in this book. At the very end of the story we will hear the first voice to ever be recorded, that of Thomas Edison.

Backwards history

No other chapter in this book spans so long a historical period. The history of acoustical recording extends from the 1920s back to 1877, that is, from the Weimar republic to the first decade after the American Civil War. This was the age of empire, and the European powers were still stronger than the USA in both the economic and military sense (Hobsbawm 1989). The British Empire stretched all across the globe, with India as the jewel in Queen Victoria's crown. The economic historian Arnold Toynbee popularized the term 'the industrial revolution' in the 1880s, and it seems like a good epithet for this period (Briggs and Burke 2002: 120). The railway, the steam engine and all kinds of industrial wonders were prevalent in society, and it was the age of natural resources, progress and technological control (Beniger 1991). In the late nineteenth century technologies were still made of wood and metal and of large moving parts, and involved all kinds of grinding, welding and fine-tuning of the equipment. It was all quite heavy and solid, in contrast to the later electronic technologies.

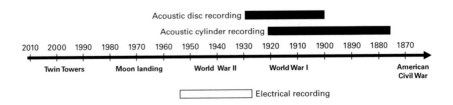

Figure 11.1 Timeline of acoustic recording media.

As a way of introducing the culture of early recording I will refer to the experimental methods of late nineteenth-century inventors. Modern industry and mechanization had influenced innovators for decades, but Thomas Edison and other American inventors developed this into a science. This period marked 'the invention of the method of invention' (Schafer [1977] 1994: 72), and the mindset of inventors had great influence on developments in the mass media. There was keen experimentation with new technologies across all industries. There was brutal competition in a fluctuating market and patent wars lasted for decades, but there was great optimism through it all. The drive towards the electrification of society is of special importance, since it bears on all the electronic media that came after acoustic recording. Edison invented a functional light bulb in the 1890s and promoted electricity as a domestic infrastructure for lighting. The Niagara Falls were harnessed for electrical power by Nikola Tesla also in the 1890s, and Alexander Graham Bell invented the telephone and started building networks in the 1880s. Ordinary people really became aware of the change towards electrical platforms when brightly coloured neon signs were introduced on the streets of New York in 1904 (Briggs and Burke 2002: 340). Although there was no electricity involved, acoustic recording also impressed the public. The fact that sound signals could be transported through time and space on a feeble disc was a scientific miracle just as impressive as the telephone, the electric light and the movies.

Figure 11.1 shows that acoustic recording dominated for over fifty years, from 1877, when Edison first proved its functionality, to the mid-1920s, when the microphone and electric recording techniques replaced it. Notice that Berliner's rotating disc was the really successful recording platform. And although it had a relatively short life as a strictly acoustic technology, the rotating disc lived on first as 78 with electrical pick up and later in the form of singles, LPs and indeed CDs in our own time. While Edison's cylinder phonograph was the only platform for several decades in the late nineteenth century it never became a mass medium, and became obsolete in the early 1920s (for detailed accounts of early recording, see Sterne 2003; Millard 2005; Wurtzler 2007).

The strongest mass medium in the 1910s was the movies. We call them silent movies, but Rick Altman (2004) has clarified that there were all kinds of sounds being made in the movie theatres, from piano playing and orchestras to sound effects made by local staff. The first Hollywood studio was built in 1911 (Briggs and Burke 2002: 340), and there were countless improvements and innovations to the silver screen in the decades to come.

Most of the media we live with in the 2000s had not yet been invented. In 1914, at the outbreak of World War I, there was no radio broadcasting, and private homes were very quiet at night. In 1901, at the time of Caruso's international debut, the phonograph was so new and expensive that it was still a showcase item and not a consumer appliance. The only widespread sound medium at the turn of the century was the telephone. But in 1888, at the time of the oldest recording on the soundtrack to this book, not even the telephone had anything resembling a regular function in society.

The recording artist, 1924

Acoustic recording was at its technological and cultural pinnacle in the early 1920s. By this time a prominent new profession had emerged alongside those of the operatic singer, the virtuoso instrumentalist and the cabaret artist – that of the recording artist. The most famous recording artist of them all was Enrico Caruso, to whom I will return later in the chapter. Popular music was now available to music lovers on disc, and not just at concerts or in the form of sheet music. Records sold in the hundreds of thousands and far outstripped the audience reach of the concert scene. With recording came a democratization of the means of production because musicians without formal training now had a better chance of a genuine career. Simon Frith (1998: 231) suggests that acoustic recording was instrumental in the emergence of jazz, basically because aspiring artists could learn from records and expand on what they heard, regardless of their social status or where they lived .

In the USA African-American singers and players had a chance to achieve real artistic success (Kennedy 1994). The first case study in this chapter is a recording with Bessie Smith singing 'St Louis Blues', a standard song that is associated equally with blues and jazz. W. C. Handy's original version (1922) was orchestrated for a big band and was full of instrumental embellishments. Bessie Smith's version is simpler and more intense. The recording was made on acoustic gramophone in 1925.

Track 33: Bessie Smith: St Louis Blues, 1925 (1:37).

> St Louis woman, with her diamond rings,
> Pulls my man around by her apron strings.
> Wasn't for powder and this store-bought hair,
> That man I love wouldn't go nowhere, nowhere [she shouts].

I got this St Louis blues, just as blue as I can be.
He's got a heart like a rock cast in the sea,
Or else he wouldn't have gone so far from me.

This is a band of three musicians, with Bessie Smith being accompanied by Louis Armstrong on cornet and Fred Longshaw on harmonium. All through the recording there is a beautiful duet between the voice and the cornet which sometimes sounds like two cornets, partly because Smith and Armstrong aligned their performances to create this effect, and partly because the acoustic horn distorts Smith's voice so much that it almost sounds like a cornet anyway.

Bessie Smith sings with an intensity that resembles that of Edith Piaf and Billie Holiday, but it is the way that personal character is project in the singing rather than the sound of the voice that is similar (McClary 2003). She has a strong, determined voice that projects the blues mood very well. Her intensity falters at one point in the performance, during the line 'That man I love wouldn't go nowhere, nowhere!', for the repetition of 'nowhere' is shouted in a quite vulgar way that does not conform to the mood of the song. Louis Armstrong also has a strong presence on the recording. It sounds as if he sings along with Bessie Smith, and that the cornet is an extension of his voice. 'St Louis Blues' and the various performances by Bessie Smith and Louis Armstrong have been analysed prolifically by musicologists over the years.

The Bessie Smith recording demonstrates the type of documentary realism that was widespread in the 1920s and before. In acoustic recording there were obviously no microphones or electrical amplification, instead there was a quite big acoustic horn which funnelled the sound to the disc-cutting machine. The acoustic gramophone recorded events exactly as they occurred in a locale, except that high and low frequencies were missing and there were a range of disturbances on account of resonance and other technical shortcomings (Gronow and Saunio 1998: 56). This means that, although the signal was a poor reflection of the sound quality of the performance, it was a highly credible reflection of the event of the performance. Nobody would dispute that these events had actually happened, and furthermore had happened exactly as they were heard on the disc. Bad sound could not alter this basic fact.

Spinning the disc

In 1913 Claude Debussy wrote: 'In a time like ours, when the genius of engineers has reached such undreamed of proportions, one can hear famous pieces of music as easily as one can buy a glass of beer' (quoted in Eisenberg 1987: 55). The really big cultural innovation that sound recording introduced was that opportunity to enjoy the sounds themselves without regard to the musicians or their feelings. The music lover could play the discs whenever they wanted, providing a brand new way of relating to music.

Figure 11.2 Bessie Smith in the studio.

The next case study is a Swedish folk song called 'Ack Wärmeland du sköna', and it was recorded in 1914 by the international operatic star Ellen Gulbranson. The melody is well known and very touching to many Swedes because of its national-romantic melody and lyrics. Notice that in this case I have played the 78 rpm on a 1904 Victrola (and re-recorded it to computer file). This process makes the playback sound as similar as possible to the way it would have sounded when it was released and played by music lovers in the 1910s. In this reproduction Gulbranson sounds very far away, and there is something unnerving and unpleasant about the sound.

Track 34: Ellen Gulbranson: Ack Wärmeland du sköna, 1914 (1:09).

> Oh Wärmeland, what a beautiful, wonderful land,
> The crown among the counties of Sweden.
> And if I were to reach the promised land,
> To Wärmeland I would return.
> Yes, there I will live, and there I will die.
> If ever I found a girl from Wärmeland,
> I know I would never leave her.

Gulbranson sings to piano accompaniment. The recording is shrill, and it seems as if she has to sing as loudly as she can to get through, which makes her voice sound quite strained and in addition means it is difficult to make out the words. Adding to these technical limitations, she sings in a very neutral way, especially if compared with charismatic singers such as Bessie Smith and Enrico Caruso. Like Charles Panzéra, Gulbranson was an art singer, and there was no expectation that she might be singing about her own life. There are no assumptions of truly personal emotions in this type of singing.

In Sweden the audience would nevertheless be satisfied, because they would in any event recognize the song and know the lyrics. It was quite typical for record companies to release 'standard songs', where the attraction was to hear a well-known hymn, lullaby or chanson. In such cases the listener would know the lyrics and the melody from before, so it wouldn't matter that it was difficult to distinguish the words. We can imagine a hundred situations in which this Swedish ballad was played and where no one was really concerned about the sound quality. The gramophone was not so much a device for listening to pleasant music as a device for a pleasant sing-along. On many a summer night people would gather around the gramophone to sing in approximately the way that Sergei Prokofiev describes in 1909:

> One of the peasants has bought himself a gramophone. And now every evening this invention of the devil is placed outside his hut, and begins to gurgle its horrible songs. A crowd of spectators roars with delight and joins in with their own false renditions of the songs, dogs bark and wail, the cows returning from the fields moo and run in all directions, and someone in a neighboring hut accompanies in a wrong key on his accordion.
> (quoted in Eisenberg 1987: 70)

Simon Frith argues that 'we express ourselves through our deployment of other people's music' (1998: 237). His point is that people shape the musical experience as much by their own desires and purposes as those of the people who actually made the music. With gramophone recording this interpretative freedom was greatly expanded at the expense of the musician's control over how music was to be experienced, and this is probably the reason why Prokofiev describes the peasant's activities in such a condescending way. The musician has become a tool for generalized participation in music. Anecdotal evidence suggests that listeners were not satisfied with the sound quality of the gramophone/phonograph. In 1923 *The Gramophone* published an article called 'A Defence of the Gramophone', wherein it was pointed out that fidelity had improved more than most members of the audience realized. 'To them it is an infernal machine which makes all music sound as if it is being played by nursery soldiers. They decry it.' The writer admits that the full volume of an orchestra or a piano cannot yet be rendered satisfactorily. Nearly always the piano resembles a banjo, and the time restriction entails that, 'far too often, the music has been ruthlessly cut'. But mainly the writer praises the results of the 'incessant search for improvement', and he is confident that these deficiencies will be diminished in the near future. And even now, he concludes: 'it is possible to be altogether absorbed in a fine piece of music which is being performed by means of the gramophone – to be moved by it and absorbed in it as one would be in the concert hall' (Gelatt 1977: 202–3). The last sentence is a recommendation of causal listening, which means that one should listen for the traces of the *external source*. Perhaps the writer in *The Gramophone* thought it absurd to listen to the quality of the recorded sounds themselves as long as the technical quality was so poor.

Pop idol, 1901

The recordings of Enrico Caruso demonstrate a musical and technical craft that is complete. There are no weaknesses, no clumsiness or amateurship in these recordings; rather, there is great skill in making the equipment perform maximally within its limited potential. By the early 1900s the skills and innovations in engineering had made the gramophone into a proper medium, that is, an industrial, conventionally regulated medium for making and selling music. Operatic recordings by Caruso and artists such as Nellie Melba, Lauritz Melchior and John McCormack sold in the millions during the 1900s and 1910s (Gelatt 1977: 142). They were the culmination of a practice that had been refined for more than twenty years.

The last musical example was made backstage at the New York Metropolitan Opera in 1901 (sleeve notes to the LP *20 Great Tenors in Recording History*, Tap records, T-303). After setting up the equipment and perhaps rehearsing the performance, the recordist would signal for Caruso and the piano player to begin, and they would have rehearsed the timing so that the aria was completed before the needle neared the end of the disc. This is continuity realism in its natural form.

Track 35: Enrico Caruso: The Siciliana, 1901 (1:08).

> Ntra la porta tua lu sangu è sparsu,
> E nun me mporta si ce muoru accisu
> E si ce muoru e vaju' n paradisu
> Si nun ce truovo a ttia, mancu ce trasu.
> E si ce muoru e vaju' n paradisu
> Si nun ce truovo a ttia, mancu ce trasu.

This sounds wonderful! To my ears Caruso's voice is so rich in emotion that it doesn't matter what he is singing about. This recording from 1901 has none of the weaknesses of the Gulbranson recording from 1914, and is due to the wonderful pitch and timbres of Caruso's voice and the skills of the acoustic technicians who made the recording. Caruso's voice carries much better across the hundred years of technological innovation than those of many of his contemporaries who also released recordings (for a description of Caruso's early career, see Millard 2005: 59–60).

My point is that there is nothing lacking in this recording. The frequency spectrum of Caruso's voice fits perfectly with the frequency spectrum that could be recorded with the early gramophone. 'Caruso's strong voice and slightly baritonal quality helped drown out the surface noise inherent in the early discs, and his vocal timbre seemed peculiarly attuned to the characteristics of the acoustic recording diaphragm' (Gelatt 1977: 115).

With the new recording practices there was a change in the focus of listening among artists. With recording it would not be the natural sound of the orchestra in a concert hall that mattered most, but the sounds from the acoustic horn. The recordist did not attend to *musical* qualities, only to qualities of volume, dynamic range and balance or distinctiveness of instruments in relation to each other. But still the work of technicians resembled the work of conductors, except that the sound went directly to the cutting machine, and not to a resonant concert hall full of people. It was always a matter of balancing the instruments in relation to each other.

The acoustic disc medium

The techniques I have described took place in a medium that was incredibly simple compared with the magnetic and digital media that came later. This simplicity is important, because it displays the most basic functionalities that must be there for mass communication to come about. The historical accumulation of equipment and creative techniques on top of this basic platform is remarkable. In the remainder of this chapter I will describe its first functionalities in detail, but since the invention of acoustic recording is in two separate trajectories, I will describe first Berliner's gramophone and at the very end Edison's phonograph.

Figure 11.3 shows the interface, platform and signal carrier for the acoustic gramophone. It is easy to see how exposed the components of the technology are compared with later versions, where electrical amplification and miniaturization of the components made it natural to encase them for protection. The acoustic horn had approximately the same function as the microphone has today, but it was almost self-explanatory in comparison. The singer would literally project his voice into a funnel, which focused the sound waves and caused them to set a thin pointed stylus into motion.

One feature in particular defined the gramophone as a proper platform of mass communication. It was from the beginning split in two distinct interfaces: the complicated and sensitive process of engraving musical vibrations as grooves on a disc and the simple act of playing records on the consumer turntable. The process of communication consisted of two completely opposing physical functions: one stored sound waves, the other radiated sound waves. On the basis of this double interface the gramophone could become a mass medium in the true sense.

It is important to describe the simple and robust way in which this industrialization could take place. The gramophone was invented in the 1890s and is commonly credited to Emile Berliner. As I have already mentioned, the gramophone

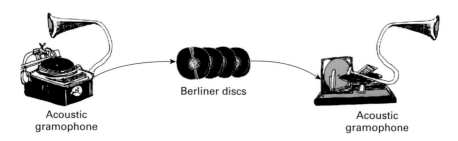

Berliner discs

Acoustic
gramophone

Acoustic
gramophone

Figure 11.3 Model of acoustic disc recording.

was based on the principle that a sharp needle made a trace on the surface of a
wax disc which rotated at 78 revolutions per minute. The flat disc rotated horizontally on a turntable, and this principle made it feasible for it to be copied
industrially, while Edison's cylinder was much larger and inconvenient for
industrial copying (more about this later). From the original recording several
matrices could be made, so that it was possible to press the copies of a particular performance at record factories in different cities and countries more or less
simultaneously (Gronow and Saunio 1998: 10). By 1897 Berliner had added a
clockwork motor to make the machine rotate independently of the shaky hand
of the operator (Moore 1999: 28). The listener had to crank the handle approximately thirty times to make a three minute recording come out at the correct
speed, and was instructed that the needle should be replaced after each playing.
Music lovers were also warned that the discs were easily broken and had to be
handled with great care.

The signal carrier was a round disc in which the signal was carved with a
stylus. Roland Gelatt points out that such acoustic recordings played back on
mechanical equipment could only reproduce the range from 168 Hz to 2,000
Hz, while the full-body range of sound is 20 Hz to 20,000 Hz. 'This did not
augur well for an expansive or vivid kind of sound. But it was recognizable as
the sound of an orchestra; it was music, not tooting; and it gave pleasure' (Gelatt
1977: 204). Since acoustic recording was strictly a mechanical technology it was
also more resistant to human control than any later sound medium. Michael
Chanan (1995: 131) refers to the mechanical limitations as 'the tyranny of the
needle'. There was no amplification of sound at any point between recording
and playback. It was the sheer force of the sound pressure coming from the
singers and instrumentalists that carved the groove. More precisely the acoustic
horn funnelled the sound pressure down onto a sensitive diaphragm that caused
a crystal needle to engrave the vibrations into the surface of a rotating disc
(MacFarlane 1917: 24). This meant that a loud sound would make a wide tracing that would take up much space on the disc, while a soft sound would make
a narrower tracing. In the beginning there was no standardized signal; rather, the

very characteristics of the musical instrument would determine the fluctuations of the needle. Steve Jones (1992: 22) observes that 'it would be possible to fit ten minutes of a piccolo solo on a disc, whereas it would be possible to fit only five minutes of the same part performed on bassoon.' Loud pieces would be recorded more distinctly than quiet ones, and this was important for the listening conventions of the early acoustic gramophone.

Balancing the recording

The only thing recordists could do was to balance the sound sources in relation to each other. Notice that this was a well-established practice in concert halls and at the opera. The different voices, for instance, soprano and baritone, would have to be perfectly balanced, and the different parts of the orchestra would require different volume levels, which meant that the musicians had to stand at different distances from the acoustic horn. The early recordings sound so straightforward that it is hard to appreciate the careful work that has gone into them. Listening again to Bessie Smith, Ellen Gulbranson and Enrico Caruso you will notice that the intended solo voices are actually in focus, the intended background sounds are actually in the background, and, most importantly, there are no unwanted sounds (except the noises of the recording itself). The people in charge of balancing the recording had to work hard if the listener was to have a pleasurable and harmonious musical experience. Indeed, the record would not have been released at all without the balance being adequate.

To achieve such a balance the band members had to be placed in unconventional ways around the horn in a manner that Lindsay Buick (1927: 102) called the 'grotesque pantomime of the old recording studios'. Since there was only one acoustic horn for each recording machine, and since it was highly impractical to mix partial recordings on a new disc, every instrumentalist had to orient themselves to the single pickup. The instruments had to be positioned according to their natural volume and whether they were to have a prominent or background role in the piece.

There are contemporary descriptions of the musicians' behaviour in the studio that display the characteristics of the acoustic production technique. Musicians had to stand in the weirdest positions in order for the recording to sound good. Columbia's London studio was made for operatic or classical music recording. A description from 1911 tells how there were platforms of varying heights to allow the instruments to project their sound on top of each other in a cone-like arrangement towards the horn. The violins were nearest the horn. 'The French horns, having to direct the bells of their instruments towards the recording horn, would turn their backs on it and were provided with mirrors in which they could watch the conductor' (quoted in Gelatt 1977: 180). In the Gennett studio in Richmond, Indiana, there was a parallel practice in the early 1920s. 'Certain musicians, such as banjo players, sat on high stools in front of the horns. Naturally, louder brass players were positioned in the back' (Kennedy 1994: 31).

Furthermore, musicians had to move back and forth according to the role of their instrument during the course of the piece. The director had to motion to vocalists when to lean in close and when to duck or step away from the horn to allow instrumental solos. 'Inexperienced phonograph singers who had not yet learned how to control their voices or step back during loud passages had to be physically jerked to and fro during recording sessions to ensure a good product' (Morton 2000: 21). According to Lindsay Buick, 'No artist could give of his or her best under such conditions. We can only marvel that records in the past have been so good, and admire the skill of the singers and the recording experts who made them' (1927: 102–3).

Again I will return to the ideal of documentary realism. Nothing was to destroy the listener's illusion that they were sitting in Philharmonic Hall rather than their living room. 'The art of recording was not to compete for the public's aesthetic attention to the art that was being recorded' (Kealy [1979] 1990: 211). The sound engineers' greatest achievement came about if their work was completely inaudible, and Edward Kealy refers to this objective as 'concert hall realism'. Unwanted sounds were not to be recorded, or at least were to be minimized, and desired sounds were to be recorded without distortion and with satisfying balance of volume and pitch. Between 1915 and 1925 the Edison Company embarked on a series of public demonstrations called 'tone tests'. 'These tests challenged the audience to detect the difference between the sound of new Diamond Disc records and the sound of the performers who made them' (Morton 2000: 22). There was little scientific credibility to these tests, and they were invariably staged for optimal results. Edison tried to convince the public that the phonograph, unlike a real instrument, had no 'tone' and instead faithfully reproduced the original sound without adding or subtracting anything. In short, the record was supposed to sound just like the original event (ibid.: 23). This was a clear articulation of the quest for 'perfect' or transparent sound.

Artists with an interest in experimentation had difficulties making use of the recording platform. 'The central artistic problem that they all faced was the weight of the documentary status of the recorded sound, the vocation of the recording for overt mimesis: its dogged faithfulness to the original, its empirical matter-of-factness' (Chanan 1995: 139). The gramophone reinforced ideals of musical presentation that existed in the concert hall, albeit with far inferior sound quality. Theodore Adorno ([1934] 1990: 57) criticized gramophone recording in light of its function as a mere transport medium. He said that the disc stores and reproduces 'a music that is deprived of its best dimension, a music, namely, that was already in existence before the phonograph record and is not significantly altered by it'.

Analytic listening

I have discussed the technique of analytic listening before, and now I will describe its very first appearance. One of the interesting new experiences that came about with the gramophone was the opportunity of hearing one's own voice without speaking, or for that matter of hearing oneself playing the piano without playing. Neither the telephone nor the wireless could do this. Sound recording made it possible to hear one's own voice 'infused with a lesser distribution of body because it will be a voice heard without bone conduction' (Kahn 1999: 7). It seems reasonable to say that such lack of bone conduction created a reflexive, distanced and also potentially more critical way of relating to one's own performance.

A magazine advertisement from the 1900s shows the self-confident way in which 'the Great Coquelin' related to this feature of repetition. 'Your wonderful Gramophone has at last given me what I have so much desired, the surprise and (shall I confess it?) the pleasure of hearing myself.' The third-person perspective on himself did not put Coquelin off, rather it made him identify all the more with the perspective of his audience. 'I have heard the recitation "Les Limaçons" [...] and my word ... I did what I have seen the public do for a long time, I laughed' (quoted in Gelatt 1977: 64).

The opportunity to hear one's performance over and over again of course made performers and technicians aware of all kinds of ways in which to improve the quality of the recording. All the time it would be the sound qualities *as contained on the disc* that mattered, and nothing else. Musicians have always wanted to sound good, but now this ambition had to be directed to the functionalities of the gramophone. The artists and producers would listen intently to the recording to find out what worked well and what worked poorly, and how to improve matters in the next session.

Performers and technicians learnt to notice whether a sound was suitable for recording. 'As one learns what to listen for, and as one understands more about sound and how it is used, his or her ability to remember material increases proportionally' (Moylan 1992: 153–4). People who are accomplished singers know what to listen for when they evaluate a singer's competence, and those who are accomplished recording artists know what to listen for when evaluating a recording. Certain sound qualities can only be appreciated if a parallel sound-producing practice is mastered. This training process is similar to learning a foreign language. First people can barely express themselves, but if they are clever they may learn not just to make themselves understood but to express themselves more thoroughly, and continue to expand their knowledge for years and decades to come.

Analytic listening presumes a highly specific perceptual knowledge acquired by trial and error, recording and playback evaluations and public response. This technique of listening evolved along with a vocabulary and tacit understanding that only other professionals would hear and appreciate. A new expressive field was identified in this process, and it was largely internal to the medium. There was no other creative practice where things were done in the same way (remember that sound film was not yet a reality).

On record forever

The phonograph's first practical function was as a showcase item. An advertisement for an Edison trade show in 1878 refers to 'The Miracle of the 19th

Century' and the 'Talking Machine'. 'It will Talk, Sing, Laugh, Crow, Whistle, Repeat Cornet Solos, imitating the Human Voice, enunciating and pronouncing every word perfectly, IN EVERY KNOWN LANGUAGE' (quoted in Gelatt 1977: 64). The Edison laboratory conceived of the phonograph mainly as a speech dictation machine that would be useful in offices, and also as a device for reinforcing long-distance telephone signals at relay stations (Welch and Burt 1994: 13). Notice that these are functions that do not require copies, and which have nothing to do with mass mediation.

In 1888 Edison was on a publicity tour to London, where he gathered together a group of important gentlemen for an elegant supper. They were presumably discussing more ways of promoting Edison's device, and the prospect of recording and distribution music must have been high on the agenda. The final case study is of Thomas Edison and the British composer Arthur Sullivan speaking into the horn. First they have enjoyed the excellent dinner, and now it is time for a practical demonstration of the new wonder. This recording was not intended as a public document; rather it was a gimmick for the people gathered there and then. The main attraction was that the speakers and the other dinner guests could hear their own voices played back from the machine right away.

Track 36: Thomas Edison with Arthur Sullivan, 1888 (1:28).

> Edison: Little Menlo, October 5, 1888, register. Continuation of introduction of friends. Now listen to the voice of Sir Arthur Sullivan:
> Sullivan: Dear Mr Edison, if my friend Edmund Yates has been a little incoherent it is in consequence of the excellent dinner and good wines that he has drunk. Therefore I think you will excuse him. He has his lucid intervals. For myself, I can only say that I am astonished and somewhat terrified at the result of this evening's experiments: astonished at the wonderful power you have developed, and terrified at the thought that so much hideous and bad music may be put on record for ever. But all the same I think it is the most wonderful thing that I have ever experienced, and I congratulate you with all my heart on this wonderful discovery. Arthur Sullivan.

Thomas Edison sounds quite relaxed in comparison with the composer. He has introduced many other friends before, and does it in a business-minded way without any high-flying eloquence. Arthur Sullivan, on the contrary, conceives of this as a solemn occasion and speaks with typical British solemnity. This is the first time his voice was being recorded, and Sullivan must have been acutely aware that he was speaking into the future. In light of the fact that he was putting himself on record forever, he might have chosen his words more carefully. At the beginning of his address he makes fun of one of the other dinner guests for his drunken behaviour, and it sounds as if there is general laughter among the guests. Nevertheless, Sullivan has an interesting objection to the

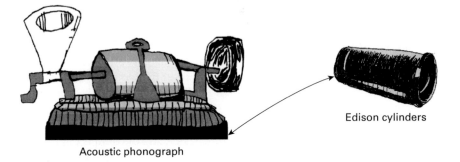

Acoustic phonograph

Edison cylinders

Figure 11.4 Model of acoustic cylinder recording.

invention of the phonograph. He is 'terrified at the thought that so much hideous and bad music may be put on record for ever'.

Sullivan is a composer, and naturally he would be concerned with the musical uses of the phonograph. And, indeed, Edison's phonograph is commonly conceived of as the fundamental technology for music recording, at least in the Anglo-American context. But this is a later interpretation that doesn't sit well with the facts. Because of the difficulty in making copies, the cylinder phonograph was ill-suited to becoming a mass medium, and it went out of prodcution around 1920 (Morton 2000: 20–2).

Figure 11.4 displays the interface, platform and signal carrier of Edison's phonograph. It is easy to see how simple the technology is compared with the later versions, where microphones, mixing boards and not least a large number of discs are part of the set-up. But the most striking difference from the other medium models is that there is only one platform involved. The cylinder phonograph did not rely, like all other recording media discussed in this book, on two different platforms for production and for reception, but could record and play back the sound on one and the same piece of machinery. Notice also that the cylinder signal carrier is quite large and unwieldy compared to the rotating disc of Berliner's gramophone.

Every cylinder was an original, and in order to make ten recordings of a performance ten phonographs would have to be placed in front of the singer and cranked by ten assistants (Gronow and Saunio 1998: 4). In later and more developed versions, Edison found a way of copying the cylinders with wax coating, but this was cumbersome and could not compete with the industrial copying of discs for the gramophone. Furthermore, the cylinder machine had very bad sound quality, and none of the moving parts were standardized. This meant that, if Edison cranked the handle unevenly while recording, to make the results sound natural he had to crank it with the same unevenness during playback. Furthermore the grooves were impermanent on account of the soft material used to coat the cylinder, and would be ground down quickly in playback. The dynamic range and volume of the sound were poor because of the primitive diaphragm technology, and great care had to be taken to avoid blasting and hissing noises (MacFarlane 1917: 37).

Although Edison's phonograph was not a true mass medium, it was clearly an enormous technological breakthrough. In the literature of sound studies the story about Edison's first successful recording in 1877 figures prominently. At the fifty-year anniversary celebration in 1927 Lindsay Buick tells the story about the first recording:

> The final adjustments having been made, Edison took hold of the crank and gave the cylinder a few turns, then spoke into the recording tube the first verse of Sarah J. Hale's nursery classic: 'Mary had a little lamb, Its fleece was white as snow, And everywhere that Mary went, The lamb was sure to go'. So far as the human eye could discern, all that had happened was that there was a slight scratch on the surface of the tinfoil, but to Edison, with his previous experience of paper records, that scratch meant much. When the crank of the machine was turned back, and this little groove was placed opposite the reproducing needle, it was found that Mary had the lamb all right. No sooner had Edison, with bated breath, begun to turn the handle again, than there came back to him his very words clothed in his very accent. Not, it is true, so loudly as he had pronounced them, but loud enough and clear enough to leave no doubt that the machine had spoken and that the problem of reproducing the human voice was indisputably solved.
>
> (Buick 1927: 40)

Before this invention was made people had lived without reproduction of human voices. Going backwards through history there are fewer and fewer users until there are none at all. The technology is less well functioning and less complex until there are only first-generation prototypes in the laboratory. Ultimately the backwards history brings us to a time when there were no sound media, and the story ends.

References

Aarseth, Espen (1993) 'Postindustriell kulturindustri' [Post-industrial culture industry] in
Rasmussen, Terje, and Søby, Morten (eds) *Kulturens digitale felt*. Oslo: Aventura.

Åberg, Carin (1999) *The Sounds of Radio: On Radio as an Auditive Means of Communication*.
Stockholm: Department of Journalism, Media and Communication, Stockholm
University.

Adorno, Theodore W. ([1934] 1990) 'The Form of the Phonograph Record', trans. Thomas
Y. Levin. *October*, no. 55.

Aitken, Hugh (1976) *Syntony and Spark: The Origins of Radio*. Princeton, NJ: Princeton
University Press.

—— (1985) *The Continuous Wave: Technology and American Radio 1900–1932*. Princeton,
NJ: Princeton University Press.

Alderman, John (2001) *Sonic Boom: Napster, mp3, and the New Pioneers of Music*. New York:
Basic Books.

Altman, Rick (1992a) 'The Material Heterogeneity of Recorded Sound', in Altman (ed.)
Sound Theory: Sound Practice. New York: Routledge.

—— (1992b) 'Sound Space', in Altman (ed.) *Sound Theory: Sound Practice*. New York: Routledge.

—— (2004) *Silent Film Sound*. New York: Columbia University Press.

Arnheim, Rudolf ([1936] 1986) *Radio*, trans. Margaret Ludwig and Herbert Read. Salem,
NH: Ayer.

Attali, Jacques (1985) *Noise: The Political Economy of Music*, trans. Brian Massumi.
Minneapolis: University of Minneapolis Press.

Auslander, Philip (1999) *Liveness: Performance in a Mediatized Culture*. New York: Routledge.

Barnett, Kyle S. (2006) 'Furniture Music: The Phonograph as Furniture 1900–1930', *Journal
of Popular Music Studies*, 18(3): 301–24.

Barnouw, Erik (1966) *A Tower in Babel: A History of Broadcasting in the United States*, Vol. 1:
To 1933. New York: Oxford University Press.

—— (1968) *The Golden Web: A History of Broadcasting in the United States*, Vol. 2: *1933 to
1953*. New York: Oxford University Press.

—— ([1975] 1990) *Tube of Plenty: The Evolution of American Television*. New York: Oxford
University Press.

Barthes, Roland (1977) 'The Grain of the Voice', in *Image, Text, Music*, trans. Stephen Heath.
London: Fontana.

Barthes, Roland ([1972] 1993) *Mythologies*, trans. Annette Lavers. London: Vintage.

Bastiansen, Henrik Grue (1994) *'Live from Moon': En case-studie i fjernsynets historie* [Live from
the moon: A case study in the history of television]. Oslo: Norwegian Research Council.

Beniger, James (1991) 'The Control Revolution', in Crowley, David, and Heyer, Paul (eds) *Communication in History: Technology, Culture, Society*. New York: Longman.

Bergmeier, Horst, and Lotz, Rainer (1997) *Hitler's Airwaves: The Inside Story of Nazi Radio Broadcasting and Propaganda Swing*. New Haven, CT: Yale University Press.

Berry, Richard (2006) 'Will the iPod Kill the Radio Star? Profiling Podcasting as Radio', *Convergence*, 12(2): 143–62.

Bitzer, Lloyd ([1968] 1991) 'The Rhetorical Situation', in Medhurst, M. J., and Benson, T. W. (eds) *Rhetorical Dimensions in Media: A Critical Casebook*. Dubuque, IA: Kendall/Hunt.

Blesser, Barry, and Salter, Linda-Ruth (2007) *Spaces Speak, Are You Listening? Experiencing Aural Architecture*. Cambridge, MA: MIT Press.

Blondheim, Menahem (2003) 'Harold Adams Innis and his Bias of Communication', in Katz, Elihu, *et al.* (eds) *Canonic Texts in Media Research: Are There Any? Should There be Any? How About These?* Cambridge: Polity.

Bolter, J. David, and Grusin, Richard (1999) *Remediation: Understanding New Media*. Cambridge, MA: MIT Press.

Boorstin, Daniel ([1961] 1985) *The Image: A Guide to Pseudo-Events in America*. New York: Atheneum.

Borgmann, Albert (1984) *Technology and the Character of Contemporary Life*. Chicago: University of Chicago Press.

—— (1999) *Holding on to Reality: The Nature of Information at the Turn of the Millennium*. Chicago: University of Chicago Press.

Boyd, Andrew (1988) *Broadcast Journalism: Techniques of Radio and TV News*. Oxford: Heinemann.

Brand, Graham, and Scannell, Paddy (1991) 'Talk, Identity and Performance: *The Tony Blackburn Show*', in Scannell (ed.) *Broadcast Talk*. London: Sage.

Brecht, Bertolt ([1932] 2001) 'The Radio as a Communications Apparatus', in Silberman, Marc (ed.) *Brecht on Film and Radio*. London: Methuen.

Briggs, Asa (1965) *The Golden Age of Wireless: The History of Broadcasting in the United Kingdom*. Vol. 2. London: Oxford University Press.

—— (1970) *The War of Worlds: The History of Broadcasting in the United Kingdom*, Vol. 3. London: Oxford University Press.

—— ([1961] 2000) *The Birth of Broadcasting: The History of Broadcasting in the United Kingdom*, Vol. 1. London: Oxford University Press.

Briggs, Asa, and Burke, Peter (2002) *A Social History of the Media: From Gutenberg to the Internet*. Cambridge: Polity.

Brooks, John (1975) *Telephone: The First Hundred Years*. New York: Harper & Row.

Brummett, Barry (1991) *Rhetorical Dimensions of Popular Culture*. Tuscaloosa: University of Alabama Press.

Bruzelius, Margaret (2001) 'What to Say when You Talk to Yourself: The Tower of Psychobabble', in Salamensky, S. I. (ed.) *Talk, Talk, Talk: The Cultural Life of Everyday Conversation*. New York: Routledge.

Buick, T. Lindsay (1927) *The Romance of the Gramophone*. Wellington: Ernest Dawson.

Bull, Michael (2000) *Sounding out the City: Personal Stereos and the Management of Everyday Life*. Oxford: Berg.

—— (2003) 'Soundscapes of the Car: A Critical Study of Automobile Habitation', in Bull, Michael, and Black, Les (eds) *The Auditory Culture Reader*. Oxford: Berg.

Bull, Michael, and Black, Les (eds) (2003) *The Auditory Culture Reader*. Oxford: Berg.

Burke, Kenneth ([1950] 1969) *A Rhetoric of Motives*. Berkeley: University of California Press.

Cantril, Hadley, and Allport, Gordon ([1935] 1986) *The Psychology of Radio*. New York: Peter Smith.

Carey, James (1989) 'A Cultural Approach to Communication', in *Communication as Culture: Essays on Media and Society*. New York: Routledge.

Carey, James, and Quirk, John (1989) 'The Mythos of the Electronic Revolution', in Carey, *Communication as Culture: Essays on Media and Society*. New York: Routledge.

Carpenter, Edmund ([1960] 1979) 'The New Languages', in Gumpert, Gary, and Cathcart, Robert (eds) *INTER/MEDIA: Interpersonal Communication in a Media World*. New York: Oxford University Press.

Carpentier, Nico (2005) 'Identity, Contingency and Rigidity: The (Counter-)hegemonic Constructions of the Identity of the Media Professional', *Journalism*, 6(2): 199–219.

Carter, Harold (1995) *The Study of Urban Geography*. London: Arnold.

Chanan, Michael (1995) *Repeated Takes: A Short History of Recording and its Effects on Music*. New York: Verso.

Chion, Michel (1994) *Audio-Vision: Sound on Screen*. New York: Columbia University Press.

Connell, John, and Gibson, Chris (2003) *Sound Tracks: Popular Music, Identity and Place*. London: Routledge.

Couldry, Nick (2004) 'Liveness, "Reality", and the Mediated Habitus from Television to the Mobile Phone', *Communication Review*, 7: 353–61.

Coyle, Rebecca (2000) 'Observations from an Experiment in "Internet radio"', *Convergence*, 6(3): 57–75.

Crisell, Andrew (1994) *Understanding Radio*. London: Routledge.

—— (1997) *An Introductory History of British Broadcasting*. London: Routledge.

Cunningham, Mark (1998) *Good Vibrations: A History of Record Production*. London: Sanctuary.

Dahl, Hans Fredrik (1999a) *Hallo – hallo! Kringkastingen i Norge 1920–1940*. [Hello – hello! Norwegian broadcasting 1920–1940]. Oslo: Cappelen.

Dahl, Hans Fredrik (1999b) *Dette er London: NRK i krig 1940–1945*. [This is London: NRK at war 1940–1945]. Oslo: Cappelen.

Dahlén, Peter (1999) *Från Vasaloppet till Sportsextra*. [From the Vasa Race to Sports Extra]. Värnamo: Stiftelsen Etermedierna i Sverige.

Danielsen, Anne (2006) *Presence and Pleasure: The Funk Grooves of James Brown and Parliament*. Middletown, CT: Wesleyan University Press.

Danielsen, Anne, and Maasø, Arnt (forthcoming) 'Mediating Music: Materiality and Silence in Madonna's Don't Tell Me', *Popular Music*.

Day, Timothy (2000) *A Century of Recorded Music: Listening to Musical History*. London: Yale University Press.

Dayan, Daniel, and Katz, Elihu (1992) *Media Events: The Live Broadcasting of History*. Cambridge, MA: Harvard University Press.

Delys, Sherre, and Foley, Marius (2006) 'The Exchange: A Radio-Web Project for Creative Practitioners and Researchers', *Convergence*, (12)2: 129–35.

DeNora, Tia (2000) *Music in Everyday Life*. Cambridge: Cambridge University Press.

Douglas, Susan (1987) *Inventing American Broadcasting 1899–1922*. Baltimore: Johns Hopkins University Press.

—— (1999) *Listening In: Radio and the American Imagination*. New York: Times Books.

—— (2002) 'Letting the Boys be Boys: Talk Radio, Male Hysteria, and Political Discourse in the 1980s', in Hilmes, Michele, and Loviglio, Jason (eds) *Radio Reader: Essays in the Cultural History of Radio*. New York: Routledge.

Dymling, Carl Anders (ed.) (1934) *Röster om radio: Intryck och erfarenheter av tio års svensk rundradio*. [Voices about radio: Impressions and experiences after ten years of Swedish broadcasting]. Stockholm: P. A. Norstedt.

Eisenberg, Evan (1987) *The Recording Angel: Explorations in Phonography*. New York: McGraw-Hill.

Ellis, John (1999) 'Television as Working-Through', in Gripsrud, Jostein (ed.) *Television and Common Knowledge*. London: Routledge.

—— (2000) *Seeing Things: Television in the Age of Uncertainty*. London: I. B. Tauris.

Ellul, Jacques (1964) *The Technological Society*, trans. John Wilkinson. New York: Vintage Books.

Enli, Gunn (2007) *The Participatory Turn in Broadcast Television: Institutional, Editorial and Textual Challenges and Strategies*. Oslo: Unipub.

Fafner, Jørgen (1982) *Tanke og Tale: Den retoriske tradition i Vesteuropa*. [Thought and speech: The rhetorical tradition in Western Europe]. Copenhagen: C. A. Reitzel.

Feuer, Jane (1983) 'The Concept of Live Television: Ontology as Ideology', in Kaplan, Ann E. (ed.) *Regarding Television: Critical Approaches*. Frederick, MD: American Film Institute.

Fornatale, Peter, and Mills, Joshua (1980) *Radio in the Television Age*. Woodstock, NY: Overlook Press.

Foss, Sonja K. (1996) *Rhetorical Criticism: Exploration & Practice*. Prospect Heights, IL: Waveland Press.

Frith, Simon (1981) *Sound Effects: Youth, Leisure, and the Politics of Rock*. New York: Pantheon Books.

—— (1998) *Performing Rites: Evaluating Popular Music*. Oxford: Oxford University Press.

Gauntlett, David (ed.) (2000) *Web.studies: Rewiring Media Studies for the Digital Age*. London: Arnold.

Gelatt, Roland (1977) *The Fabulous Phonograph: From Edison to Stereo*. New York: Appleton-Century.

Genosko, Gary (1999) *McLuhan and Baudrillard: The Masters of Implosion*. New York: Routledge.

Gentikow, Barbara (2007) 'The Role of Media in Developing Literacies and Cultural Techniques', *Nordic Journal of Digital Literacy* 2(2): 78–96.

Gibson, James J. (1966) *The Senses Considered as Perceptual Systems*. Boston: Houghton Mifflin.

Giddens, Anthony (1991) *Modernity and Self-Identity: Self and Society in the Late Modern Age*. Cambridge: Polity.

Gitlin, Todd (2002) *Media Unlimited: How the Torrent of Images and Sounds Overwhelms our Lives*. New York: Henry Holt.

Goffman, Erving (1981) 'Radio Talk', in *Forms of Talk*. Philadelphia: University of Pennsylvania Press.

—— ([1959] 1990) *The Presentation of Self in Everyday Life*. New York: Anchor Books.

Goldsmith, Alfred, and Lescarboura, Austin (1930) *This Thing Called Broadcasting*. New York: Henry Holt.

Goodwin, Andrew (1990) 'Sample and Hold: Pop Music in the Digital Age of Reproduction', in Frith, Simon, and Goodwin (eds) *On Record: Rock, Pop & the Written Word*. London: Routledge.

Goodwin, Robert (ed.) (1999) *Apollo 11: The NASA Mission Reports*, Vol. 1 Ontario: Apogee.

Gould, Glenn (1984) *The Glenn Gould Reader*, ed. Tim Page. New York: Vintage Books.

Gracyk, Theodore (1996) *Rhythm and Noise: An Aesthetics of Rock*. London: I. B. Tauris.

Gronow, Pekka, and Saunio, Ilpo (1998) *An International History of the Recording Industry*, trans. Christopher Moseley. London: Cassell.

Grosswiler, Paul (1998) *The Method is the Message: Rethinking McLuhan through Critical Theory*. Montreal: Black Rose Books.

Gumbrecht, Hans, and Pfeiffer, K. Ludwig (eds) (1994) *Materialities of Communication*, trans. William Whobrey. Stanford, CA: Stanford University Press.

Gumpert, Gary (1979) 'The Ambiguity of Perception', in Gumpert and Cathcart, Robert (eds) *INTER/MEDIA: Interpersonal Communication in a Media World*. New York: Oxford University Press.

Gumpert, Gary, and Cathcart, Robert (eds) (1979) *INTER/MEDIA: Interpersonal Communication in a Media World*. New York: Oxford University Press.

Hacker, Scot (2000) *MP3: The Definitive Guide*. Sebastopol, CA: O'Reilly.

Hall, Edward T. (1969) *The Hidden Dimension: Man's Use of Space in Public and Private*. London: Bodley Head.

Handel, Stephen (1989) *Listening: An Introduction to the Perception of Auditory Events*. Cambridge, MA: MIT Press.

Harley, Robert (1998) *The Complete Guide to High-End Audio*. Albuquerque, NM: Acapella.

Head, Sydney, and Sterling, Christopher (1978) *Broadcasting in America: A Survey of Television, Radio, and New Technologies*. Boston: Houghton Mifflin.

Head, Sydney, Sterling, Christopher, and Schofield, Lemuel (1996) *Broadcasting in America: A Survey of Electronic Media*. Boston: Houghton Mifflin.

Hendy, David (2000) *Radio in the Global Age*. Cambridge: Polity.

—— (2007) *Life on Air: A History of Radio Four*. Oxford: Oxford University Press.

Herbert, John (2000) *Journalism in the Digital Age*. Oxford: Focal Press.

Herman, Andrew, and Swiss, Thomas (eds) (2000) *The World Wide Web and Contemporary Cultural Theory*. New York: Routledge.

Hill, Annette (2005) *Reality TV: Audiences and Popular Factual Television*. London: Routledge.

Hobsbawm, Eric (1989) *The Age of Empire 1875–1914*. London: Cardinal.

—— (1994) *Age of Extremes: The Short Twentieth Century, 1914–1991*. London: Michael Joseph.

Honeybone, Andy, *et al.* (1995) *What's MIDI*. Swanley: Nexus.

Hornby, Nick (1995) *High Fidelity*. London: Gollancz.

Horton, Donald, and Wohl, Richard ([1956] 1979) 'Mass Communication and Para-Social Interaction: Observations on Intimacy at a Distance', in Gumpert, Gary, and Cathcart, Robert (eds) *INTER/MEDIA: Interpersonal Communication in a Media World*. New York: Oxford University Press.

Hutchby, Ian (1991) 'The Organization of Talk on Talk Radio', in Scannell, Paddy (ed.) *Broadcast Talk*. London: Sage.

—— (2001) *Conversation and Technology: From the Telephone to the Internet*. Cambridge: Polity.

Ihde, Don (1990) *Technology and the Lifeworld: From Garden to Earth*. Indianapolis: Indiana University Press.

—— ([1976] 2007) *Listening and Voice: A Phenomenology of Sound*. Albany: State University of New York Press.

Inglis, Andrew F. (1990) *Behind the Tube: A History of Broadcasting Technology and Business*. Boston: Focal Press.

Innis, Harold ([1951] 1991) *The Bias of Communication*. Toronto: University of Toronto Press.

Jauert, Per, and Lowe, Gregory F. (2005) 'Public Service Broadcasting for Social and Cultural Citizenship: Renewing the Enlightenment Mission', in Lowe and Jauert (eds) *Cultural Dilemmas in Public Service Broadcasting*. Gothenburg: Nordicom.

Jensen, Klaus Bruhn (1995) *The Social Semiotics of Mass Communication*. London: Sage.

Johansen, Anders (1999) 'Credibility and Media Development', in Gripsrud, Jostein (ed.) *Television and Common Knowledge*. London: Routledge.

—— (2002) *Talerens troverdighet: Tekniske og kulturelle betingelser for politisk retorikk* [The speaker's credibility: Technical and cultural preconditions for political rhetoric]. Oslo: Universitetsforlaget.

Johnson, Paul (1999) *A History of the American People*. New York: Harper Perennial.

Johnson, Steven (1997) *Interface Culture: How New Technology Transforms the Way We Create and Communicate*. San Francisco: HarperEdge.

Jones, Steve (1992) *Rock Formation: Music, Technology, and Mass Communication*. Newbury Park, CA: Sage.

—— (2000) 'Music and the Internet', *Popular Music*, 19(2): 217–30.

—— (2002) 'Music that Moves: Popular Music, Distribution and Network Technologies', *Cultural Studies*, 16(2): 213–32.

Kahn, Douglas (1999) *Noise, Water, Meat: A History of Sound in the Arts*. Cambridge, MA: MIT Press.

Katz, James E. (2006) *Magic in the Air: Mobile Communication and the Transformation of Social Life*. New Brunswick, NJ: Transaction Books.

Katz, James E., and Aakhus, Mark (2002) *Perpetual Contact: Mobile Communication, Private Talk, Public Performance*. Cambridge: Cambridge University Press.

Katz, Mark (2004) *Capturing Sound: How Technology Has Changed Music*. Berkeley: University of California Press.

Kealy, Edward R. ([1979] 1990) 'From Craft to Art: The Case of Sound Mixers and Popular Music', in Frith, Simon, and Goodwin, Andrew (eds) *On Record: Rock, Pop & the Written Word*. London: Routledge.

Kennedy, Rick (1994) *Jelly Roll, Bix, and Hoagy: Gennett Studios and the Birth of Recorded Jazz*. Bloomington: Indiana University Press.

Kerckhove, Derrick de (1995) *The Skin of Culture: Investigating the New Electronic Reality*. London: Kogan Page.

Kittler, Friedrich (1999) *Gramophone, Film, Typewriter*, trans. Geoffrey Winthrop-Young and Michael Wutz. Stanford, CA: Stanford University Press.

Kretschmer, Martin, Klimis, George, and Wallis, Roger (2001) 'Music in Electronic Markets', *New Media and Society*, 3(4): 417–41.

Langer, John (1981) 'Television's Personality System', *Media, Culture & Society*, 3(4).

Lanza, Joseph (2004) *Elevator Music: A Surreal History of Muzak, Easy-Listening, and Other Moodsong*. Ann Arbor: University of Michigan Press.

Larner, Gerald (1996) *Maurice Ravel*. London: Phaidon Press.

Lastra, James (2000) *Sound Technology and the American Cinema: Perception, Representation, Modernity*. New York: Columbia University Press.

Lax, Stephen (2008) *Media and Communication Technologies: A Critical Introduction*. London: Palgrave.

Lax, Stephen, Shaw, Helen, Ala-Fossi, Marko, and Jauert, Per (2008) 'DAB – the Future of Radio? The Development of Digital Radio in Four European Countries', *Media, Culture & Society*, 30(2).

Leandros, Nicos (ed.) (2006) *The Impact of the Internet on the Mass Media in Europe*. Bury St Edmunds: Arima.

Leeuwen, Theo van (1999) *Speech, Music, Sound*. Basingstoke: Macmillan.

Levinson, Paul (1999) *Digital McLuhan: A Guide to the Information Millennium*. New York: Routledge.

Levy, Steven (2006) *The Perfect Thing: How the iPod Shuffles Commerce, Culture and Coolness.* New York: Simon & Schuster.

Lewis, Tom (1991) *Empire of the Air: The Men Who Made Radio.* New York: Edward Burlingame.

Ling, Rich (2004) *The Mobile Connection: The Cell Phone's Impact on Society.* Amsterdam: Elsevier.

Livingstone, Sonia (1999) 'New Media, New Audiences?', *New Media & Society* 1(1): 59–66.

Lowe, Greg, and Jauert, Per (eds) (2005) *Cultural Dilemmas in Public Service Broadcasting.* Gothenburg: Nordicom.

Maasø, Arnt (2002) *'Se hva som skjer': En studie av lyd som kommunikativt virkemiddel i TV.* ['See what's happening': A study of sound as a communicative means in TV]. Oslo: Unipub.

McCaffery, Steve (1997) 'From Phonic to Sonic: The Emergence of the Audio-Poem', in Morris, Adelaide (ed.) *Sound States: Innovative Poetics and Acoustical Technologies.* Chapel Hill: University of North Carolina Press.

McClary, Susan (2003) 'Bessie Smith: Thinking Blues', in Bull, Michael, and Black, Les (eds) *The Auditory Culture Reader.* Oxford: Berg.

MacFarlane, Lloyd (1917) *The Phonograph Book.* New York: Rider–Long.

McLeish, Robert (1999) *Radio Production.* Oxford: Focal Press.

McLuhan, Marshall ([1962] 1992) *The Gutenberg Galaxy: The Making of Typographic Man.* Toronto: University of Toronto Press.

—— ([1964] 1994) *Understanding Media: The Extensions of Man.* Cambridge, MA: MIT Press.

McLuhan, Marshall, and Fiore, Quentin (1967) *The Medium is the Massage: An Inventory of Effects.* New York: Bantam Books.

Manovich, Lev (2001) *The Language of New Media.* Cambridge, MA: MIT Press.

Marvin, Carolyn (1988) *When Old Technologies Were New: Thinking about Electric Communication in the Late Nineteenth Century.* New York: Oxford University Press.

Marwick, Arthur (1998) *The Sixties: Cultural Revolution in Britain, France, Italy and the United States, c. 1958–c. 1974.* Oxford: Oxford University Press.

Mathieu, W. A. (1991) *The Listening Book: Discovering your own Music.* Boston: Shambhala.

Mercer, David (2006) *The Telephone: The Life Story of a Technology.* Westport, CT: Greenwood Press.

Merleau-Ponty, Maurice ([1945] 1992) *Phenomenology of Perception*, trans. Colin Smith. London: Routledge.

Metz, Christian (1985) 'Aural Objects', in Weis, Elisabeth, and Belton, John (eds) *Film Sound: Theory and Practice*, trans. Georgia Gurrieri. New York: Columbia University Press.

Meyrowitz, Joshua (1979) 'Television and Interpersonal Behavior: Codes of Perception and Response', in Gumpert, Gary, and Cathcart, Robert (eds) *INTER/MEDIA: Interpersonal Communication in a Media World.* New York: Oxford University Press.

—— (1985) *No Sense of Place: The Impact of Electronic Media on Social Behavior.* New York: Oxford University Press.

—— (1994) 'Medium Theory', in Crowley, and Mitchell, David (eds) *Communication Theory Today.* Cambridge: Polity.

Middleton, Richard (1990) *Studying Popular Music.* Philadelphia: Open University Press.

Millard, Andre (2005) *America on Record: A History of Recorded Sound.* Cambridge: Cambridge University Press.

Miller, Daniel, and Slater, Don (2000) *The Internet: An Ethnographic Approach.* Oxford: Berg.

Miller, Jonathan (1971) *McLuhan.* London: Fontana/Collins.

Mitcham, Carl (1994) *Thinking through Technology: The Path between Engineering and Philosophy.* Chicago: University of Chicago Press.

Moore, Jerrold N. (1999) *Sound Revolutions: A Biography of Fred Gaisberg.* London: Sanctuary.

Moores, Shaun (1988) '"The Box on the Dresser": Memories of Early Radio and Everyday Life', *Media, Culture & Society,* 10(1).

—— (2000) *Media and Everyday Life in Modern Society.* Edinburgh: Edinburgh University Press.

Morley, David (2000) *Home Territories: Media, Mobility and Identity.* London: Routledge.

Morton, David (2000) *Off the Record: The Technology and Culture of Sound Recording in America.* New Brunswick, NJ: Rutgers University Press.

Moss, John, and Morra, Linda M. (eds) (2004) *At the Speed of Light There is Only Illumination: A Reappraisal of Marshall McLuhan.* Ottawa: University of Ottawa Press.

Mott, Robert L. (1990) *Sound Effects: Radio, TV, and Film.* Boston: Focal Press.

Moylan, William (1992) *The Art of Recording: The Creative Resources of Music Production and Audio.* New York: Van Nostrand Reinhold.

Murdock, Graham (2005) 'Building the Digital Commons: Public Broadcasting in the Age of the Internet', in Lowe, Greg and Jauert, Per (eds) *Cultural Dilemmas in Public Service Broadcasting.* Stockholm: Nordicom.

Naughton, John (1999) *A Brief History of the Future: The Origins of the Internet.* London: Weidenfeld & Nicolson.

Nyre, Lars (2003) *Fidelity Matters: Sound Media and Realism in the 20th Century.* Volda: Volda University College [doctorate thesis].

—— (2007a) 'Minimum Journalism: Experimental Procedures for Democratic Participation in Sound Media', *Journalism Studies* (8)3: 397–413.

—— (2007b) 'What Happens when I Turn on the TV Set?', *Westminster Papers in Communication and Culture,* 4(2).

Nyre, Lars, and Ala-Fossi, Marko (2008) 'The Next Generation Platform: Comparing Audience Registration and Participation in Digital Sound Media', *Journal of Radio and Audio Media,* no. 1.

Ong, Walter (1982) *Orality & Literacy: The Technologizing of the Word.* New York: Methuen.

O'Sullivan, Sara (2005) 'The Whole Nation is Listening to You: The Presentation of the Self on a Tabloid Talk Radio Show', *Media, Culture & Society,* 27(5): 719–38.

Pegg, Mark (1983) *Broadcasting and Society 1918–1939.* London: Croom Helm.

Perloff, Marjorie (1997) 'The Music of Verbal Space: John Cage's "What You Say …"', in Morris, Adelaide (ed.) *Sound States: Innovative Poetics and Acoustical Technologies.* Chapel Hill: University of North Carolina Press.

Peters, John Durham (1999) *Speaking into the Air: A History of the Idea of Communication.* Chicago: University of Chicago Press.

—— (2001) 'Witnessing', *Media, Culture & Society,* 23(6).

Phillips, Tony (2001) 'The Great Moon Hoax', at http://science.nasa.gov/headlines/y2001/ast23feb_2.htm (accessed 23 November 2007).

Plomp, Reinier (2002) *The Intelligent Ear: On the Nature of Sound Perception.* London: Erlbaum.

Pool, Ithiel de Sola (ed.) (1977) *The Social Impact of the Telephone.* Cambridge, MA: MIT Press.

Priestman, Chris (2002) *Web Radio: Radio Production for Internet Streaming.* Oxford: Focal Press.

Radio World (2007) 'Imus to Return to Radio', at www.radioworld.com/pages/s.0100/t.9449.html (accessed 23 November 2007)

Rheingold, Howard ([1985] 2000) *Tools for Thought: The People and Ideas behind the Next Computer Revolution.* New York: Simon & Schuster.

—— (2002) *Smart Mobs: The Next Social Revolution.* Cambridge, MA: Basic Books.

Riesman, David ([1950] 1990) 'Listening to Popular Music', in Frith, Simon, and Goodwin, Andrew (eds) *On Record: Rock, Pop & the Written Word*. London: Routledge.

Rodman, Gilbert, and Vanderdonckt, Cheyanne (2006) 'Music for Nothing, or, I Want my mp3: The Regulation and Recirculation of Affect', *Cultural Studies* 20(2–3): 245–61.

Ross, Karen (2004) 'Political Talk Radio and Democratic Participation: Caller Perspectives on Election Call', *Media, Culture & Society* 26(6): 785–801.

Salamensky, S. I. (ed.) (2001) *Talk, Talk, Talk: The Cultural Life of Everyday Conversation*. New York: Routledge.

Scannell, Paddy (ed.) (1991) *Broadcast Talk*. London: Sage.

—— (1996) *Radio, Television & Modern Life*. Oxford: Blackwell.

—— (1998) 'What Happens when I (or Anyone) Turn on the TV Set?', unpublished manuscript presented at the conference Developments in Nordic Broadcasting, Voksenaasen Hotel, Oslo, 22–4 March.

—— (2000) 'For Anyone as Someone Structures', *Media, Culture & Society*, 22(1).

—— (2005) 'The Meaning of *Broad*casting in the Digital Era', in Lowe, Greg, and Jauert, Per (eds) *Cultural Dilemmas in Public Service Broadcasting*. Gothenburg: Nordicom.

Scannell, Paddy, and Cardiff, David (1991) *A Social History of British Broadcasting*, Vol. 1: *1922–1939: Serving the Nation*. Oxford: Blackwell.

Schafer, R. Murray ([1977] 1994) *The Soundscape: Our Sonic Environment and the Tuning of the World*. Rochester, NY: Destiny Books.

Scheuer, Jeffrey (2001) *The Sound Bite Society: How Television Helps the Right and Hurts the Left*. New York: Routledge.

Schlesinger, Philip (1992) *Putting 'Reality' Together*. London: Constable.

Schudson, Michael (1991) 'Historical Approaches to Communication Studies', in Jensen, Klaus B., and Jankowski, Nicholas (eds) *A Handbook of Qualitative Methodologies for Mass Communication Research*. London: Routledge.

Schutz, Alfred (1970) *On Phenomenology and Social Relations*. Chicago: University of Chicago Press.

Schwartz, Tony (1974) *The Responsive Chord*. New York: Anchor Books.

Sconce, Jeffrey (2000) *Haunted Media: Electronic Presence from Telegraphy to Television*. Durham, NC: Duke University Press.

Sennett, Richard ([1974] 1988) *The Fall of Public Man*. London: Faber & Faber.

Shelton, Robert (1987) *No Direction Home: The Life and Music of Bob Dylan*. London: Penguin.

Shingler, M., and Wieringa, C. (1998) *On Air: Methods and Meanings of Radio*. London: Arnold.

Shuker, Roy (2001) *Understanding Popular Music*. London: Routledge.

Siapera, E. (2004) 'From Couch Potatoes to Cybernauts? The Expanding Notion of the Audience on TV Channels' Websites', *New Media & Society* 6(2): 155–72.

Simpson, Ron (1998) *Cutting Edge Web Audio*. Upper Saddle River, NJ: Prentice-Hall.

Snyder, Ross ([1966] 1979) 'Architects of Contemporary Man's Consciousness', in Gumpert, Gary, and Cathcart, Robert (eds) *INTER/MEDIA: Interpersonal Communication in a Media World*. New York: Oxford University Press.

Sterling, Christopher, and Kittross, John (1991) 'The Golden Age of Programming', in Crowley, David, and Heyer, Paul (eds) *Communication in History: Technology, Culture, Society*. New York: Longman.

Sterne, Jonathan (1997) 'Sounds like the Mall of America: Programmed Music and the Architectonics of Commercial Space', *Ethnomusicology*, 41: 22–50.

—— (2003) *The Audible Past: Cultural Origins of Sound Reproduction*. Durham, NC: Duke University Press.

—— (2006) 'The mp3 as Cultural Artifact', *New Media & Society* 8(5): 825–42.

Stott, William (1991) 'Documenting Media', in Crowley, David, and Heyer, Paul (eds) *Communication in History: Technology, Culture, Society*. New York: Longman.

Théberge, Paul (1997) *Any Sound You Can Imagine: Making Music/Consuming Technology*. Hanover, NH: Wesleyan University Press.

Thompson, Robert, and Thompson, Barbara F. (2000) *PC Hardware in a Nutshell: A Desktop Quick Reference*. Cambridge: O'Reilly.

Tolson, Andrew (2006) *Media Talk: Spoken Discourse on TV and Radio*. Edinburgh: Edinburgh University Press.

Tuchman, Gaye (1978) *Making News: A Study in the Construction of Reality*. New York: Free Press.

Turkle, Sherry (1997) *Life on the Screen: Identity in the Age of the Internet*. London: Phoenix.

Vowell, Sarah (1997) *Radio On: A Listener's Diary*. New York: St Martin's Press.

Watkinson, John (1998) *The Art of Sound Reproduction*. Oxford: Focal Press.

Watson, Ben (1993) *Frank Zappa: The Negative Dialectics of Poodle Play*. London: Quartet.

Welch, Walter, and Burt, Leah (1994) *From Tinfoil to Stereo: The Acoustic Years of the Recording Industry 1877–1929*. Gainesville: University Press of Florida.

Westergren, Tim (2007) 'The Music Genome Project©', at http://www.pandora.com/mgp.shtml (accessed October 2007).

White, Paul (1997) *Basic Digital Recording*. London: MPG Books.

Williams, Raymond ([1975] 1990) *Television: Technology and Cultural Form*. London: Routledge.

Winner, Langdon (1986) *The Whale & the Reactor: A Search for Limits in an Age of High Technology*. Chicago: University of Chicago Press.

Winston, Brian (1998) *Media Technology and Society: A History from the Telegraph to the Internet*. London: Routledge.

—— (2005) *Messages: Free Expression, Media and the West from Gutenberg to Google*. London: Routledge.

Wurtzler, Steve (1992) '"She Sang Live, but the Microphone was Turned off": The Live, the Recorded and the *Subject* of Representation', in Altman, Rick (ed.) *Sound Theory: Sound Practice*. New York: Routledge.

—— (2007) *Electric Sounds: Technological Change and the Rise of Corporate Mass Media*. New York: Columbia University Press.

Ytreberg, Espen (2002) 'Erving Goffman as a Theorist of the Mass Media', *Critical Studies in Media Communication*, 19(4).

—— (2004) 'Formatting Participation within Broadcast Media Production', *Media, Culture & Society* 26(5): 677–92.

Zielinski, Siegfried (2006) *Deep Time of the Media: Toward an Archaeology of Hearing and Seeing by Technical Means*, trans. Gloria Custance. Cambridge, MA: MIT Press.

Zinn, Howard ([1980] 2003) *A People's History of the United States: 1492–Present*. New York: HarperCollins.

Soundtrack supplement

The soundtrack CD is not a professional audio production; it is a series of historical examples relating to the academic argument of this book. No attempt has been made to polish the sound; however, on some tracks the volume has been adjusted to avoid variations in level. No changes have been made in the continuity of the recordings, except to start and stop the re-recording process. This supplement lists the source for the track, the re-recording process made for this CD publication, and the copyright situation.

The following tracks were reproduced with kind permission. While every effort has been made to trace copyright holders and obtain permission, this has not been possible in all cases. Any omissions brought to our attention will be remedied in future editions.

Track 1: Marshall McLuhan: *The Medium is the Massage*, 1967 (1:42). Source: The LP *The Medium is the Massage with Marshall McLuhan*, Columbia CS9501 (1967). Written by Marshall McLuhan, Quentin Fiore and Jerome Agel, and produced by John Simon. The track was re-recorded from the original stereo LP to wav file. Copyright: published with the kind permission of Jerome Agel.

Track 2: Cleveland Orchestra: *La Valse*, 1991 (1:13). Source: The CD *Ravel. Boléro. La Valse. Rapsodie Espagnole* (1996). Decca 448-708-2 (DDD). The recording was made in 1991 and released in 1996. The track was re-recorded from the stereo CD to wav file. Copyright: published with the kind permission of Universal Music TV.

Track 3: London Symphony Orchestra: *La Valse*, 1970 (1:18). Source: The LP *Ravel. Boléro. Rapsodie Espagnole. La Valse. Tzigane* (1970). Philips 6-580-031. The track was rerecorded from the stereo LP to wav file. Copyright: published with the kind permission of Universal Music TV.

Track 4: Orchestre Lamoureux: *La Valse*, 1931 (1:02). Source: A 78 rpm release by Polydor, F 20120 (1931). The track was re-recorded by playing the 78 rpm on a wind-up gramophone, picking up the sound with a microphone, and recording it on a wav file. Copyright: it is believed that the recording has entered the public domain, and can be used within the fair use framework for educational purposes such as criticism, comment, teaching, scholarship, and research.

Track 5: *Modem sounds* (0:27). Source: An mp3 file acquired from http://freesound.iua.upf.edu/samplesViewSingle.php?id=16475. The file was added by Jlew in March 2006. The track was rerecorded from mp3 to wav file. Copyright: If you are the owner of copyright in this material and do not consent to the use of this material within the Fair Use framework, please contact the author forthwith with a written objection and proof of ownership.

Track 6: YouTube: *Blunty3000*, 2007 (1:06). Source: A video file acquired from www.youtube.com/watch?v=QXJbXFSLT58. Blunty3000 talks about headphones working as shields. The file was published on YouTube by Blunty3000 on 23 April 2007. The track was re-recorded from video file to wav file, and the visual feed was consequently lost. Copyright: published with the kind permission of Blunty3000.

Track 7: Acidplanet: *God vs. the Internet*, 2005 (0:48). Source: An mp3 file acquired from www.acidplanet.com/artist.asp?PID=652203&T=180823. The artist *God vs. the Internet* plays 'May the Circle be Unbroken' (God vs. the Internet). The file was published on 13 October 2005. The track was re-recorded from mp3 file to wav file. Copyright: If you are the owner of copyright in this material and do not consent to the use of this material within the Fair Use framework, please contact the author forthwith with a written objection and proof of ownership.

Track 8: BBC Radio 4: *Acoustic Shadows*, 2004 (2:02). Source: An mp3 file acquired from www.bbc.co.uk/radio4/science/acousticshadows.shtml. The programme was produced by BBC journalist Robert Sandall, who presents the science of acoustic archeology with the archeologist Steve Waller. The track was re-recorded from mp3 file to wav file. Copyright: published with the kind permission of the BBC.

Track 9: This Week in Tech: *Podcast Expo*, 2006 (2:31). Source: An mp3 file acquired from www.twit.tv/71. The host Leo Laporte talks to industry people at Podcast Expo at Ontario Convention Center, Los Angeles, on 2 October 2006. The track was re-recorded from mp3 file to wav file. Copyright: If you are the owner of copyright in this material and do not consent to the use of this material within the Fair Use framework, please contact the author forthwith with a written objection and proof of ownership.

Track 10: haltKarl: *Almost Gills*, 2007 and 2005 (1:51). Source: A wav file acquired from haltKarl. Both versions of 'Almost Gills' (haltKarl) are unpublished. The tracks were in wav format from the outset, and no re-recording was necessary. Copyright: published with the kind permission of haltKarl.

Track 11: Autechre: *Dael*, 1995 (1:09). Source: The CD *tri reptae* (1995), on Warp warpcd38 (1995). 'Dael' is composed by Autechre. The track was re-recorded from stereo CD to wav file. Copyright: published with the kind permission of Warp Records.

Track 12: Portishead: *Glory Box*, 1994 (1:03). Source: The CD *Dummy* (1994), on Go! Discs/London 828553 (1994). 'Glory Box' is composed by Barrow, Gibbons, Hayes and Utley. The track was re-recorded from stereo CD to wav file. Copyright: published with the kind permission of Universal Music TV.

Track 13: 1010 WINS: *Top of the Hour*, 2001 (2:24). Source: a CD recording from the station's audio archive, supplied by 1010 WINS editor Mark Mason. Lee Harris reads the news at 7 a.m. on 2 May 2001. The track was re-recorded from CD to wav file. Copyright: published with the kind permission of 1010 WINS/Infinity Broadcasting.

Track 14: Unknown artist: *Get Mobilized*, 2000 (1:00). Source: aired on the American radio station 1010 WINS in 2000, and recorded to magnetic cassette by Lars Nyre. The song is an advertisement for Mobil Oil. The track was re-recorded from cassette to wav file.

Track 15: 1010 WINS: *Breaking news*, 2001 (1:23). Source: a CD recording from the station's audio archive, supplied by 1010 WINS editor Mark Mason. Lee Harris presents breaking news on 11 September 2001 and Joan Fleischer reports from the scene. The track was re-recorded from CD to wav file. Copyright: published with the kind permission of 1010 WINS/Infinity Broadcasting.

Track 16: 1010 WINS: *The South Tower collapses*, 2001 (2:16). Source: a CD recording from the station's audio archive, supplied by 1010 WINS editor Mark Mason. Lee Harris talks with eyewitness Joan Fleischer on 11 September 2001. The track was re-recorded from CD to wav file. Copyright: published with the kind permission of 1010 WINS/Infinity Broadcasting.

Track 17: LBC London: *Nick Ferrari with Rosemary*, 2004 (3:05). Source: Live programme aired on DAB, and recorded to minidisc by Lars Nyre. 'Nick Ferrari at Breakfast' is broadcast every weekday from 7 to 9 a.m., and this particular show was aired on 24 June 2004. The track was re-recorded from minidisc to wav file. Copyright: published with the kind permission of LBC 97.3 FM, a company in the Chrysalis Radio Group.

Track 18: BBC Radio One: *Sara Cox with Nicola and Rachel*, 2001 (3:50). Source: Live programme distributed on streaming audio from www.bbc.co.uk/

radio1, and recorded to minidisc by Lars Nyre. 'The Breakfast Show with Sara Cox' was aired on BBC Radio 1 on 24 October 2001. The track was re-recorded from minidisc to wav file. Copyright: published with the kind permission of the BBC.

Track 19: WOR New York: *Dr Joy Browne with Barney*, 2002 (3:41). Source: Live programme distributed on streaming audio on www.wor710.com, and recorded to minidisc by Lars Nyre. The psychiatry show 'Dr Joy Browne' was aired on 710 WOR, New York, on 20 February 2002. The track was re-recorded from minidisc to wav file. Copyright: published with the kind permission of WOR Radio HD.

Track 20: Residents: *Never Known Questions*, 1974 (1:20). Source: The stereo LP *Not Available* RR1174 (1978). The song 'Never Known Questions' was composed by the Residents, and although it was recorded in 1974 it was first published in 1978. The track was re-recorded from stereo LP to wav file. Copyright: published with the kind permission of the Cryptic Corporation.

Track 21: Sly and the Family Stone: *If You Want Me to Stay*, 1973 (1:26). Source: The stereo LP *Fresh*, Epic KE32134 (1973). The song 'If You Want Me to Stay' is composed by Stewart. The track was re-recorded from stereo LP to wav file. Copyright: published with the kind permission of SONY BMG Music Entertainment Norway AS.

Track 22: Traffic: *Giving to You*, 1967 (1:15). Source: The stereo LP *Mr Fantasy*, United Artists UAS 6651 (1968). The song 'Giving to You' was composed by Winwood, Capaldi, Wood and Mason. The track was re-recorded from stereo LP to wav file. Copyright: published with the kind permission of Universal Music TV.

Track 23: NASA: *Neil Armstrong on the moon*, 1969 (1:19). Source: An mp3 file acquired from the website http://161.115.184.211/teague/apollo/audio/. This was originally a live transmission by NASA, aired on 20 July 1969. The track was re-recorded from mp3 file to wav file. Copyright: Published in accordance with the NASA History Division.

Track 24: BBC Radio One: *Promo*, 1967 (0:27). Source: The CD *75 Years of the BBC: A Celebration of BBC Radio*, ZBBC 2038 (1997). This was a promotional element for the new station Radio 1, and it was aired on 30 September 1967. The track was re-recorded from CD to wav file. Copyright: published with the kind permission of the BBC.

Track 25: NBC: *The Kraft Music Hall with Bing Crosby*, 1943 (1:46). Source: an mp3 file from the Internet site www.old-time.com. This was originally a live transmission on AM radio aired on NBC on 30 December 1943. The track was re-recorded from mp3 file to wav file. Copyright: It is believed that pre-1950 radio programmes fall under the Copyright Act of 1909, and therefore have entered the public domain. If anyone has written proof that any selections are not public domain, and does not consent to the use of this material within the fair use framework, please contact the author forthwith with a written objection.

Track 26: BBC: *The Brains Trust*, 1943 (1:06). Source: The CD *75 Years of the BBC: A Celebration of BBC Radio*, ZBBC 2038 (1997). This was originally a live transmission aired on the BBC Home Service on 30 March 1943. 'The Brains Trust' panel included Lord Moran (Sir Charles Wilson), Dr C. E. M. Joad, Lt. Commander R. T. Gould, M. Jan Marsaryk and the Rt Hon. Lord Kennet. The track was re-recorded from CD to wav file. Copyright: published with the kind permission of the BBC.

Track 27: CBS: *Breaking news*, 1941 (1:34). Source: Acquired from the audio cassette *Newsbreaks as They Happened* (release date and serial number unknown). Thanks are due to Chris Swenson for making this tape available. This was originally a live news transmission on CBS on 7 December 1941. Copyright: It is believed that pre-1950 radio programmes fall under the Copyright Act of 1909, and therefore have entered the public domain. If anyone has written proof that any selections are not public domain, and does not consent to the use of this material within the fair use framework, please contact the author forthwith with a written objection.

Track 28: Swedish Radio (SR): *Sports commentary*, 1931 (1:05). Source: Acquired from the CD *Klassiska idrottsreferat* [Classic sports relays], appended to Dahlén (1999). This was originally a live transmission on Sveriges Radio [Swedish Radio Corporation] on 30 August 1931. The track was re-recorded from CD to wav file. Copyright: It is believed that pre-1950 radio programmes fall under the Copyright Act of 1909, and therefore have entered the public domain. If anyone has written proof that any selections are not public domain, and does not consent to the use of this material within the fair use framework, please contact the author forthwith with a written objection.

Track 29: Edith Piaf: *L'Accordéoniste*, 1940 (1:09). Source: A 78 rpm release by Polydor, 524 669 (1940). The song 'L'Accordéoniste' was composed by Michel Emer. The track was re-recorded by playing the 78 rpm on a wind-up gramophone, picking up the sound with a microphone, and recording it on a wav file. The lyrics in English translation were found at www.dailymotion.com/video/x2iz6n_edith-piaf-l-accordeoniste-english_music. Copyright: It is believed that this recording has entered the public domain. If anyone has written proof that any selections are not public domain, and does not consent to the use of this material within the fair use framework, please contact the author forthwith with a written objection.

Track 30: Harry Brandelius: *Spelmannen*, 1938 (0:59). Source: A 78 rpm release by His Master's Voice, ALP 3378 (1938). The song 'Spelmannen' was composed by Ågren/Andersson. The track was re-recorded by playing the 78 rpm on a wind-up gramophone, picking up the sound with a microphone, and recording it on a wav file. Copyright: It is believed that this recording has entered the public domain. If anyone has written proof that any selections are not public domain, and does not consent to the use of this material within the fair use framework, please contact the author forthwith with a written objection.

Track 31: Charles Panzéra: *Chanson triste*, 1931 (1:03). Source: A 78 rpm release by Victor Red Seal, 1892 (1931). Charles Panzéra sings 'Chanson triste' (Lahor/ Duparc) with Magdaleine Panzéra-Baillot accompanying on piano. The track was re-recorded by playing the 78 rpm on a wind-up gramophone, picking up the sound with a microphone, and recording it on a wav file. English language lyrics by Richard Stokes, found at http://www.recmusic.org/lieder/get_text.html? TextId=9772. Copyright: It is believed that this recording has entered the public domain. If anyone has written proof that any selections are not public domain, and does not consent to the use of this material within the fair use framework, please contact the author forthwith with a written objection.

Track 32: *Tuning in the AM spectrum* (1:01). This is a montage of electronic and atmospheric noises made by Lars Nyre and Kjetil Vikene in 2002. Five differ- ent noises were generated on a mono Radionette receiver, recorded to wav file, and superimposed on each other in SoundForge. The tracks were in wav for- mat from the outset, and no re-recording was necessary. Notice that no pre- sumption of historical accuracy is made. Copyright: published with the permission of Lars Nyre and Kjetil Vikene.

Track 33: Bessie Smith: *St Louis Blues*, 1925 (1:37). Source: The CD *Legends of the Blues, Volume 1*, CBS 01-467245-10 (1990). The song was composed by W. C. Handy. The track was re-recorded from CD to wav file. Copyright: It is believed that this recording has entered the public domain. If anyone has writ- ten proof that any selections are not public domain, and does not consent to the use of this material within the fair use framework, please contact the author forthwith with a written objection.

Track 34: Ellen Gulbranson: *Ack Wärmeland du sköna*, 1914 (1:09). Source: A 78 rpm release by the International Record Collector's Club, IRCC no. 222-B (no release date given). The track was re-recorded by playing the 78 rpm on a 1904 Victrola gramophone, picking up the sound with a microphone, and recording it on a wav file. Copyright: It is believed that this recording has entered the public domain. If anyone has written proof that any selections are not public domain, and does not consent to the use of this material within the fair use framework, please contact the author forthwith with a written objection.

Track 35: Enrico Caruso: *The Siciliana*, 1901 (1:08). Source: The LP *20 Great Tenors in Recording History*, Tap Records, T-303 (no release date given). Enrico Caruso made this recording backstage at the New York Metropolitan in 1901. The track was re-recorded from LP to wav file. Copyright: It is believed that this recording has entered the public domain. If anyone has written proof that any selections are not public domain, and does not consent to the use of this material within the fair use framework, please contact the author forthwith with a written objection.

Track 36: *Thomas Edison with Arthur Sullivan*, 1888 (1:28). Source: An mp3 file acquired from http://math.boisestate.edu/gas/other_sullivan/html/historic.html. This was originally recorded on a cylinder phonograph on 5 October 1888. The track was re-recorded from mp3 file to wav file. Copyright: It is believed that this recording has entered the public domain. If anyone has written proof that any selections are not public domain, and does not consent to the use of this material within the fair use framework, please contact the author forthwith with a written objection.

Index

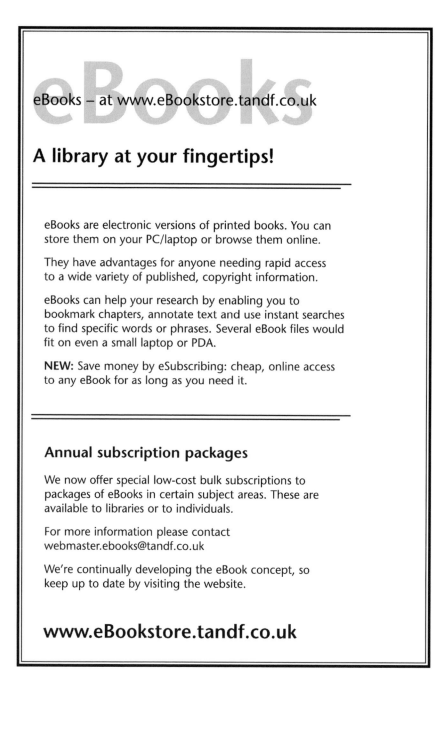